CENTRAL BANKING IN
DEVELOPING COUNTRIES

This book examines the objectives, activities and independence of central banks in developing countries. It is based on macroeconomic data from IMF and World Bank sources as well as detailed questionnaire responses from central banks in Africa, Asia, Europe, Latin America and the Caribbean. It explores the practical problems faced by these central banks over the past 15 years in confronting government demands for monetary financing, formulating and implementing monetary policy, choosing and maintaining an exchange rate regime, supervising their financial systems, as well as enhancing their status and independence.

The book covers three general topics: government financing, foreign exchange systems and the development of the domestic banking system. In all three areas central banks in developing countries face environments that differ radically from the environments faced by central banks in the richer OECD countries. In particular, they face difficulties with uncompetitive financial systems and the endemic problem of government finance. However, positive changes are now occurring, especially as the benefits of price stability become widely accepted. The book is in a clear and easy-to-use format with generous use of tables, figures and boxed material.

This book is published in association with the Bank of England and presents an authoritative assessment of the role of central banks in developing countries.

Maxwell J. Fry is Tokai Bank Professor of International Finance and Director of the International Finance Group at the University of Birmingham. **Charles A.E. Goodhart** is the Norman Sosnow Professor of Banking and Finance at the London School of Economics. **Alvaro Almeida** is affiliated with the Financial Markets Group, London School of Economics and Faculdade de Economia do Porto.

CENTRAL BANKING IN DEVELOPING COUNTRIES

Objectives, Activities and Independence

Maxwell J. Fry,
Charles A. E. Goodhart
and Alvaro Almeida

Foreword by Eddie George,
Governor of the Bank of England

London and New York

First published 1996
by Routledge
11 New Fetter Lane, London EC4P 4EE

Simultaneously published in the USA and Canada
by Routledge
29 West 35th Street, New York, NY 10001

Routledge is an International Thomson Publishing company

© 1996 The Bank of England

Typeset in Garamond by LaserScript, Mitcham, Surrey
Printed and bound in Great Britain by
TJ Press (Padstow) Ltd, Padstow, Cornwall

British Library Cataloguing in Publication Data
A catalogue record for this book is available from the British Library

Library of Congress Cataloging in Publication Data
A catalogue record for this book has been requested

ISBN 0–415–14533–3 (hbk)
ISBN 0–415–14534–1 (pbk)

CONTENTS

List of figures　　　　　　　　　　　　　　　　vii
List of tables　　　　　　　　　　　　　　　　viii
Foreword　　　　　　　　　　　　　　　　　　x
Acknowledgements　　　　　　　　　　　　　xii

1　INTRODUCTION　　　　　　　　　　　　　1

2　PRICE STABILITY, MONETARY EXPANSION
　　AND OUTPUT GROWTH　　　　　　　　　13
　　Box A Inflation and growth: the statistical relationship
　　　　for the BoE group　　　　　　　　　　16
　　Box B Monetary growth and inflation: the relationship
　　　　refined　　　　　　　　　　　　　　22

3　THE CENTRAL BANK AND THE GOVERNMENT　27
　　Seigniorage　　　　　　　　　　　　　　32
　　Financial repression　　　　　　　　　　35
　　Foreign exchange operations　　　　　　37
　　Stock and flow variables in the central bank's
　　　　relationship with its government　　　37
　　A monetary policy reaction function　　　40
　　Box C Estimates of a monetary policy reaction function
　　　　for the BoE group by independence　　41

4　CENTRAL BANKS' EXTERNAL ACTIVITIES　47
　　Box D Estimates of a monetary policy reaction function
　　　　for the BoE group by exchange rate regime　53

v

5 THE CENTRAL BANK AND THE PRIVATE
  SECTOR   56
  The payments system   56
  The banking system   58
  Other financial markets   66

6 REGULATION AND SUPERVISION   79

7 THE STATUS OF THE CENTRAL BANK   90
  The use of skilled staff by the central bank   90
  The determinants of total staff numbers   97
  Central bank independence   98
  Central bank and government cooperation   108

8 CONCLUSION   112

  APPENDIX 1
  Central bank questionnaire   114
  APPENDIX 2
  *Some macroeconomic and monetary characteristics of
    the Bank of England group, 1979–93*   119
  APPENDIX 3
  Alternative measures of per capita income in US dollars 127
  APPENDIX 4   129
  *Estimated seigniorage revenue in the Bank of England
    group, 1979–93*   130
  *Estimated seigniorage revenue/GDP in the Bank of
    England group, 1979–93*   131
  *Estimated seigniorage revenue/government revenue in
    the Bank of England group, 1979–93*   132
  APPENDIX 5
  *Estimated revenue from financial repression in the Bank
    of England group, 1979–93*   133
  SYMPOSIUM PROCEEDINGS
  *Minutes of symposium on central banking in developing
    countries held at the Bank of England, 9 June 1995* 137

  Bibliography   155
  Index   159

FIGURES

1.1 Ratio of reserve money to deposits and inflation   5
1.2 CPI inflation and government borrowing from central
     bank   6
1.3 Economic growth and government borrowing from
     central bank   6
1.4 Economic growth and government surpluses   7
2.1 Economic growth and CPI inflation   14
2.2 CPI inflation and its standard deviation   15
2.3 Nonlinear effect of inflation on economic growth   18
2.4 CPI inflation and M1 growth rates   21
2.5 Actual and predicted inflation in Argentina   24
5.1 Average settlement delay (capital)   60
6.1 Supervision staff (relative to total staff)   81
6.2 Supervision staff (relative to deposits)   82
7.1 Total graduate intake (excluding sponsored staff)   92
7.2 Total graduate intake (including sponsored staff)   92
7.3 Graduates/postgraduates ratio   95
7.4 Postgraduates in relevant fields   96
7.5 Number of governors since 1975   102
7.6 Number of governors since 1975, corrected for the age
     of the central bank   102

TABLES

1.1 The Bank of England group   2
1.2 Some macroeconomic and monetary characteristics of developing and OECD countries, 1979–93   4
1.3 Some macroeconomic and monetary characteristics of the Bank of England group, 1979–93   8
2.1 The relationship between growth and nominal variables   17
2.2 The relationship between growth and nominal variables (excluding outliers)   17
2.3 Iterative 3SLS estimates of real GDP growth, *YG*, 1971–94   18
2.4 The CPI inflation experience in the BoE group   20
2.5 Effects of monetary growth on inflation   21
2.6 Iterative 3SLS estimate of inflation, *INFG*, 1972–93   23
3.1 Iterative 3SLS estimates of monetary policy reaction function *DDCY* by independence, 1972–93   43
4.1 Foreign exchange regimes in the Bank of England group   49
4.2 Iterative 3SLS estimates of monetary policy reaction function *DDCY* by exchange rate regime, 1972–93   54
5.1 Daily turnover of payments system   58
5.2 Payments system   59
5.3 Reforms to payments system since 1975   61
5.4 Growth and monetisation   63
5.5 Monetisation and growth   64
5.6 Demand for money functions   67
5.7 Market classification   71
5.8 Market impediments   74
6.1 Ratio of staff to deposits   84
6.2 Staff/deposits ratio excluding outlier   84

TABLES

7.1 Ratio of graduates to total staff   94
7.2 Graduates/total staff ratio excluding outlier   94
7.3 Ratio of nonsupervisory staff to population   99
7.4 Government representation on the central bank's board   103
7.5 Inflation and central bank independence   104
7.6 F question correlations   106
7.7 Inflation and the status of the central bank   107

FOREWORD

During 1994, our tercentenary year, we organised a Symposium to recall the history and to review the current prospects of central banking. It involved more than 130 governors or former governors from central banks around the world. The two main papers were by S. Fischer on 'Modern Central Banking' and by Capie, Goodhart and Schnadt on 'The Development of Central Banking'. These papers, together with the comments of their distinguished discussants, were published under the title *The Future of Central Banking* by Cambridge University Press later that year.

It was natural, indeed almost inevitable, that these papers concentrated primarily on the history and circumstances of central banks in the developed countries. This was pointed out in the discussion by Dr Courtney Blackman of Barbados, who said that the papers failed to address the particular problems of central banks in developing countries. We therefore decided to address this lacuna at the next appropriate occasion, which was the meeting in 1995 of governors from central banks drawn mainly from the erstwhile Sterling Area. This group, like so many other financial groupings nowadays, has never had hard and fixed boundaries, and we took the opportunity to invite a rather wider range of colleagues from central banks from many continents who would, we hoped, be interested in discussing central banking in developing countries.

In order to provide a focus for this discussion, we asked Professor Maxwell Fry, the Tokai Professor of International Finance at the University of Birmingham, and Professor Charles Goodhart, the Norman Sosnow Professor of Banking and Finance at the London School of Economics, to prepare a paper. This they did, assisted by Alvaro Almeida, a Ph.D. student at the London School of Economics. The resulting monograph forms the main part of this book, together with their discussants' comments. We are grateful to Dr Chakravarthi Rangarajan, Governor of the Reserve Bank of India, Dr Matthew Chikaonda, Governor of the Reserve Bank of Malawi, and Professor Stanley Fischer, First Deputy Managing Director of the International Monetary Fund, for acting as discussants.

Despite the extensive knowledge that the authors of the main paper already had on central banking in many countries, historical periods and circumstances, the task of preparing a paper that would address issues relevant to such a widely disparate audience was a daunting one. How can an academic fully understand, and usefully comment on, the diverse concerns of, for example, Chile, India, Sierra Leone, Singapore, the Solomon Islands, and Trinidad and Tobago, all at the same time and in one paper?

The authors felt that it was simply not realistic for them to try to become expert on the individual circumstances in the large number, and considerable variety, of countries whose central bank governors would form their audience. Faced with this problem, they decided to ask the real experts, the central banks themselves, to describe what they were doing. So the authors prepared a questionnaire for the participating central banks. The authors have expressed their thanks to the many responding central banks for their care and courtesy in completing this lengthy task, and I should like to join them in this. The questionnaire itself is reproduced as Appendix 1 in the book.

The timetable for this exercise was quite short. The questionnaire was designed in December and dispatched in January; most of the responses arrived in March/April; the paper was drafted in May for the Conference in early June. The greater part of the monograph builds on the data thereby obtained, as well as on a wider statistical base obtained from IMF and World Bank publications.

The authors use these databases to report how central banks have fared in their main objective of achieving price stability and in their relationships with their governments, the external and private sectors. We and our audience at the Symposium found this a useful and interesting exercise. I hope that readers of this book will find it interesting too.

Eddie George
Governor of the Bank of England

ACKNOWLEDGEMENTS

Central bankers do not seek the limelight. First and foremost, therefore, we are grateful to the 40 central banks that returned answers to our questionnaire. We are particularly appreciative of the care and effort they took in preparing their replies to this long and detailed questionnaire. The extraordinarily high 90 per cent response rate was in no small part due to the concomitant invitation from the Bank of England to attend its Symposium on Central Banking in Developing Countries. Secondly, therefore, we extend our thanks to the many members of the Bank of England who were involved not only in arranging the Symposium but also in administering the questionnaire. In particular, our thanks go to Eddie George for inviting us to prepare this monograph for the Symposium and to Lionel Price for supervising the questionnaire transmittal and replies as well as his efforts to make the Symposium such an enjoyable and worthwhile occasion.

Many individuals helped by providing information for and comments on earlier drafts, as well as administrative assistance in various aspects of this project. Here our thanks go to Salem Abdul Aziz Al-Sabah, William Allen, Peter Burridge, Christine Chaplin, Carlo Cottarelli, José De Gregorio, Stanley Fischer, Victoria Fleming, John Footman, John Hawkins, Peter Hayward, Nicholas Horsewood, Anthony Latter, Roberto Marino, Enrique Matayoshi, Archibald Meredith, Leora Meridor, Shahnaz Moore, S. Narube, Carron Robson, Michelle Scudder, Ananthanarayanan Seshan, Andrew Sheng, Terry Smeeton, David Strachan and Lorraine Yuille.

1

INTRODUCTION

This book examines central banking in 44 developing countries that appear to be reasonably representative of central banks in developing countries as a whole. The study starts by examining the achievement of this group of central banks in maintaining price stability, their primary stated objective. Because success has been elusive, we then examine the relationship between central banks and government financing, as fiscal exigencies certainly explain a considerable part of the difficulties central banks have faced in their price stability objectives. This analysis is followed by an examination of central banking activities in the foreign exchange markets, including the nature of the foreign exchange regime, why such a regime was chosen and what functions central banks perform in this area. The remaining chapters of the book examine the relationships between the central bank and the private sector. Here we cover both the implementation of monetary policy and the prudential regulation and supervision of the financial system. In all three general areas – government financing, foreign exchange systems and the domestic banking system – we find that central banks in developing countries face environments that differ radically from the environments faced by central banks in the richer OECD countries. Nevertheless, we detect some distinct changes over the past 25 years.

This study, undertaken at the invitation of the Bank of England (BoE) for its Symposium on Central Banking in Developing Countries on 9 June 1995, relies on several sources of information. Most of the quantitative work is based on data from *International Financial Statistics (IFS)* and the World Bank's *Socio-economic Time-series Access and Retrieval System: World Tables*. In addition to publicly available data from the *IFS* and *World Tables*, we

1

supplemented the factual basis for this book through responses to a questionnaire, which we devised, on a variety of central banking topics. The Bank of England sent the questionnaire to and collected the responses from the central bank governors who were invited to the Symposium. This questionnaire is reproduced in Appendix 1 and the countries to which it was sent are listed in Table 1.1.[1] Clearly, these countries, referred to hereafter as the BoE group, were not randomly selected; the group consists predominantly of Commonwealth countries and under-represents Francophone and East Asian countries.

The typical central bank of a developing country operates under several conditions that contrast with those in the OECD countries.[2] First and foremost, central banks in developing countries tend to dominate their countries' financial sectors to a larger extent than do central banks in the OECD countries. Rather than acting as *primus inter pares*, the typical developing country central bank dictates the terms and conditions under which other financial institutions may operate. Partly as a consequence of this role, central banks in these

Table 1.1 The Bank of England group

Africa	Asia	Middle East and Europe	Western Hemisphere
Botswana	Bangladesh	Cyprus	Argentina
Gambia	Brunei	Israel	Bahamas
Ghana	Fiji	Jordan	Barbados
Kenya	Hong Kong	Kuwait	Belize
Lesotho	India	Malta	Chile
Malawi	Malaysia	Saudi Arabia	·Guyana
Mauritius	Pakistan	United Arab Emirates	Jamaica
Namibia	Papua New Guinea		Mexico
Nigeria	Singapore		St Lucia
Sierra Leone	Solomon Islands		Trinidad and
South Africa	Sri Lanka		Tobago
Swaziland			
Tanzania			
Uganda			
Zambia			
Zimbabwe			

countries have assumed an enhanced responsibility for fostering the structural development of their financial systems, a subject covered in Chapter 5.

At least until very recently, market forces were fragile or even nonexistent in many developing countries, in part due to financial repression. Hence, developing country central banks were relieved from the attendant problems of operating within a market framework. However, thriving parallel and noninstitutional markets circumvented controls over the formal financial system. In recent years, therefore, most central banks in developing countries have been struggling to move from a regulatory or control mode, which was becoming increasingly ineffective, to indirect market-based techniques of implementing monetary policy, as discussed in Chapter 5.

Table 1.2 compares some salient variables across developing and OECD countries. The sample consists of 122 developing countries and 20 OECD countries, all countries for which reasonably comprehensive data sets are available from *IFS* and *World Tables*.[3] The 122 developing countries are split into two groups: a control group of 79 countries and 43 countries of the BoE group.[4]

Table 1.2 shows that the ratio of money (M2) to GDP (M/Y) in developing countries is barely above one-half of the money/income ratio in OECD countries. At the same time, however, the data in Table 1.2 support our assertion that central banks dominate their financial systems to a considerably greater extent in developing countries than they do in the OECD countries. Specifically:

- The ratio of central bank liabilities in the form of reserve money (currency in circulation plus bank deposits at the central bank) to M2 (H/M) is almost three times higher in developing countries than in the OECD countries.[5]
- The ratio of bank reserves to bank deposits (R/D) is five times higher in developing countries than in the OECD countries.
- M2 represents a larger percentage of total financial assets in developing countries than in the OECD countries.

Table 1.2 also shows, somewhat surprisingly, that while developing countries differ from OECD countries the BoE group possesses the same characteristics as the developing country population as a whole. For example, in both the BoE group and all other developing countries:

Table 1.2 Some macroeconomic and monetary characteristics of
developing and OECD countries, 1979–93 (per cent)

Variable	Developing countries (122)	Control group (79)	BoE group (43)	OECD countries (20)
YG	2.9	2.7	3.3	2.5
INF	29.4	27.7	32.2	7.3
M/Y	38.9	35.7	44.2	67.6
H/M	40.3	44.2	33.2	13.7
R/D	28.6	33.8	19.1	5.7
CBCG	45.2	52.2	32.6	2.9
CGDC	21.2	21.0	21.6	15.9
GS/Y	–5.9	–6.4	–5.0	–3.8
GR/Y	25.2	24.2	26.8	32.8
DT/Y	68.6	69.3	67.2	n.a.
PCY	$1,149.0	$1,000.0	$1,440.0	$21,083.0

Key:
	YG	Trend growth rate in GDP at constant prices.
	INF	Consumer price inflation.
	M/Y	Money (M2)/GDP.
	H/M	Reserve money/M2.
	R/D	Bank reserves/bank deposits.
	CBCG	Central bank net credit to government/net domestic credit to government.
	CGDC	Net domestic credit to government/aggregate domestic credit.
	GS/Y	Government deficit (–)/GDP.
	GR/Y	Government revenue/GDP.
	DT/Y	Foreign debt/GDP.
	PCY	1992 per capita income in US dollars (exchange rate based, geometric averages).

- Inflation (*INF*) averaged 30 per cent over past 15 years.
- The ratio of money to income (*M/Y*) averaged 40 per cent.
- The ratio of reserve money to M2 (*H/M*) averaged 40 per cent.
- The ratio of bank reserves to deposits (*R/D*) averaged 25 per cent.
- Government deficits averaged 6 per cent of GDP (*–GS/Y*).
- Foreign debt averaged 70 per cent of GDP (*DT/Y*).

In other words, the BoE group appears to represent developing countries reasonably well. We hope, therefore, that our findings from this group apply more broadly to developing countries in general.

The macroeconomic data for the BoE group presented in Table 1.2 exhibit some simple statistical associations:[6]

- The ratio of reserve money to M2 (H/M) is positively related to inflation (INF) and government deficits ($-GS/Y$).
- The ratio of bank reserves to deposits (R/D) is positively related to inflation (Figure 1.1) and to government deficits ($-GS/Y$).
- Inflation (INF) is positively related to the proportion of government borrowing met by the central bank ($CBCG$) (Figure 1.2) and to the proportion of government borrowing in total domestic credit ($CGDC$).
- Economic growth (YG) is negatively related to the proportion of government borrowing met by the central bank ($CBCG$) (Figure 1.3) and to the proportion of government borrowing in total domestic credit ($CGDC$).
- Economic growth (YG) is negatively related to both government deficits ($-GS/Y$) (Figure 1.4) and foreign debt (DT/Y). David Ricardo (1817) explains why foreign debt accumulation is inimical to growth by encouraging capital flight.[7]
- Inflation (INF) is negatively related to economic growth (YG).

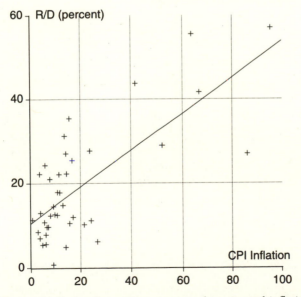

Figure 1.1 Ratio of reserve money to deposits and inflation

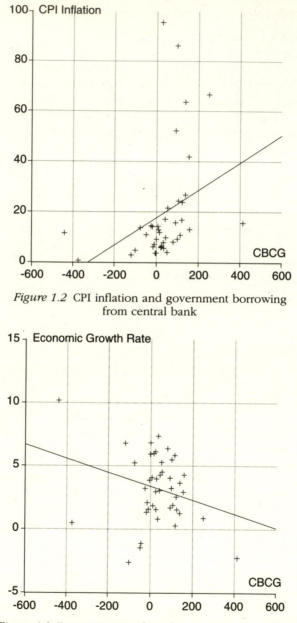

Figure 1.2 CPI inflation and government borrowing
from central bank

Figure 1.3 Economic growth and government borrowing
from central bank

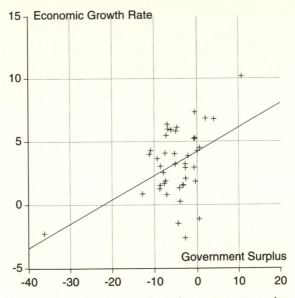

Figure 1.4 Economic growth and government surpluses

Most of these relationships are relevant, either directly or indirectly, to central banking and monetary policy implementation in developing countries. They are therefore considered again in more detail in appropriate chapters later in this book.[8]

While Table 1.2 demonstrates that developing countries differ from OECD countries in some important respects, it also suggests the BoE group does not diverge greatly from the developing country population as a whole, at least in terms of these variables. In other words, the BoE group appears to represent developing countries reasonably well. Nevertheless, the BoE group is far from homogeneous, another accurate reflection of developing countries as a whole. Appendix 2 provides data for individual countries in this group on the same basis as Table 1.2. Average rates of economic growth over the period 1979–93 range from –2.3 per cent in Guyana to 10.2 per cent in Botswana. Inflation averaged 0.7 per cent in Saudi Arabia compared with 556 per cent in Argentina. Per capita income comparisons also reveal large disparities. However, the results vary enormously depending on the basis used for such comparisons. For this reason, we present three alternative sources of per capita income estimates for the BoE group in Appendix 3.[9]

When we look at trends over the past 15 years, we detect a shift from a *dirigiste* environment of administratively fixed interest rates, credit rationing and directed credit policies towards financial liberalisation and the use of indirect market-based techniques of monetary control. Table 1.3 presents the results of splitting the observation period into three five-year sections. The data are not strictly comparable to those in Table 1.2 because only countries with observations for all three periods are used in calculating the averages presented in Table 1.3.

Table 1.3 shows that while growth rates and money/income ratios have risen over the past 15 years in the BoE group, inflation has risen. When Argentina is excluded, average inflation for the remaining countries remained virtually unchanged at around 20 per cent. The financial-fiscal variables, however, indicate a consistent trend:

Table 1.3 Some macroeconomic and monetary characteristics of the Bank of England group, 1979–93 (per cent)

Variable	1979–83	1984–88	1989–93
YG	1.9	3.8	3.7
INF	22.4	30.4	43.6
M/Y	42.0	50.2	51.1
H/M	36.3	33.5	29.6
R/D	21.6	19.6	16.0
CBCG	42.4	35.7	21.1
CGDC	26.4	30.1	22.1
GS/Y	−4.9	−3.7	−3.8
GR/Y	28.2	27.6	26.6
DT/Y	42.3	76.5	86.6

Key:
YG	Trend growth rate in GDP at constant prices.
INF	Consumer price inflation.
M/Y	Money (M2)/GDP.
H/M	Reserve money/M2.
R/D	Bank reserves/bank deposits.
CBCG	Central bank net credit to government/net domestic credit to government.
CGDC	Net domestic credit to government/aggregate domestic credit.
GS/Y	Government deficit (−)/GDP.
GR/Y	Government revenue/GDP.
DT/Y	Foreign debt/GDP.

- A falling ratio of reserve money to M2 (H/M).
- A falling reserve ratio (R/D).
- A falling proportion of the government's total bank borrowing provided by the central bank ($CBCG$).
- A falling proportion of total domestic credit appropriated by government ($CGDC$).

These changes are themselves consistent with the decline in government deficits from 5 to 4 per cent of GDP. However, this decline has been achieved not by an increase in revenue but rather by a decline in expenditure. Indeed, government investment expenditure in a number of developing countries has been cut drastically in the aftermath of the foreign debt crisis. Despite the improved fiscal situation, the final variable in Table 1.3 shows that the ratio of foreign debt to GDP has continued to rise.

In Chapter 2 we note that the primary objective of central banks, in both developing and developed countries, has generally moved towards the attainment of price stability. Considering that growth is negatively associated with inflation (Barro 1995; De Gregorio 1994; Fischer 1994) and inflation is disliked for its own sake, the achievement of price stability would seem, subject to the transitional costs of getting there, self-evidently desirable. Since inflation is a monetary phenomenon, as we document once more, and central banks should be able to control monetary conditions, why is inflation still so high in so many countries?

One reason may be that central banks have been persuaded by their governments to pursue other objectives. In particular, in some developing as well as developed countries the government's capacity and discipline to raise funds from non-bank sources (by taxation or borrowing) is limited. Hence short-sighted governments have in many cases effectively used their central bank as a fiscal milch cow. We discuss this issue in Chapter 3. Having addressed the relationship between the central bank and the government in Chapter 3, we then describe the relationships between the central bank and the other two sectors: the external sector in Chapter 4 and the private sector in Chapter 5.

The two main interrelated objectives of central banks in all countries are the macro-objective of providing an anchor of nominal price stability and the micro-objective of preserving and enhancing the structural stability of the payments, banking and financial system. We discuss some aspects of this latter micro-function, e.g., the development of the payments system and of a range of financial markets, as carried out by the BoE group, in Chapter 5. In Chapter 6 we examine their supervisory and regulatory role.

In Chapters 2 to 6 we document what the BoE group of central banks have been doing. In Chapter 7, however, we explore whether their differing constitutional and professional status has made a significant difference to their behaviour, especially with respect to their relative rate of monetary expansion and inflation. The subject matter of this chapter falls mainly within the rapidly expanding field of central bank independence and covers much the same ground as Alex Cukierman (1992, Chs 18–23), Cukierman *et al.* (1992, 1993) and José De Gregorio (1994). However, we also obtained some additional and distinct (but adjunct) data on the professional qualifications of new recruits to the BoE group of central banks.

NOTES

1 The *aggregated* raw data on which our analysis is based can be obtained from the authors. However, the individual questionnaire responses are confidential and could be released only with each central bank's agreement. Although the Eastern Caribbean Central Bank is located on St Kitts, we use St Lucia in our quantitative analysis because it is the largest country served by this central bank. Unfortunately, data deficiencies prevented the inclusion of Brunei in the quantitative analysis presented here.

2 The 20 OECD countries used for comparison throughout this book are Australia, Austria, Belgium, Canada, Denmark, Finland, France, Germany, Iceland, Ireland, Italy, Japan, the Netherlands, New Zealand, Norway, Spain, Sweden, Switzerland, the United Kingdom and the United States.

3 Data for Hong Kong were obtained from local sources and Asian Development Bank, *Key Indicators of Developing Asian and Pacific Countries* (annual).

4 The countries in the control group, which consists of all other developing countries for which a reasonably complete data set is available, are Afghanistan, Algeria, Antigua and Barbuda, Aruba, Bahrain, Benin, Bhutan, Bolivia, Brazil, Burkina Faso, Burundi, Cameroon, Cape Verde, Central African Republic, Chad, China, Colombia, Comoros, Congo, Costa Rica, Côte d'Ivoire, Djibouti, Dominica, Dominican Republic, Ecuador, Egypt, El Salvador, Equatorial Guinea, Ethiopia, Gabon, Greece, Grenada, Guatemala, Guinea-Bissau, Haiti, Honduras, Indonesia, Iran, Korea, Lebanon, Liberia, Libya, Madagascar, Maldives, Mali, Mauritania, Morocco,

Mozambique, Myanmar, Nepal, the Netherlands, Antilles, Nicaragua, Niger, Oman, Panama, Paraguay, Peru, Philippines, Portugal, Qatar, Rwanda, St Kitts and Nevis, St Vincent and the Grenadines, Senegal, Seychelles, Somalia, Sudan, Suriname, Syria, Thailand, Togo, Tonga, Tunisia, Turkey, Uruguay, Vanuatu, Venezuela, Western Samoa and Zaïre.

5 For consistency with the ratio of bank reserves to bank deposits, reserve money is defined here as bank reserves plus currency in circulation (*IFS* lines 14a + 20). In Chapter 3, however, *IFS* line 14 is used for the definition of reserve money. Textbooks generally define reserve money as the sum of currency in circulation and bank reserves. In practice, however, the *IFS* definition of reserve money is not identical to currency in circulation plus bank reserves (International Monetary Fund 1984). On the one hand, reserve money can include private sector and public enterprise deposits at the central bank, as well as restricted deposits of commercial banks that are not included in the definition of bank reserves; these inclusions may produce a reserve money total that exceeds currency in circulation plus bank reserves. On the other hand, bank reserves can include money market paper issued by the central bank, foreign currency holdings, private bank notes and various other assets which may cause currency in circulation plus bank reserves to exceed reserve money. The only large (over 25 per cent) discrepancies for the BoE group occur in Chile and Ghana. In Chile's case, 'other liabilities to deposit money banks' included in the definition of reserve money causes reserve money to be about five times larger than the sum of currency in circulation plus bank reserves. In the case of Ghana, the sum of currency plus reserves is half the size of reserve money.

6 All the relationships reported in this paragraph are significant at the 95 per cent confidence level. Figures 1.1 and 1.2 exclude Argentina and Figure 1.3 excludes Guyana because they are extreme outliers.

7 'A country which has accumulated a large debt is placed in a most artificial situation; and although the amount of taxes, and the increased price of labour, may not, and I believe does not, place it under any other disadvantage with respect to foreign countries, except the unavoidable one of paying those taxes, yet it becomes the interest of every contributor to withdraw his shoulder from the burthen, and to shift this payment from himself to another; and the temptation to remove himself and his capital to another country, where he will be exempted from such burthens, becomes at last irresistible, and overcomes the natural reluctance which every man feels to quit the place of his birth, and the scene of his early associations. A country which has involved itself in the difficulties attending this artificial system, would act wisely by ransoming itself from them, at the sacrifice of any portion of its property which might be necessary to redeem its debt' (Ricardo 1817, p. 338).

8 In addition, data in Table 1.2 show that the ratio of money to GDP (*M/Y*) is positively related to the natural logarithm of per capita income (*PCY*); in other words, the income elasticity of demand for M2

11

exceeds 1; we analyse the determinants of money demand more fully in Chapter 5. Furthermore, M/Y and inflation (INF) are negatively related. Not surprisingly, the ratio of reserve money to M2 (H/M) is negatively related to the natural logarithm of per capita income. The ratio of bank reserves to bank deposits (R/D) is positively related to the foreign debt ratio (DT/Y). The government deficit is negatively related to M/Y, but positively related to the foreign debt ratio DT/Y which, in turn, is positively related to R/D and negatively related to economic growth.

9   As anticipated, the estimates of 1993 per capita incomes adjusted for purchasing-power parity shown in Appendix 3 (column 6 headed 'PPP') tend to raise low per capita incomes relative to higher per capita incomes. These estimates indicate a range from $770 in Sierra Leone to $23,390 in the United Arab Emirates. For a consistency check, we provide 1985 PPP per capita incomes (column 3 headed 'SH') estimated by Robert Summers and Alan Heston (1991), together with exchange-rate based estimates of per capita income for 1985 and 1992 (columns 2 and 5). While there are large differences between PPP and exchange-rate based per capita income estimates, comparing the ratios of PPP and exchange-rate based estimates for 1985 with the ratios calculated for 1992/3 suggests that roughly the same degree of difference occurs for each country. For example, in both years the PPP estimates for Bangladesh and Sri Lanka are almost six times higher than the exchange-rate based estimates, while for higher income countries such as Hong Kong and Singapore the differences are 1.4 and 1.3, respectively.

2

PRICE STABILITY, MONETARY EXPANSION AND OUTPUT GROWTH

In the 1960s, much of the economics profession accepted the finding that a trade-off existed between inflation and growth. In the 1970s, more sophisticated expectations-augmented Phillips curves became popular. Ironically, one of the clearest expositions of the expectations-augmented Phillips curve was provided by David Hume in 1752:

> Accordingly we find, that in every kingdom, into which money begins to flow in greater abundance than formerly, every thing takes a new face; labour and industry gain life; the merchant becomes more enterprizing; the manufacturer more diligent and skillful; and even the farmer follows his plough with greater alacrity and attention . . . To account, then, for this phænomenon, we must consider, that tho' the high price of commodities be a necessary consequence of the encrease of gold and silver, yet it follows not immediately upon that encrease; but some time is requir'd before the money circulate thro' the whole state, and make its effects be felt on all ranks of people. At first, no alteration is perceiv'd; by degrees, the price rises, first of one commodity, then of another; till the whole at last reaches a just proportion, with the new quantity of specie, which is in the kingdom. In my opinion, 'tis only in this interval or intermediate situation, betwixt the acquisition of money and rise of prices, that the encreasing quantity of gold and silver is favourable to industry.
>
> (Hume 1752, pp. 46–47)

In fact, simple bivariate regressions, cross-section and pooled time-series, indicate negative relationships between inflation and growth for the BoE group in both long and short runs. Figure 2.1 shows the average inflation-average growth rate relationship for the BoE group, but we find a much more significant relationship when we use inflation and growth rates for each year for each country in a pooled time-series estimate as detailed in Box A.[1] Negative sloping long-run expectations-augmented Phillips curve relationships between inflation and growth have also been found, particularly in developing countries (Fry 1995, Ch. 10).

Far from there being any exploitable trade-off in the medium and longer term between inflation and higher output levels, the accepted view now is that in the longer term this relationship is negative, i.e., more inflation is associated with lower growth (Barro 1995; De Gregorio 1994; Fischer 1994). The deleterious effects of hyper-inflation on growth, with the dislocations caused to saving patterns and to the monetary and pricing mechanisms, are fairly obvious. But inflation has, so it is claimed, a negative effect on growth even at low or moderate levels.

In part, this latter effect may be because a higher level of inflation is generally associated with a greater variability of inflation

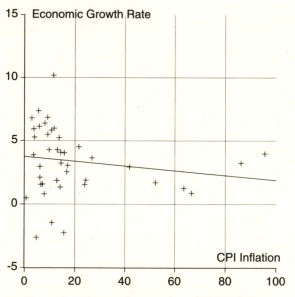

Figure 2.1 Economic growth and CPI inflation

14

and hence a greater riskiness of longer-term unindexed contracts. As John Locke wrote:

> I see no reason to think, that a little bigger or less size of the pieces coined is of any moment, one way or the other . . . The harm comes by the change, which unreasonably and unjustly gives away and transfers men's properties, disorders trade, puzzles accounts, and needs a new arithmetic to cast up reckonings, and keep accounts in; besides a thousand other inconveniencies.
>
> (Locke 1695, p. 189)

We find that the correlation between the level and standard deviation of inflation averaged over the last 15 years for the BoE group was +0.961; the observations shown in Figure 2.2 lie closely along the 45° line.[2] The variability in inflation is also associated within this group with high variability in monetary expansion (correlation +0.879) and in both nominal and real exchange rates *vis-à-vis* the US dollar, with correlations of +0.516 and +0.347 respectively on a cross-country 15-year basis. Similarly, the

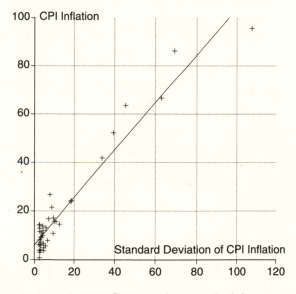

Figure 2.2 CPI inflation and its standard deviation

15

variability in real interest rates (lending rate) was significantly positively correlated with the variability in both M2 growth, +0.742, and in inflation, +0.879 (all significant at the 99 per cent confidence level).[3] Thus instability in nominal variables, money and inflation, is associated with higher variance (and presumably less predictability) in certain key *real* prices, i.e., real exchange and interest rates, another channel whereby inflation may depress growth.[4]

There are many different potential channels for both negative and positive effects running from inflation to growth, and vice versa. In developing countries, fixed nominal interest and exchange rates may have been particularly harmful (Fry 1995, Ch. 8). As inflation rises, lower real interest rates resulting from fixed nominal rates reduce credit availability and distort resource allocation, while a fixed exchange rate prices exports out of world markets. Both effects are growth-reducing. Box A presents findings for the BoE group, which are consistent with the present consensus view, that the longer-term effect of inflation on output growth is negative, though the strength of the relationship is variable.[5]

With inflation also being disliked for its own sake, the natural implication is that the objective of a central bank must be to achieve price stability. This objective has come to be widely, if not generally, accepted among central banks in OECD countries. For example, the protocol of the European System Central Banks (ESCB) in the Maastricht Treaty makes price stability the primary objective, with support for other governmental objectives only possible when price stability has been attained (a lexicographic ordering). The statutes of other European central banks, both in the West (e.g., France, Spain and Sweden), and in the East (e.g., the Czech Republic and Hungary) (Hochreiter 1994), have been altered consonantly.[6]

Box A Inflation and growth: the statistical relationship for the BoE group

The coefficients of inflation in the growth equations are always negative, but in the first set of simple tests run here only sometimes significant. In this first exercise, we examined the relationships over an averaged 15-year period (1979–93), over the last of the constituent five-year averaged periods (1989–93) and using annual data for 1991, the latest year for which a complete data set is available. We also regressed output growth both against inflation and the growth rates of M1 and M2 (measured in percentage points); Table 2.1 gives the results (t values in brackets). The negative relationship appears to be slightly stronger in the short run, in part because of outliers, notably Zambia and Sierra Leone, both with low growth and high inflation. Partly to remove cases of (incipient) hyperinflation, where the negative relationship may well be stronger, we re-ran the test excluding all countries in which inflation over the relevant period exceeded 50 per cent.

These latter tests reported in Table 2.2 indeed suggested, as has been also found elsewhere, that the strength of the negative relationship (between growth and nominal variables) is greater in absolute terms among the inflationary outliers. None of the above simple relationships is significantly different from zero but, apart from the relationship between the growth of output and nominal money in 1991, which may have been influenced by very short-term cyclical factors, all the coefficient signs remain negative.

The use of averages means that some information is not fully used. To use all the available data and to confront the problem that inflation and money growth rates have been far more variable (heteroscedastic) in some countries than in others, we also estimated the relationships between growth and inflation and growth and

Table 2.1 The relationship between growth and nominal variables

| Explanatory variable | Coefficient in growth equation with | | |
	15-year average	1989–93	1991
Inflation	−0.023	−0.050	−0.059
	(−1.17)	(−2.72)	(−2.82)
M1	−0.018	−0.084	−0.027
	(−0.76)	(−2.52)	(−1.52)
M2	−0.005	−0.015	−0.034
	(−0.30)	(−1.14)	(−1.47)

Table 2.2 The relationship between growth and nominal variables (excluding outliers)

| Explanatory variable | Coefficient in growth equation with | | |
	15-year average	1989–93	1991
Inflation	−0.074	−0.053	−0.104
	(−1.25)	(−1.03)	(−1.49)
M1	−0.063	−0.054	+0.011
	(−1.17)	(−1.08)	(−0.18)
M2	−0.023	−0.065	+0.068
	(−0.43)	(−1.16)	(−1.39)

Table 2.3 Iterative 3SLS estimates of real GDP growth,
YG, 1971–94

Explanatory variable	Coefficient
$INFG^2$	–0.029
	(–6.852)
$INFG^3$	0.008
	(5.411)
$\bar{R}^2$	0.154
MG^2	–0.018
	(–4.125)
MG^3	0.003
	(1.684)
$\bar{R}^2$	0.142

Key: YG   Continuously compounded rate of change in real GDP.
$INFG^2$ Square of continuously compounded rate of change in GDP deflator.
$INFG^3$ Cube of continuously compounded rate of change in GDP deflator.
MG^2 Square of continuously compounded rate of change in M2.
MG^3 Cube of continuously compounded rate of change in M2.

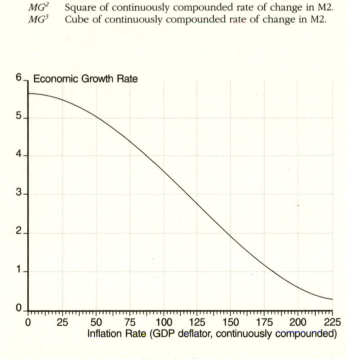

Figure 2.3 Nonlinear effect of inflation on economic growth

money growth using iterative three-stage least squares on a system of equations with the same slope parameters but different intercepts for each country. Furthermore, we deal with the problem of simultaneity by treating inflation and money growth as endogenous variables.[7] Initial tests for nonlinearities indicated that the inclusion of both squared and cubed inflation ($INFG^2$ and $INFG^3$) and money growth rates (MG^2 and MG^3) as explanatory variables for ecónomic growth produced better results than levels ($INFG$ and MG). Table 2.3 reports these estimates (with t values in parentheses) for 41 of the BoE group for the period 1971–94 (860 observations for the inflation estimate and 820 observations for the money growth estimate);[8] Figure 2.3 illustrates the growth–inflation estimate. These latter results give a firmer basis for accepting the growing consensus that inflation reduces growth.

In virtually all cases, the statutory objectives of the central banks in the BoE group include the preservation of the (external and internal) value of the currency; this was mentioned in 28 out of the 33 responses to question F5 of the questionnaire, but only four countries – Argentina, Chile, Cyprus and Mexico – gave it the same priority as the ESCB. In part this is because central bank statutes are amended only at long intervals. Were all the countries in the BoE group to revise their central bank statutes today, we surmise that a larger proportion would give primacy to the achievement of price stability.

Whether the priority given to price stability would or would not be taken as absolute, it is generally given a high priority by the central banks in the BoE group. Yet the results have been mixed in this respect. On average, the experience of the BoE group has been slightly worse than the control group of 79 other developing countries. In both groups, however, it has been much worse than the developed OECD countries, as shown in Table 1.2. That table shows the average mean level of inflation over the last 15 years. Average mean values are, however, susceptible to large outliers. A variety of additional data on CPI inflation are given in Table 2.4 for the BoE group. These data indicate that the disappointing inflation figures are not just the result of a few very high inflation countries distorting the average value. The problem is much more widespread.

Nor is there much evidence that inflationary problems have diminished over time in the BoE group. We compare the same statistical data on inflation for the last five years, 1989–93, with those already shown for 1979–93 in Table 2.4. The mean inflation rate has increased, while the median has diminished slightly. The distribution and standard deviation have become more dispersed and skewed.

Moreover the problem is one of monetary control; inflation is a monetary phenomenon. We rehearse once again, here for the BoE group, the familiar strong positive relationship between inflation and monetary expansion. We regressed inflation against the growth of M1 and M2 as alternative explanatory variables on a cross-country basis over a variety of periods: 15-year average (1979–93), each of the constituent five-year averages and 1991 taken by itself. We show the coefficient on monetary growth, its t value (in parentheses) and the $\bar{R}^2$ (in square brackets) in each case (but not the constant term to save space).

A scatter diagram for the 15-year average (M1) is shown in Figure 2.4. The relationship for 1991 is comparatively much weaker. Evidently the relationship between inflation and monetary expansion is stronger in the medium than in the shorter run. However, the analysis of the relationship between money growth and inflation can be extended and improved by examining an inverted money demand function. This we do in Box B.

Some might argue, though it is not an argument that we ourselves would support, that the responsibility of a central bank for monetary control is less immediate when monetary expansion (or variability) is caused by changes in the money multiplier than when it derives from changes in the reserve base. In fact, as

Table 2.4 The CPI inflation experience in the BoE group

Statistic	15-year average 1979–93	5-year average 1989–93
Mean	32.20	43.56
Median	12.36	11.41
Standard deviation	85.64	171.86
Average in bottom quartile	4.34	3.50
Average in top quartile	103.68	154.12
Maximum	555.84	1,120.19
Minimum	0.68	1.79
Top of Q.1/Q.3	6.57/21.53	5.54/18.92

Table 2.5 Effects of monetary growth on inflation

Explanatory variable	1979–93	1979–83	1984–88	1989–93	1991
M1	1.059	1.127	1.093	1.038	0.730
	(74.9)	(20.9)	(44.1)	(64.6)	(7.0)
	[0.993]	[0.916]	[0.980]	[0.990]	[0.566]
M2	1.258	0.577	1.074	1.456	0.980
	(30.9)	(10.2)	(24.5)	(20.8)	(10.1)
	[0.959]	[0.721]	[0.937]	[0.913]	[0.726]

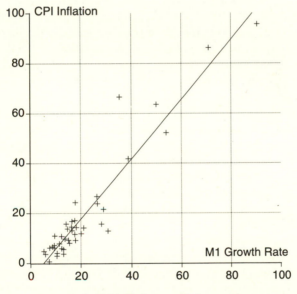

Figure 2.4 CPI inflation and M1 growth rates

expected, the correlations between cross-country changes in the reserve base and in inflation are also very high (1979–93, +0.971; 1989–93, +0.990). A decomposition of monetary expansion (M1 and M2) into that part caused by increases in the reserve base or in the money multiplier revealed no systematic effects (data available on request). Correlations between the *variability* in monetary

21

growth (M1 and M2) and in both the reserve base and the money multiplier revealed that the former at +0.998 and +0.913 respectively were much larger than the latter (+0.009 and +0.038).

During the 15 years of our data period, the median level of inflation in the BoE group was 12.4 per cent, falling to 11.4 per cent over the last five-year average; this compares with 6.4 per cent and 3.6 per cent for the OECD countries. There is perhaps one encouraging feature. Among the worst performers in terms of inflation over the data period were the Latin American countries Argentina, Chile and Mexico. In recent years Argentina and Chile have shown remarkable progress in reducing inflation, as a result of political and economic reforms. Unfortunately, a similar improvement in Mexico was set back by the recent crisis.

Nevertheless the inflationary experiences of the BoE group have been, at best, patchy. Moreover, since inflation is a monetary phenomenon, central banks must bear a considerable share of the responsibility for this state of affairs. Yet, as already noted, most of the BoE group had a statutory requirement to maintain the value of the currency. So why did most of them fail to meet this requirement?

One likely explanation is that central banks were under pressure, for a variety of reasons, to help finance their governments, and those to whom their governments wished to provide financial subsidies. Central banks were not well placed to repel such pressures. Of those who answered question F7, 72 per cent stated that the government could require the central bank to finance its deficit. Of those who answered question F8, 41 per cent stated that central bank financing of that part of the deficit *not* covered by bond sales was automatic, although there were in all cases some statutory limits, as discussed in Chapter 7. Moreover governments, perhaps more so in developing than in OECD countries, have a variety of incentives for, and means of, persuading central banks to provide them with quasi-fiscal services. Therefore, we now turn to this fiscal connection in Chapter 3.

**Box B Monetary growth and inflation:
the relationship refined**

We now refine our analysis of the relationship between monetary expansion and inflation. As discussed further in Chapter 5, the demand for money is a function of the level of prices, real incomes

---

and the rate of inflation, with this latter being a proxy for the relative cost of holding money (rather than other assets). Assuming that the supply of money is affected by a separate (exogenous) set of variables, e.g., government financing needs, we can invert the demand for money function in first difference form to provide an estimate of the rate of inflation as a function of the growth rates of money, real incomes and the change in inflation.

Heteroscedasticity can also be confronted by estimating inflation using iterative three-stage least squares, as we did for the growth rate equations shown in Table 2.3. Table 2.6 reports such an estimate (with t values in parentheses) for 41 of the BoE group for the period 1972–93 (783 observations).[9]

The explanatory variables used in Table 2.6 are taken from a simple money demand function in which real money balances m^d are a positive function of real GDP y and a negative function of the inflation rate π: $m^d = y^\alpha \cdot e^{\beta\pi}$ (Cagan 1956). The variable m^d equals M^d/P, where M^d is the demand for money in nominal terms and P is the price level. The equilibrium condition in the money market can be expressed $M^s = M^d$ or $M^s = P \cdot m^d$, where M^s is the nominal money supply. By combining this market equilibrium condition with the money demand function, $M^s = P \cdot y^\alpha \cdot e^{\beta\pi}$, converting this equation into first difference logarithmic form and rearranging, we obtain: $INFG = b_1(MG) + b_2(YG) + b_3(DINFG)$, where $INFG$ is π, MG is $\Delta\log M$, YG is $\Delta\log Y$ and $DINFG$ is $\Delta\pi$. This inverted money demand function predicts the value of b_1 to equal 1, b_2 to be negative and b_3 to be positive. Evidently, the estimate presented in Table 2.6 is consistent with these theoretical expectations and provides another monetary explanation of inflation.

Table 2.6 Iterative 3SLS estimate of inflation, *INFG*, 1972–93

Explanatory variable	Coefficient
MG	0.909
	(97.201)
YG	−0.510
	(−31.581)
DINFG	0.244
	(27.767)
$\overline{R}^2$	0.818

Key: INFG   Continuously compounded rate of change in GDP deflator.
      MG   Continuously compounded rate of change in M2.
      YG   Continuously compounded rate of change in real GDP.
      DINFG   Change in inflation rate.

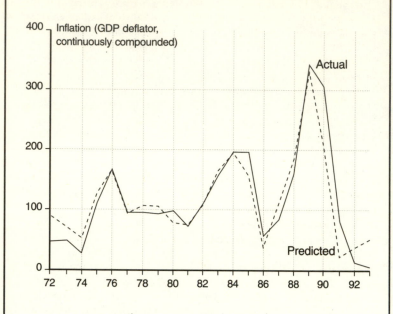

Figure 2.5 Actual and predicted inflation in Argentina

To illustrate the general applicability of the estimate in Table 2.6 to the developing country inflation experience, we re-estimated the equation for only 40 countries of the BoE group and deliberately excluded Argentina. Figure 2.5 shows actual and predicted inflation for Argentina using the estimate in which Argentinian data are excluded. The ability of this estimate to track Argentinian inflation using an estimate based on behaviour in a group of 40 other countries is slightly better than its ability to track inflation in the 40 countries used in the estimate (the $\bar{R}^2$ of an OLS regression of actual on predicted inflation in Argentina is 0.848 compared with the $\bar{R}^2$ of 0.818 for iterative three-stage least squares estimate reported above).

NOTES

1 Figures 2.1 and 2.2 exclude Argentina because it is an extreme outlier.
2 Whereas the mean and the standard deviation of inflation are strongly positively correlated, there is very little correlation between the mean of inflation and its coefficient of variation, i.e., the standard deviation

divided by the mean. The question of what relative weight we should place on the standard deviation or the coefficient of variation can be given a concrete example. Would we regard a move from an average inflation of 1 per cent (or 10 per cent) to 0.8 per cent (or 8.0 per cent) as disturbing and dislocating as a move to 80 per cent from an average inflation of 100 per cent? If we held very long-term assets, the answer could be yes. But once inflation runs at even a moderate level, the length of contracts, asset durations, etc., tend to shorten, so that the standard deviation is more relevant. Furthermore, our main concern is with real variables, real interest and exchange rates. To estimate the future expected level of such real variables, we have to use our best point estimate of future inflation. Hence *both* the coefficient of variation and standard deviation of such *real* variables will be a positive function of the standard deviation (but not of the coefficient of variation) of inflation.

3 The correlations shown in this paragraph were all estimated excluding Argentina whose extraordinary average inflation rate makes it an extreme outlier. If Argentinian data are included, all the correlations rise, with the exception of those between the variability in inflation and the variability in both nominal and real exchange rates. These latter fall sharply towards zero and are no longer significant.

4 Besides the nexus of interrelationships between the variability exhibited in money, inflation and both nominal and real exchange and interest rates, there is a second set of such interrelationships among the BoE group between the variability of the government deficit and the variability in real interest rates, +0.499, in real (but *not* nominal) exchange rates, +0.340, and in output growth, +0.313.

5 The data in Table 2.1 again exclude Argentina for which country we did not obtain all the relevant data until a late stage in the exercise. Argentina is an anomaly in this respect since it combines an extremely high inflation rate with a moderate rate of growth. If Argentina was included with the other countries in Table 2.1, all the coefficients would become less negative, and none would then be significant. The Argentina case clearly weakens the claim that inflation reduces growth, but the experience of this country may be considered an outlier and *sui generis*.

6 Governments, and their central banks, in developing countries are more concerned to foster growth than those in the OECD countries. Consequently they might be more prepared to adopt policies which might seem to promise higher growth but which also risk higher inflation, even though such higher inflation would have an inimical effect on growth. Indeed, an excessively aggressive push for growth at all costs might even lead, counterproductively, to higher inflation and lower growth. In Chapter 7 we seek to assess which of our BoE group of countries might place, *ex ante*, most weight on growth by examining which countries explicitly required their central banks to pursue growth in their statutes.

7 The instruments are lagged inflation, lagged money and output growth rates, oil inflation and the OECD growth rate. The estimation

procedure, which is asymptotically full-information maximum likelihood, automatically corrects for heteroscedasticity across equations and therefore, in this case, across countries (Johnston 1984, pp. 486–490).

8 The necessary data were not available, at least for a sufficiently long time period, for Brunei, Hong Kong and Namibia.

9 All the explanatory variables are treated as endogenous. The instruments are the lagged explanatory variables, oil inflation, the OECD growth rate and the world real interest rate.

3

THE CENTRAL BANK AND
THE GOVERNMENT

The previous chapter has demonstrated a great variety of inflationary and monetary experiences across the BoE group. As we
have already conjectured, might some large part of this variation
be due to the differing pressures that governments have placed on
their central banks? In the OECD countries such pressures are often
ascribed to the myopic desire of governments to engender a
short-term feel-good factor for electoral purposes. In developing
countries such pressures are, perhaps, caused more by the perceived objective of filling a fiscal hole.

Be that as it may, relationships between central banks and their
respective governments differ in their nature, scope and direction.
Some central banks can decline their government's requests for
credit, others cannot (Cottarelli 1993). Some central banks perform
a range of quasi-fiscal activities on behalf of their governments,
while others are prevented from doing so by statute. Given the
symbiotic relationship between a country's monetary and exchange
rate policy regimes, governments constrain central bank behaviour
for better or worse by their choice of exchange rate regime, as
discussed in Chapter 4. In many cases, however, the choice of
exchange rate regime itself is determined by fiscal exigencies.
Fiscal discipline enables greater choice of exchange rate regime,
although an exchange rate regime may be chosen to force fiscal
discipline on future governments. In general, the fiscal stance
determines the viable choice of exchange rate regimes, which in
turn determines the consistent set of monetary policies. In this
view, even the most independent central bank is still constrained
by prior choices of fiscal stance and exchange rate regime.

One reason for the greater prominence of central bank to
commercial bank liabilities in developing countries lies in the

greater use of currency in these countries. However, this fails to explain the extraordinarily high levels of bank reserves in developing countries. While holdings of vault cash are typically higher in developing than in OECD countries, the main explanation lies in the use of financial systems in developing countries as a source of government revenue. In effect, high reserve requirements enable governments to borrow at a zero interest rate through their central banks, either directly or through higher central bank profits. The reliance of developing country governments on their financial systems as a source of revenue is consistent with the higher ratios of government deficits to GDP and the lower ratios of government revenues to GDP in developing countries compared with the OECD countries.

As the Radcliffe Committee (1959, p. 276) recognised, 'monetary policy is now so inextricably connected with the Government's fiscal operations and with the management of debt' that all monetary policy activities have an important fiscal content. The relationship between central banks and governments has received some attention (Majumdar 1974; Mittra 1978; Skanland 1984). Until recently, however, central banks' quasi-fiscal activities and the fiscal aspects of monetary operations have generally been ignored. They cannot be ignored in any analysis of central banking in developing countries simply because in many developing countries they are so large. Their importance is attested by the fact that the government is represented, usually by the most senior civil servant in the Ministry of Finance, on the board of directors in 23 out of 37 central banks in the BoE group.

Table 1.2 shows that consumer price inflation averaged 30 per cent in developing countries compared with 7 per cent in OECD countries over the period 1979–93. Table 1.2 also shows that governments in developing countries borrow a higher proportion from their central banks than from their banking systems as a whole than they do in the OECD countries. Whereas governments in OECD countries borrow 3 per cent of their requirements from their central banks, developing country governments borrow 45 per cent. These comparisons should be set in the context of overall borrowing requirements: governments in the developing countries appropriate 21 per cent of total domestic credit compared with 16 per cent in the OECD countries.

While Table 1.3 indicates that changes have occurred in the BoE group, it also indicates that substantial differences still remain between a representative country in the BoE group and a typical OECD country: the proportion of government borrowing requirements met by the central bank ($CBCG$) seven times higher, inflation six times higher and the reserve/deposit ratio (R/D) almost three times higher, the ratio of reserve money to M2 (H/M) twice as high, and the proportion of total domestic credit appropriated by government ($CGDC$) still 40 per cent higher. Many of these differences reflect not only the less developed nature of the financial sectors in the BoE group but also the greater reliance by their governments on seigniorage and financial repression as revenue sources. While institutional factors are discussed in Chapter 5, this chapter concentrates on the fiscal connection.

Several central bank instruments can serve more than one purpose. Indeed, a number of techniques can be aimed at either monetary control, prudential regulation or implicit taxation of financial intermediation. Reserve requirements and minimum liquid asset ratios can serve all three purposes. While most of the BoE group have imposed or are in the process of imposing the BIS risk-weighted capital adequacy ratio requirements for the purpose of depositor protection, very few have substituted capital adequacy for reserve and liquid asset requirements. Among the respondents to our questionnaire, only Hong Kong, Kuwait and Saudi Arabia stated explicitly that no cash reserve requirement existed.

As anticipated by the fiscal approach, cash reserve requirements are low in countries, such as Kuwait, with ample government revenue. They are also low in countries, such as Bahamas, Fiji, Malta and Singapore, that are competing as international financial centres; noninterest reserve requirements impose a discriminatory tax on financial intermediation. Bangladesh, Barbados, Namibia and Nigeria also impose required reserve ratios in the 5–6 per cent range. A few countries – Chile, Cyprus, Fiji, Malta and South Africa – reimburse part of the reserve requirement tax by paying interest on required reserves. Central banks in Guyana, Hong Kong, Israel and Swaziland pay interest on excess but not required reserves.[1] At the other extreme, however, some countries clearly rely on reserve requirements as an interest-free loan to the government. Noninterest-earning cash reserve ratios of 33 per cent in Argentina, 30 per cent in Lesotho, 25 per cent in Jamaica, 24 per cent in Gambia, 20 per cent in Trinidad and Tobago, 17.5 per cent in Zimbabwe, 16 per cent in Guyana, and 15 per cent in India and Sri Lanka are difficult to interpret in any other way.

A rather similar pattern emerges in comparing required liquid asset ratios, which in many developing countries imply holding treasury bills at below-market yields. Among the questionnaire respondents, Chile, Israel and the United Arab Emirates impose no liquid asset ratio requirements. Elsewhere, these ratios appear high: 50 per cent in Jamaica; 40 per cent in Sierra Leone; 35 per cent in Malawi; 31.5 per cent in India; 30 per cent in Gambia, Jordan and Nigeria; 27 per cent in Barbados and Cyprus; 25 per cent in Guyana, Hong Kong and Pakistan; 24 per cent in Belize; 23 per cent in Mauritius; 20 per cent in Bahamas, Namibia, Sri Lanka, Uganda and Zambia; 18 per cent in Singapore; 17.5 per cent in Swaziland; 17 per cent in Malaysia; 16 per cent in Fiji; 15 per cent in Bangladesh and Saudi Arabia; although only 5 per cent in South Africa and 3 per cent in Kuwait.[2]

Interest rate controls can be designed to prevent cutthroat competition, to dampen money and credit expansion, to stimulate investment in priority sectors and to raise revenue for governments at below-market rates of interest. Enthusiasm over selective, directed or priority credit schemes in the BoE group has waned. Only Bangladesh, Cyprus, Fiji, India, Malaysia, Nigeria and Pakistan maintain controls over their banking systems designed to influence credit allocation to priority sectors. Only in Barbados, Belize, Cyprus, India, Jordan and Singapore does the central bank offer special rediscount facilities for priority sector lending. Implicit subsidies are somewhat more widespread, since the central banks of Bangladesh, Barbados, Nigeria, Pakistan, St Lucia, Solomon Islands, Sri Lanka, Swaziland, Uganda and Zimbabwe guarantee some categories of domestic loans. Fiscal exigencies, however, still appear to constitute the main reason for the maintenance of balance-sheet ratio and interest rate controls. Hence, this chapter focuses on the fiscal or implicit tax use of such instruments.

Governments generally expect to benefit financially from the monopoly privilege over fiat money that they grant to their central banks. Revenue raising activities of central banks have included the collection of seigniorage by issuing currency and imposing reserve requirements, demonetising currency notes of particular denominations, forcing unfavourable conversions of old for new currency after a currency reform, setting interest rate ceilings on financial assets that compete with government bonds, requiring import predeposits, administering multiple exchange rate systems in which exporters are obliged to sell their foreign exchange earnings to the central bank at lower prices than some importers can buy foreign exchange from the central bank, as well as collecting miscellaneous fees (Robinson and Stella 1988, 22–23). Central bank profits and losses can also be affected by revaluations of foreign exchange assets and liabilities. Central banks in some of the BoE countries have generated revenue equal to the government's explicit tax revenue; central bank profits are by no means small beer.

Over the past 25 years, a number of governments have required their central banks to undertake various additional quasi-fiscal activities. These have included allocating subsidised credit to agriculture, exports and development finance institutions through selective credit policies, providing explicit or implicit (below-cost) deposit insurance and bailing out insolvent financial (or even nonfinancial) institutions when necessary, and providing exchange rate subsidies or guarantees, particularly for debt service and essential imports. Interest rate ceilings imposed and enforced by central banks constitute both taxes and subsidies. The taxes are imposed on depositors/lenders, who subsidise priority borrowers.

Not only are central bank quasi-fiscal activities generally both large and opaque to outside observers, they are also extremely difficult to quantify. Even at a conceptual level, several issues emerge. For example, difficulties arise over the measurement of contingent liabilities, as in the case of deposit insurance or loan guarantee programmes. Other problems at this level involve the central bank's accounting conventions, which differ from those of the central government, and the valuation of foreign currency-denominated claims. The most fundamental problem of all concerns the distinction between quasi-fiscal and monetary activities. Central banks may make or lose money in their open-market operations conducted solely for monetary policy purposes. In effect, someone is taxed when the central bank makes a profit, while someone is subsidised when it makes a loss. Inevitably, the distinction between monetary and quasi-fiscal activities is blurred. Therefore, estimating the magnitude of a central bank's quasi-fiscal activities has to involve the formulation and application of accounting conventions that are unique to central banking.

A central bank that is obliged to carry out a wide range of quasi-fiscal activities can hardly aspire to the same degree of independence from government as one which has not been required to assume such activities. Furthermore, quasi-fiscal activities are likely to jeopardise monetary policy designed to maintain price stability. Where quasi-fiscal expenditures exceed seigniorage revenue consistent with a stable price level, the central bank must either resort to the inflation tax or, if price stability is to be maintained, the government must make annual budgetary appropriations to keep the central bank afloat, as has happened in Chile.

SEIGNIORAGE

Issuing currency and providing noninterest-earning bank reserves in the form of deposits held at the central bank is clearly an essential monetary activity of all central banks. However, monetary and fiscal aspects of the monopoly power over currency issue are inextricably intertwined. It is well recognised that this monopoly is a source of government revenue and that the objectives of monetary control conflict with any fiscal objective requiring an issue of reserve money in excess of the amount appropriate for monetary stability. Incompatible monetary and fiscal aspects of issuing reserve money are almost always resolved in favour of the fiscal exigencies, at least in the short run. Thereafter, fiscal reform as part of a stabilisation programme may attempt to reduce or eliminate the conflict.

An analytically intriguing aspect of seigniorage as a tax lies in the ability of the central bank to raise the tax rate by expanding the currency issue. A faster rate of growth in currency issue raises the inflation rate which, in turn, raises nominal interest rates. Hence, the opportunity cost of holding currency in the form of interest forgone rises. From the fiscal perspective, an increase in currency issue of $1 can be treated analytically as $1 borrowed. Implicit tax revenue is raised by the 100 per cent tax on the interest. This tax revenue shows up as central bank profits. The financing item – $1 increase in currency issued – has no net effect on the income statement; the central bank uses the $1 to purchase an interest-earning asset. Increased resort to this form of financing, however, leads to a higher tax rate. Whether it leads to more or less tax revenue in the long run depends, of course, on whether or not the inflation rate is initially above or below its revenue-maximising rate (Friedman 1971).

In the context of the prospective European Central Bank, Martin Klein and Manfred Neumann (1990) and Casper Van Ewijk and Lambertus Scholtens (1992) make the point that not all seigniorage revenue generated by the central bank is automatically transferred to its government.[3] For example, the central bank may retain some profit accruing from seigniorage rather than remit it all to its shareholder(s). In the present context, we show that there are three distinct ways in which a government can appropriate seigniorage. While they produce no fundamental difference in final outcomes, each has a distinct effect on government and central bank accounts.

In the first and simplest way, a central bank holds assets earning market interest rates and liabilities paying no interest; the assets might all be private sector bonds. In this case, the central bank profits should be comparable to seigniorage revenue in the way we calculate it. Implicitly, this allows the central bank to absorb all the real interest rate to cover its costs. Here seigniorage revenue becomes government nontax revenue when the central bank's profits are transferred to the government.

In the second way of appropriating seigniorage revenue, which makes the government accounts look better, the government takes interest-free loans from the central bank. In this case, central bank profits are always zero: no interest is earned on assets, no interest is paid on liabilities. Of course, however, seigniorage revenue now reduces government interest costs rather than raising its revenue.

In the third and final way, the government can reduce its recorded *primary* deficit, the noninterest component of its deficit regarded as particularly important by the International Monetary Fund in its Stand-by negotiations, by requiring its central bank to undertake various fiscal activities on its behalf. In this case, the first call on the seigniorage revenue is the central bank's own expenditures of a fiscal nature.

Whichever way it uses to extract seigniorage, the government can accumulate undistributed seigniorage revenue in its central bank or it can reduce the central bank's net worth by appropriating explicitly or implicitly more than the flow of seigniorage revenue produced over the relevant time period. If the central bank starts any period under analysis with some balance-sheet impairment in the form of substandard assets or assumed liabilities not matched by assets of equal market value, its profits will necessarily be less than seigniorage revenue estimated using the fiscal approach.

One approach to measuring seigniorage is based on a cash flow basis – the increase in reserve money made available as a residual budgetary financing item (Fischer 1982). The fiscal approach, however, treats seigniorage in terms of tax base and tax rate (Bailey 1956; Friedman 1971; Phelps 1973):

As in the usual tax theory, the revenue from the inflation tax is simply the excess of the consumer's price over the producer's price (that is, price including tax less marginal cost) *times* the amount produced and purchased – just like the revenue from any other sort of tax. Hence, in the case where liquidity is costless, it is equal to the money rate of interest times real cash balances.

(Phelps 1973, p. 70)

To provide some orders of magnitude, we estimate seigniorage revenue in the BoE group over the period 1979–93. Several authors have pointed out that there is no unique 'correct' measure of government revenue from inflation (Drazen 1985; Van Ewijk and Scholtens 1992). Here we follow William Easterly, Paolo Mauro and Klaus Schmidt-Hebbel (1995) in defining the tax rate on reserve money as $\pi/(1 + \pi)$, where π is the rate of change in consumer prices from December of the previous year to December of the year in question. The tax base is the December value of the central bank's liabilities in the form of reserve money deflated by the December CPI.[4] The product of the tax rate and the real tax base is then divided by real GDP, where the GDP deflator is re-based, where necessary, to equal 100 in 1990, which is the base year for the CPI.

The two differences between seigniorage revenue from currency and bank reserves are: (a) bank reserves held almost exclusively as deposits in the central bank involve infinitesimal maintenance costs compared with the note issue; and (b) interest may be paid on such deposits so reducing the tax rate. In those countries in the BoE group for which the information has been provided, the range of interest rates paid on required reserves runs from zero in nominal terms to 1.8 per cent in real terms.[5] Where possible, we have adjusted the calculated seigniorage revenue for interest payment on bank reserves. Clearly, however, where indexation is not applied and where nominal interest rates (if any) are sticky, the tax rate on required reserves rises with inflation.

Appendix 4 provides our estimates of seigniorage revenue expressed both as a percentage of GDP and as a percentage of the government's current revenue. On average, the estimated seigniorage revenue equalled 1.5 per cent of GDP in the BoE group over the period 1979–93. Where it yielded an above-average amount, it contributed a proportionally larger amount of government revenue.

On average, a one percentage point increase in the inflation tax in relation to GDP corresponds to an increase in the inflation tax in relation to government current revenue of eight percentage points.

From the commercial banks' viewpoint, required reserves constitute a forced acquisition of an asset on which all interest is taxed away. Under competitive conditions, banks pass the reserve requirement tax on to depositors and borrowers, the incidence depending on relative demand elasticities, in the form of lower deposit rates and higher loan rates (Fry 1995, Ch. 7). Fiscal analysis of this tax is simplified for a small country in which businesses can borrow from the domestic banks or abroad at the world interest rate; in other words, the demand for bank loans is perfectly interest elastic. In this case, the incidence of the reserve requirement tax is borne entirely by depositors. Similarly, currency holders bear the inflation tax on their currency holdings.

FINANCIAL REPRESSION

High inflation and low nominal interest rates are symptoms of financial repression. From the fiscal viewpoint, interest rate ceilings are imposed to stifle competition to public sector fund raising from the private sector. Measures such as the imposition of foreign exchange controls, interest rate ceilings, high reserve requirements and the nondevelopment, or even the suppression, of private capital markets can all increase the flow of domestic resources to the public sector without higher tax, inflation or interest rates (Fry 1973; Nichols 1974).

Selective or sectoral credit policies are common components of financial repression. The techniques employed to reduce the costs of financing government deficits can also be used to encourage private investment in what the government regards as priority activities. Interest rates on loans for such approved investment are subsidised. Selective credit policies necessitate financial repression, since financial channels would otherwise develop expressly for rerouting subsidised credit to uses with highest private returns. For selective credit policies to work at all, financial markets must be kept segmented and restricted.

Nominal interest rate ceilings established to limit competition for government borrowing are highly destabilising in the face of inflationary shocks. Just as deposit rate ceilings in the United States and other OECD countries caused disruptive disintermediation in periods of rising inflation and rising free-market interest rates, so all-embracing interest rate ceilings in developing countries cause destabilising portfolio shifts from financial to tangible assets when inflation accelerates (Lee 1980; Shaw 1975). Clearly such reaction magnifies the initial inflationary shock. Often financial repression in extreme form appears to be the unintended consequence of low, fixed nominal interest rates combined with high and rising inflation.

In countries where there are virtually no markets for direct financial claims, the implicit tax derived from financial repression can be estimated using domestic credit as the tax base and the difference between the exchange rate-adjusted world interest rate and the average domestic rate on the components of domestic credit as the tax rate.[6] Following Alberto Giovannini and Martha de Melo (1993), Appendix 5 presents two estimates of the tax revenue from financial repression, one using a treasury bill or bond yield and the stock of government domestic debt and the other based on a representative lending rate and domestic credit to the private sector. Government revenue from financial repression in the countries for which data exist on treasury bill/bond yields and government debt averaged 2.2 per cent of GDP over the period 1979–93 compared to the inflation tax revenue of 1.5 per cent of GDP. The tax-cum-subsidy involved in institutional lending rates differing from world interest rates adjusted for exchange rate changes averaged 0.6 per cent of GDP.

In the BoE group, instruments of financial repression include liquid asset requirements, priority sector credit allocation, preferential rediscount facilities and credit guarantee schemes. Loan rate ceilings have also been imposed in some of the BoE group: Chile, Cyprus, India, Kuwait, Malta, Nigeria, Solomon Islands and South Africa.[7] In the majority of the BoE group, government bill or bond rates and discount rates are administratively determined. However, there are no administratively set interest rates in Botswana, Brunei, Gambia, Guyana, Mauritius, Mexico, Namibia, Trinidad and Tobago, and Zambia. In Mauritius, for example, Bank Rate is set automatically in relation to the treasury bill auction rate. Changes over the past two decades in the BoE group suggest that financial repression is on the wane as a source of government revenue, perhaps in part as a result of the accumulated evidence of its deleterious effect on economic growth (Fry 1995, Part II).

36

FOREIGN EXCHANGE OPERATIONS

A central bank's foreign exchange activities may also involve both tax and subsidy elements. Foreign exchange has been so undervalued in some developing countries that provision of foreign exchange at the official rate was tantamount to a gift. If the central bank does not make a loss in managing undervalued foreign exchange, much of the cost is borne by exporters. Hence, even with a single exchange rate, the central bank could be imposing taxes and providing subsidies. Given the plethora of distortions that accompany substantial exchange rate disequilibrium, calculation of effective tax and subsidy rates is virtually impossible.

In general, serious central bank losses have occurred from foreign exchange operations, thereby providing a subsidy to someone, only when the timing of domestic currency receipts has been divorced from the timing of foreign currency payments. One feature of the foreign debt problem in a number of developing countries is that debt service payments have been made to the central bank in domestic currency but the central bank has not simultaneously made the corresponding payments in foreign exchange. In the interim, the central bank assumes the foreign exchange liabilities. In this and other ways, foreign exchange liabilities of central banks in a number of developing countries have risen above their foreign exchange assets. Servicing these foreign exchange liabilities eats into seigniorage revenue. The subsidy consists of accepting payment in domestic currency at a nonmarket-clearing exchange rate.[8] Although in no case were crippling foreign exchange losses reported by the BoE group, the central banks of Belize, Fiji, Guyana, India, Jamaica, Malaysia, Malta, Pakistan, Solomon Islands, Swaziland, Uganda and Zambia experienced some losses.[9]

STOCK AND FLOW VARIABLES IN THE CENTRAL BANK'S RELATIONSHIP WITH ITS GOVERNMENT

Fiscal analysis tends to concentrate on flow variables. It is therefore natural to examine central bank quasi-fiscal activities using income statements. Hence, one might be tempted to believe that effects of such activities are confined to the income period under review. The balance-sheet approach, however, shows how central bank quasi-fiscal activities can have a permanent effect on the central bank's profitability (Fry 1995, Ch. 17). A government may use its central bank to bail out a failed financial institution by buying financial assets at greatly inflated values. For any given inflation rate, it makes no difference in present value terms whether the government or the central bank provides the funds. What the government saves today it loses in the future through the reduced profits of its central bank. Conversely, retaining profits and increasing its net worth enables the central bank to provide more resources to the government without increasing inflation at some future time.

The balance-sheet approach illustrates the proposition about the permanent effect of a quasi-fiscal activity that impairs its balance sheet in terms of the reduced net worth of the central bank. Thus, there can be, and often is, an inverse relationship between the current flow of revenue to the government from the central bank's operations and its underlying balance sheet and profitability in the long run. When the central bank's net worth is positive, profits concomitant with this positive net worth necessarily absorb reserve money and so impart a deflationary bias. Conversely, negative net worth necessitates the expansion of reserve money to finance the central bank's deficit. In other words, a healthy central bank balance sheet enables greater noninflationary finance of a government's deficit than can be achieved when the central bank's balance sheet has already been impaired. Some governments appear not to have recognised this fact.[10]

In *flow* terms, we can think of the central bank as the government's golden goose. With an unimpaired balance sheet:

- The free-range goose conducting conservative monetary policy with a fair degree of independence, produces golden eggs in the form of seigniorage worth 0.5 to 1 per cent of GDP (Bahamas, Belize, Hong Kong, Kuwait, Namibia, Papua New Guinea, Saudi Arabia, United Arab Emirates).
- The battery farm goose, bred specially for intensive egg-laying, can produce golden eggs in the form of an inflation tax yielding 5 to 10 per cent of GDP (as has happened in Chile, Guyana, Mexico, Sierra Leone).
- The force-fed goose can produce revenue of up to 25 per cent of GDP for a limited period before the inevitable demise of the goose and collapse of the economy (Argentina until 1991, Chile in the early 1970s).

All three forms of central bank geese have been sighted in recent years.

In *stock* terms, the central bank is an asset whose value derives from its monopoly over legal tender. With an unimpaired balance sheet and an obligation to maintain price stability, governments could privatise their central banks expecting to achieve a price in the region of 50 per cent of GDP. This figure is produced by discounting 1 per cent of GDP forever at a 2 per cent discount factor derived from a 5 per cent real interest rate and 3 per cent growth rate. Under an obligation to maintain inflation stability (i.e., no surprise inflation), a typical central bank with a revenue-maximising inflation rate of, say, 20 per cent a month could be sold for about 350 per cent of GDP (based on same discount factor as before).

Many central banks are no longer in the pristine textbook condition in which they hold assets earning market-determined interest rates and have liabilities on which they pay no interest. In part as a response to IMF pressures to reduce fiscal deficits, a number of governments have required their central banks to undertake various quasi-fiscal activities, such as operating directed credit policies with subsidised rediscount rates, subsidising implicit or explicit deposit insurance, bailing out insolvent financial institutions, providing exchange rate guarantees, etc. Obviously, if the government expropriates central bank assets or burdens it with additional liabilities in these ways, the central bank's present value falls and, of course, its ability to lay golden eggs is thereby reduced.

Indeed, not only can and do central banks make losses, they can go bust if their governments burden them with sufficient quasi-fiscal activities. At the extreme, a central bank's balance sheet could become sufficiently impaired to ensure negative net worth at all steady-state inflation rates. The Central Bank of Argentina was essentially in this position at the end of 1989. In a case like this, the government has killed the golden goose that laid the golden eggs.

In several developing countries, central banks are no longer profitable even with double-digit inflation. Appendix 4 shows that central bank profits are typically well below our estimates of seigniorage revenue.[11] Indeed, losses were reported in their most recent accounting period by Chile, Guyana, Jamaica, Malaysia, Sierra Leone and Uganda. While 1993 inflation was only 7.7 per cent in Guyana, 3.5 per cent in Malaysia and 6.1 per cent in Uganda, it was 12.7 per cent in Chile, 22.1 per cent in Jamaica and

22.2 per cent in Sierra Leone. Sharp reductions in inflation, except in Chile and Malaysia, have exposed the fact that the central banks in these countries have become unprofitable at more moderate inflation rates. The Banco Central de Chile is still subject to the effects of recapitalising the banking system after its renationalisation in 1983, and Bank Negara Malaysia suffered extraordinary foreign exchange losses, unrelated to foreign exchange guarantees, in 1993 and 1994.

In general, the differences between reported profits and estimated seigniorage revenues in Appendix 4 are far larger than any conceivable expenditure on normal central banking activities, such as maintaining the quality of the note issue. In most cases, even the most extravagant expenditure on salaries and staff benefits could account for only a small fraction of this discrepancy. In fact, the lion's share of the difference is due to the impairment of central banks' balance sheets by the acquisition of substandard assets and of liabilities not matched by assets of equal value. Many central banks have acquired substandard assets through preferential rediscount policies and by bailing out insolvent financial institutions. They have also acquired liabilities not matched by assets of equal value in accepting domestic currency payments for foreign debts when not possessing the corresponding foreign exchange. Illustrating the proposition that quasi-fiscal activities can have permanent effects on central bank profitability, five of these central bank golden geese have expired under a costly burden of quasi-fiscal activities and those of Argentina, Botswana, India, Jordan, Pakistan, Zambia and Zimbabwe have gone broody.[12]

When a central bank is solvent, its profits can supplement government revenue. When a central bank is insolvent, defined here as the inability to be profitable at any steady-state inflation rate, the government will eventually have to transfer resources in the opposite direction (Fry 1992). In other words, the government will have to remove at least part of the quasi-fiscal burden previously placed on the central bank. Even when it comes to the central bank's money monopoly, resources are finite: there is still no such thing as a free lunch.

A MONETARY POLICY REACTION FUNCTION

While this chapter may have implied so far that central banks are impotent in the face of rapacious financing demands from

40

government, there exists one degree of freedom in their balance sheets which central banks may exploit, at least to some extent. To pursue a monetary target, the central bank in any open economy operates to control domestic credit expansion. Hence, if the government's demands would otherwise produce inflationary domestic credit expansion, the central bank could react by reducing credit to the private sector. In Mauritius, for example, the government is confronted with this stark choice at each monthly meetings of the Monetary Policy Committee. Within the accepted financial programming framework for the year, excessive government borrowing must be countered by a credit squeeze, with all its economic and political ramifications, on the private sector. In Box C we estimate the extent to which BoE central banks have neutralised government credit expansion by reducing credit to the private sector.

The estimated monetary policy reaction function presented in Table 3.1 of Box C indicates that collectively the BoE group has not neutralised the impact of increased government borrowing on aggregate domestic credit expansion. Another study of monetary policy reaction functions for 27 developing countries reports similar findings (Fry 1995, p. 250). In this latter study, the summed coefficient of current and lagged changes in the government borrowing requirement indicates that aggregate domestic credit is expanded by 85 per cent of any increase in net domestic credit to the government for a control group of 21 countries. However, in six Pacific Basin developing countries (Indonesia, Korea, Malaysia, Philippines, Taiwan and Thailand), aggregate domestic credit was increased by only 33 per cent of the increase in net domestic credit to the government. In other words, the central banks of these Pacific Basin developing countries reduced domestic credit to the private sectors by 67 per cent of any increase in their governments' credit requirements.

Box C Estimates of a monetary policy reaction function for the BoE group by independence

To examine the extent to which central banks in the BoE group have neutralised government credit expansion by reducing private sector credit, we estimate a monetary policy reaction function for the BoE group. Following the early work on monetary policy reaction functions by Grant Reuber (1964) and Richard Froyen

---

(1974), central bank objectives have typically been taken to include a balance-of-payments target, an inflation target and possibly some response to exogenous shocks such as changes in the terms of trade. Here, we include a variable that enables us to measure the extent to which the central banks in the BoE group have neutralised increased credit requirements of the government by concomitantly squeezing private sector credit availability.

We specify this particular monetary policy reaction function in terms of the change in domestic credit scaled by GDP *DDCY*, the intermediate target of monetary policy in most open economies. As the first explanatory variable, we include the change in net foreign assets of the banking system adjusted for exchange rate changes and scaled by GDP *DNFAY* to detect any systematic sterilisation of the effects of such asset acquisition on the money supply. Complete sterilisation implies a coefficient of −1. The monetary authorities might squeeze domestic credit in response to a widening gap between domestic inflation and inflation in the United States *INFGAP*. If they do, the coefficient of this variable would be negative. Finally, the monetary authorities might squeeze domestic credit to the private sector when the credit requirements of the government, as measured by the change in net domestic credit to the government scaled by GDP *DDCGY*, increase. A complete neutralisation of the government's extra borrowing requirements would imply a coefficient of zero for *DDCGY* in this monetary policy reaction function. Partial neutralisation would produce a coefficient greater than zero but less than 1.

The equations reported in Table 3.1 are estimated using iterative three-stage least squares. The variables *DNFAY* and *INFGAP* are treated as endogenous; the instruments are the remaining explanatory variables, lagged *DNFAY*, lagged *INFGAP*, the lagged money growth rate, oil inflation, the OECD growth rate and the world real interest rate. The estimation procedure is, asymptotically, full-information maximum likelihood.

Column 2 shows the estimate using a system of 41 equations with the same slope parameters but different intercepts for each country using data for the period 1972–93. The necessary data were not available, at least for a sufficiently long time period, for Brunei, Hong Kong and Namibia. Of note here is the fact that there is no sign of any neutralisation of additional government borrowing through credit squeezes on the private sectors in these 41 countries. Indeed, the summed coefficients of the current and lagged changes in the government borrowing requirement indicate that domestic credit is expanded by 112.5 per cent of any increase in net domestic credit to the government.

Table 3.1 Iterative 3SLS estimates of monetary policy reaction function *DDCY* by independence, 1972–93

(1) Explanatory variable	*(2)* All (776 obs.)	*(3)* No gov. rep. (256 obs.)	*(4)* Gov. rep. (416 obs.)	*(5)* No auto (394 obs.)	*(6)* Auto (278 obs.)
DNFAY	−0.056	−0.047	−0.190	−0.054	−0.175
	(−11.963)	(−3.098)	(−12.737)	(−5.022)	(−6.118)
DNFAY$_{t-1}$	0.074	0.007	0.047	0.010	0.047
	(19.341)	(0.548)	(3.935)	(1.025)	(2.318)
INFGAP	0.047	0.013	0.023	0.011	0.022
	(23.579)	(1.782)	(5.343)	(1.929)	(3.976)
DDCGY	1.084	0.987	0.824	0.964	0.846
	(191.259)	(53.550)	(45.072)	(69.526)	(26.195)
DDCGY$_{t-1}$	0.041	−0.005	−0.046	−0.001	−0.039
	(8.399)	(−0.315)	(−2.835)	(−0.057)	(−1.442)
$\bar{R}^2$	0.934	0.952	0.773	0.940	0.776

Key:
No gov. rep.	No government representative on central bank Board.
Gov. rep.	Government representative appointed to central bank Board.
No auto	Government deficit not automatically financed by central bank.
Auto	Government deficit automatically financed by central bank.
DDCY	Change in domestic credit/GDP.
DNFAY	Change in net foreign assets (adjusted for exchange rate changes)/GDP.
INFGAP	Difference between domestic and US inflation.
DDCGY	Change in net domestic credit to the government/GDP.

We split the BoE group into sub-groups classified by characteristics that might affect the extent to which government borrowing would be neutralised. Dividing the BoE group into sub-groups characterised by high and low reserve ratio requirements, high and low liquid asset ratio requirements and the existence, or not, of open-market operations produced estimates that were not significantly different from one another. However, the estimate for 23 central banks that have government officials on their Boards does differ from the estimate for 13 central banks that do not. We also find the estimate for 14 central banks that meet their governments' borrowing needs automatically differs significantly from the estimate for 22 central banks that do not.[13]

The estimates presented in Table 3.1 show that central banks *without* government officials on their Boards allowed aggregate domestic credit to increase by 99 per cent of any increase in government borrowing, whereas central banks with government officials on their Boards permitted aggregate domestic credit to increase by 82.4 per cent of any increase in government borrowing in the current year and reduced aggregate domestic credit by 4.6 per cent in the following year. This implies that credit to the private sector was reduced by 22.3 per cent of the increased government borrowing in this sub-group. Similarly, we find that central banks that do *not* lend automatically to meet their governments' financing requirements allowed aggregate domestic credit to rise by 99 per cent of any increase in government borrowing, whereas central banks that do lend automatically permit aggregate domestic credit to expand by 84.6 per cent of increased government borrowing in the current year and reduce it by 3.9 per cent in the next year, implying a reduction in credit to the private sector of 19.3 per cent of any increased government borrowing.

While evidence of neutralisation by some sub-groups of BoE central banks exists, the magnitudes are by no means large, particularly in comparison with neutralisation coefficients estimated for the six Pacific Basin developing countries mentioned above. The somewhat paradoxical conclusion of this empirical work is that greater government involvement in and control over central banks may result in greater recognition of the need to trade-off government and private sector credit allocation within a noninflationary framework. On the other hand, it may be that, in countries where governments are not so dependent on their central banks, increased government borrowing requirements can be met without squeezing the private sector because these requirements remain within an expansion of aggregate domestic credit that does not jeopardise monetary control. In fact, the former explanation seems more plausible than the latter.

For all 41 countries used in this analysis, the mean value of the annual increase in domestic credit averaged 8.3 per cent of GDP. Differences in mean values of domestic credit expansion for countries with low and high required reserve and liquid asset ratios and for countries that conduct and do not conduct open-market operations are insignificant. However, the mean value of domestic credit expansion for countries *without* government officials on their central bank Boards is 11.9 per cent, while the mean value of domestic credit expansion for countries with government officials on their central bank Boards is only 4.6 per cent. Similarly, the mean value of domestic credit expansion for countries *without* automatic government borrowing rights from their central bank is 8 per cent, while the mean value of domestic credit expansion for countries with automatic government borrowing rights from their central bank is 6.3 per cent. In other words, greater govern- ment involvement in and control over central banks is associated with lower rates of domestic credit expansion, in part due to the neutralisation of government borrowing on aggregate domestic credit expansion through reductions in private sector credit.

NOTES

1 Since, in the absence of rapid compilation of monetary statistics, fluctuating excess reserve holdings can jeopardise monetary control, we assume that data compilation is rapid or that monetary policy is not aimed at controlling monetary aggregates in countries paying interest on excess reserves.

2 One problem that we have been unable to resolve is that some liquid asset ratios are inclusive of cash reserves, as in Malawi and Sierra Leone, while most are not, as in India and Mauritius.

3 In his comment on our presentation at the Bank of England Symposium, Stanley Fischer also stressed the fact that tax paid does not necessarily equal tax received.

4 This is line 14 'reserve money' in *International Financial Statistics*. In Israel's case, however, we subtract the foreign currency component (line 14cf) of reserve money.

5 Brazil's central bank has paid 7.3 per cent after monetary correction (indexation) in the case of the 20 per cent reserve requirement against savings deposits. In this case, the tax on these required reserves must be zero if not negative at all rates of inflation.

6 In Turkey, for example, lending interest rates were held at least 20 percentage points below world rates in 1979. With domestic credit averaging TL715 billion, the financial repression tax was TL143 billion or 6.5 per cent of GDP. Clearly, this was also the value of the interest rate subsidy to borrowers, including the government.

7 In Kuwait, loan rate ceilings of 2.5 per cent above the discount rate for short-term loans and 4 per cent above the discount rate for long-term loans are instruments of prudential regulation rather than financial repression.

8 One example of central bank foreign exchange losses is provided by the Central Bank of Turkey's foreign exchange risk insurance scheme. The central bank absorbed the foreign exchange rate risk by passing on foreign exchange loans to borrowers in domestic currency at an interest rate averaging 29.7 per cent over the period 1984–88, 15

percentage points below the average annual rate of depreciation of the Turkish lira over the same period. In 1988, the subsidy involved in this foreign exchange scheme represented 0.6 per cent of GDP. The buildup of foreign exchange liabilities was simply not matched by the acquisition of assets of equal value. Venezuela initiated a similar foreign exchange rate guarantee scheme in 1983. Registration of private external debt was completed in 1986, just prior to a 93 per cent devaluation of the bolívar from B7.50 to B14.50 to the US dollar in December 1986. The Venezuelan authorities maintained a rate of B4.30 for registered private sector debt service and B7.50 for 'essential' imports. The switch from central bank profit on foreign exchange operations in 1986 to losses in 1987 represented 3.2 per cent of GDP. In Venezuela's case, the central bank's profits and losses from foreign exchange operations were consolidated with the central government's accounts.

9 Another quasi-fiscal activity that has been used surprisingly little by the BoE group involves deposit insurance schemes. To the extent that the insurance premiums (zero where no explicit deposit insurance exists) do not cover the risk, the central bank provides a subsidy to the banking industry. Since the subsidy takes the form of a contingent liability for the central bank, the outlays in the form of recapitalising insolvent financial institutions tend to be very uneven. In fact, central banks have not borne the costs of recapitalising insolvent financial institutions in all countries. In any event, however, the costs borne by central banks in some developing countries have been a relatively high fraction (over 10 per cent in Chile) of GDP. This subject is discussed at greater length in Chapter 6.

10 The US government provides an example in the case of the savings-and-loan débâcle.

11 While a variety of methods exist for estimating seigniorage revenue, the one adopted here deliberately provides figures at the lower end of the range.

12 This classification is based on inflation tax revenue exceeding profits by more than 1 per cent of GDP over the period 1989–93.

13 Of the 39 respondents to the questionnaire from which we obtained data on Board representation and automatic government access to its central bank, one did not answer these questions and three (Brunei, Hong Kong and Namibia) were excluded because of other data deficiencies. Hence, these sets of estimates include 35 countries in the BoE group.

4

CENTRAL BANKS' EXTERNAL ACTIVITIES

Monetary and exchange rate policies are closely related in all countries:

> Monetary policy determines the value of domestic money in terms of domestic goods. Foreign exchange rate policy determines the value of domestic money in terms of foreign goods. These two values of money must eventually coincide. In the absence of free capital mobility, the identity between monetary and exchange rate policies is likely to hold only in the very long run. But when capital movements are unrestricted – a condition toward which many countries are now moving – monetary and exchange rate policies become inextricably linked, even in the short run.
>
> (Cottarelli 1994, p. 331)

In some countries the foreign exchange rate regime dominates or constrains monetary policy, while in others the opposite is true. In a number of countries fiscal exigencies are the overriding determinant of the monetary–foreign exchange regime choice: rapid and uncontrollable monetary expansion makes a float virtually inevitable. In all countries fiscal stance, monetary policy and the foreign exchange rate regime are closely intertwined.

All central banks conduct at least some foreign exchange operations for their clients. Most central banks also undertake foreign exchange operations on their own account to influence the domestic currency's value in the foreign exchange markets. Only in the case of a pure float does the central bank not intervene for this purpose. Since a pure float is incompatible with any exchange controls, only one country in the BoE group (Gambia) can be identified as a pure floater.

Central bank intervention in the country's foreign exchange markets takes a variety of forms in the BoE group. Some central banks act as market maker, in effect requiring all purchases and sales of foreign exchange to pass through the central bank at its announced price. Such market making occurs in both spot and forward markets in several countries of the BoE group. In contrast, some central banks intervene as a market player in a passive mode without announcing any price but rather choosing when and at what price to take up offers from other participants. In some cases, passive intervention may be conducted anonymously through dealers acting in confidence on the central bank's behalf.

Table 4.1 illustrates the variety of foreign exchange regimes in the BoE group.[1] Column 2 indicates whether the country has signed the International Monetary Fund's Article VIII agreement on currency convertibility for current account transactions. In this group, 27 countries are Article VIII countries, while 16 are not. Column 3 attempts to classify the present exchange rate regime in terms of a fixed exchange rate *vis-à-vis* a single currency 'A',[2] a managed exchange rate possibly targeted on the value of a basket of currencies 'B', or a floating exchange rate 'C'. Some countries, e.g., Argentina and Mexico, have adopted their present regime only very recently and are classified under their earlier regime for analytical purposes.[3] In some cases, the classification is not clear cut, e.g., Nigeria has both fixed and floating exchange rates. In others, the same classification is associated with different objectives. For example, Israel and Singapore both manage their exchange rates. However, Israel sets a depreciation rate in line with the difference between domestic and foreign inflation, while Singapore has appreciated its exchange rate to achieve price stability. Over the period 1979–93, fixed exchange rate countries devalued by 21 per cent, managed exchange rate countries by 56 per cent and floaters by 92 per cent against the US dollar. The devaluation by fixed exchange rate countries was in large part due to the inclusion of countries with currencies fixed to the South African rand which has itself been devalued against the dollar. Real exchange rates were substantially less volatile under fixed and managed exchange rate regimes than they were under floating exchange rate regimes.

Columns 4 and 5 indicate whether there are restrictions on current account payments and surrender requirements for export proceeds. Eighteen of the group impose some restrictions on current account payments, while 25 do not. Thirty-two countries

Table 4.1 Foreign exchange regimes in the Bank of England group

Country	Article VIII	Forex regime	CA restric.	Export surr.	Forward market	CB cover	Forex control
Argentina	Yes	C	No	No	Yes	No	Yes
Bahamas	Yes	A	No	Yes	Yes	No	Yes
Bangladesh	No	B	Yes	Yes	Yes	Yes	Yes
Barbados	Yes	A	No	Yes	Yes	Yes	Yes
Belize	Yes	A	No	Yes	No	No	Yes
Botswana	No	B	Yes	Yes	Yes	No	Yes
Chile	Yes	B	Yes	Yes	No	No	Yes
Cyprus	Yes	A	No	Yes	Yes	Yes	Yes
Fiji	Yes	B	No	Yes	Yes	No	Yes
Gambia	Yes	C	No	Yes	No	No	No
Ghana	No	C	Yes	Yes	No	No	Yes
Guyana	Yes	C	No	Yes	No	No	Yes
Hong Kong	Yes	A	No	No	Yes	No	No
India	No	B	Yes	Yes	Yes	Yes	Yes
Israel	Yes	B	No	Yes	Yes	No	Yes
Jamaica	Yes	C	Yes	No	Yes	Yes	Yes
Jordan	No	B	Yes	Yes	Yes	No	Yes
Kenya	No	C	Yes	Yes	Yes	No	Yes
Kuwait	Yes	B	No	No	Yes	Yes	No
Lesotho	No	A	No	Yes	Yes	No	Yes
Malawi	No	C	Yes	Yes	No	No	Yes
Malaysia	Yes	B	No	Yes	Yes	No	Yes
Malta	No	B	Yes	Yes	Yes	Yes	Yes
Mauritius	Yes	B	No	Yes	Yes	No	No
Mexico	Yes	B	No	No	Yes	No	No
Namibia	No	A	Yes	Yes	Yes	Yes	Yes
Nigeria	No	C	Yes	Yes	No	No	Yes
Pakistan	No	B	Yes	Yes	Yes	Yes	Yes
Papua New Guinea	Yes	B	No	Yes	Yes	Yes	Yes
St Lucia	Yes	A	No	Yes	No	No	Yes
Saudi Arabia	Yes	A	No	No	Yes	No	Yes
Sierra Leone	No	C	Yes	Yes	No	No	Yes
Singapore	Yes	B	No	No	Yes	No	No
Solomon Islands	Yes	B	No	Yes	Yes	Yes	Yes
South Africa	Yes	B	No	Yes	Yes	Yes	Yes
Sri Lanka	Yes	B	No	No	Yes	No	Yes
Swaziland	Yes	A	No	Yes	Yes	No	Yes
Tanzania	No	C	Yes	No	Yes	No	Yes
Trinidad and Tobago	Yes	C	No	No	Yes	No	Yes
Uganda	Yes	C	Yes	Yes	Yes	No	Yes
United Arab Emirates	Yes	A	No	No	Yes	Yes	No
Zambia	No	C	Yes	Yes	No	No	Yes
Zimbabwe	No	B	Yes	Yes	Yes	Yes	Yes

Key: A – fixed; B – managed; C – floating.

require export proceeds to be surrendered to authorised foreign exchange dealers, while 11 countries have no such requirement. Column 6 provides information about the existence of markets in forward foreign exchange transactions; 33 countries permit at least some authorised foreign exchange dealers to operate in forward markets, while there are no forward foreign exchange markets in 10 countries. Column 7 indicates that 14 central banks offer forward cover, while 29 do not. Finally, column 8 shows that foreign exchange controls exist in 36 of 43 countries in the BoE group.

Table 4.1 demonstrates that the group is fairly evenly divided among fixed (11), managed (19) and floating (13) exchange rate regimes. While 22 out of 40 questionnaire respondents indicate that the exchange rate regime was decided, at least in part, by the central bank (question C2), it was determined solely by the government in 11 cases. In the other cases, it was a matter of historical accident or inheritance.[4]

Perhaps of more interest is the reason behind the choice of exchange rate regime. Optimum currency area or dominance by a large neighbour explains most cases of definitively fixed exchange rates (Bahamas, Barbados, Belize, Cyprus, Lesotho, Namibia, St Lucia and Swaziland). However, its use as a nominal anchor lies behind Hong Kong's choice of a fixed exchange rate and oil exports priced in US dollars behind the same choice by Saudi Arabia and the United Arab Emirates. Interestingly, only Israel and Hong Kong appear to use the exchange rate explicitly (although Singapore uses it implicitly) as a nominal anchor. Argentina adopted its recent fixed exchange rate regime 'as the only way to guarantee its [the peso's] use by the public and allow the government to collect seigniorage' in the aftermath of hyperinflation and currency substitution in the 1980s.

Various reasons were given for the choice of a managed but not fixed exchange rate. Perhaps the greater flexibility it provides lay behind the responses from Bangladesh and Sri Lanka that the choice was dictated by the liberalisation process. Other reasons include balance-of-payments equilibrium (Chile and South Africa), maintaining export competitiveness (India and Pakistan), unspecified trade-related advantages (Botswana, Malaysia, Malta and Solomon Islands), and exchange rate stability (Jordan and Kuwait).[5] As already pointed out above, Israel uses its managed exchange rate as a nominal anchor through a crawling peg designed to decelerate domestic inflation towards the world average.

Floating exchange rates were chosen on the grounds of balance-of-payments equilibrium (Gambia and Malawi), liberalisation (Jamaica, Uganda and Zambia), avoidance of speculative attacks (Mexico), avoidance of appreciation in the real exchange rate (Nigeria), and consistency with market-based economic policy (Sierra Leone).

Intervention in the foreign exchange market is decided by the central bank in most of the BoE group, in four cases after consultation with the government. In Argentina, Hong Kong and South Africa, the government takes responsibility for this decision. There was however more involvement by governments in the decisions over exchange controls, although 19 out of 27 central banks played some role in these decisions. Of 12 in the BoE group, this question was not applicable since there are no exchange controls. Almost invariably the central bank administers exchange controls, the exceptions being the Eastern Caribbean Central Bank (St Lucia). In Nigeria and South Africa, both the central bank and the government administer controls.

Governments are responsible for their foreign borrowing decisions in all the BoE group respondent countries, except Kuwait. In the main, governments also make their own arrangements for borrowing abroad; the exceptions are Barbados, Cyprus, Malaysia, Namibia and Saudi Arabia. In Malawi and Zambia, the central bank and the government work together in arranging foreign loans.

Foreign exchange guarantees are provided by Belize, Cyprus, Guyana, Malta, Pakistan, Singapore and Swaziland. Foreign exchange losses by central banks have been associated with foreign exchange guarantees, but in some countries also with other events, in Belize, Chile, Fiji, Guyana, India, Jamaica, Malta, Pakistan, Solomon Islands, Swaziland and Zambia.

Perhaps of greatest significance is the fact that the choice of exchange rate regime is associated with the size of the government's deficit. Using average deficits over the period 1979–93, countries with fixed exchange rates posted deficits of 1.6 per cent of GDP compared with 8.9 per cent in countries with floating exchange rates; countries with managed exchange rates averaged government deficits of 4.1 per cent of GDP.[6] The exchange rate regime is also associated with a country's foreign debt level: fixed exchange rate countries averaged foreign debts equal to 38 per cent of GDP compared with 101 per cent of GDP for floating exchange rate countries. Again, managed exchange rate countries are between the two, but nearer the fixed rate countries, with debt/GDP ratios averaging 47 per cent of GDP.

The exchange rate regime is also associated with differences in the ratio of reserve money to M2, inflation and economic growth. The ratios of reserve money to M2 for fixed, managed and floating exchange rate countries averaged 24, 30 and 45 per cent, respectively, over the period 1979–93.[7] For the same country groups, inflation averaged 8, 16 and 74 per cent, while growth averaged 3.7, 4 and 1.7 per cent. Countries with export surrender requirements experienced growth averaging 1.8 per cent annually compared with growth averaging 3.7 per cent in countries without such restrictions. Given the well-documented link between export and output growth rates (Dollar 1992; Feder 1982), this association could be due to overvalued exchange rates and hence slower export growth in those countries that impose export surrender requirements.

The monetary policy reaction function presented in Chapter 3 can also throw light on the extent to which the central banks in the BoE group have sterilised the impact of changes in net foreign assets on the money supply and have reacted to terms-of-trade changes and foreign debt buildup. Estimates for this purpose are presented in Box D.

The estimates presented in Table 4.2 of Box D suggest that the BoE central banks as a whole have not sterilised the impact of changes in net foreign assets on the money supply by changing domestic credit in the opposite direction. However, central banks under fixed exchange rates have sterilised 26.5 per cent of any change in net foreign assets compared with 3.2 per cent for floaters and 10.4 per cent for managed exchange rate central banks. Furthermore, fixed-rate central banks neutralised 26.2 per cent of any increase in net domestic credit to the government by reducing domestic credit to the private sector compared with –12.5 per cent for managed-rate and 6.8 per cent for floaters. Central banks under fixed exchange rates increased domestic credit after improvements in terms of trade by less than the other groups. Finally, their reaction to foreign debt buildup has been substantially greater than the reactions of the other two sub-groups.

While the estimates presented in Table 4.2 of Box D suggest that central banks operating under fixed exchange rates reacted more conservatively and in a less inflationary manner to shocks in the forms of changes in net foreign assets, government borrowing requirements, terms of trade and foreign debt ratios, an explanation for these consistently different responses requires additional information. On the one hand, conservative central banks may have enabled the adoption of fixed exchange rate regimes. On the other hand, fixed exchange rate regimes may have forced central banks to adopt more conservative monetary policy stances. In our view, both explanations are probably correct, since the choice of fixed exchange rate regimes and the ability of central banks to pursue conservative monetary policy are interdependent and both influenced to a large extent by the country's fiscal stance. Nevertheless, fixed exchange rate regimes are associated with more conservative monetary policy stances than those adopted by central banks under managed or floating exchange rate regimes.

Box D Estimates of a monetary policy reaction function for the BoE group by exchange rate regime

Table 4.2 presents four estimates of the monetary policy reaction function. In addition to the explanatory variables used in the reaction functions presented in Table 3.1, these estimates also include the lagged rate of change in the terms of trade *TTG* and the lagged ratio of foreign debt to GDP *DTY*. The estimate in column 2 for all 41 countries indicates that the group as a whole has not sterilised the impact of changes in net foreign assets on the money supply by changing domestic credit in the opposite direction; complete sterilisation implies a coefficient of −1. However, the central banks in the BoE group as a whole decrease domestic credit expansion in response to a deterioration in their terms of trade. Rather than accommodating higher world-market oil prices through monetary expansion, for example, the BoE group reacted by tightening monetary policy to resist incipient inflationary pressures.[8] Finally, the BoE group also tightened credit conditions significantly, but to only a small extent, when foreign debt ratios rose.

Again, these results are similar to those reported elsewhere for a sample of 27 developing countries (Fry 1995, p. 250). The control group in that sample sterilised only 12 per cent of any change in net foreign assets, while the six Pacific Basin developing countries sterilised 41 per cent of any increase in the banking system's net foreign assets. The small sterilisation coefficient for this control group and non-existent sterilisation coefficient for the BoE group may be due to the fact that some countries actually increased domestic credit when net foreign assets rose. Arturo Porzecanski (1979, pp. 434–435) found that Mexico and Venezuela accelerated domestic credit expansion when net foreign assets increased; the

Table 4.2 Iterative 3SLS estimates of monetary policy reaction function *DDCY* by exchange rate regime, 1972–93

(1) Explanatory variable	(2) All (780 obs.)	(3) Fixed (155 obs.)	(4) Managed (360 obs.)	(5) Floating (261 obs.)
DNFAY	−0.048	−0.328	−0.090	−0.030
	(−10.219)	(−9.338)	(−4.418)	(−2.293)
DNFAY$_{t-1}$	0.074	0.063	−0.014	−0.002
	(18.493)	(2.043)	(−0.812)	(−0.171)
INFGAP	0.049	0.040	0.012	0.023
	(21.646)	(1.647)	(1.549)	(3.815)
DDCGY	1.093	0.713	1.086	0.962
	(187.734)	(17.252)	(47.339)	(44.383)
DDCGY$_{t-1}$	0.061	0.025	0.039	−0.030
	(12.266)	(0.674)	(1.875)	(−1.459)
TTG$_{t-1}$	0.024	0.010	0.028	0.019
	(17.411)	(0.893)	(4.869)	(4.863)
DTY$_{t-1}$	−0.014	−0.058	0.000	−0.008
	(−13.370)	(−4.743)	(0.049)	(−3.440)
$\bar{R}^2$	0.936	0.894	0.929	0.954

Key:
DDCY   Change in domestic credit/GDP.
DNFAY   Change in net foreign assets (adjusted for exchange rate changes)/GDP.
INFGAP   Difference between domestic and US inflation.
DDCGY   Change in net domestic credit to the government/GDP.
TTG   Rate of change in terms of trade.
DTY   Foreign debt/GDP.

same phenomenon has been detected in Turkey (Fry 1988, pp. 90–98). In these countries, domestic credit was increased when foreign exchange receipts rose so that a larger volume of capital equipment and raw material imports could be financed. Rather than contracting domestic credit to sterilise foreign exchange inflows, these central banks reacted by expanding domestic credit to stimulate investment and growth. Apparently, the inflationary consequences of the concomitant monetary expansion were either ignored or considered a price worth paying.

Table 4.2 also provides separate estimates of monetary policy reaction functions for sub-groups of countries classified by their exchange rate regime: for fixed exchange rate countries in column 3, managed exchange rate countries in column 4 and floating exchange rate countries in column 5. Evidently, monetary policy reactions of central banks operating under a fixed exchange rate regime differ substantially from reactions of central banks under floating exchange rates. As might be expected, the reactions of central banks under managed exchange rate regimes lie between the fixed and floating extremes.

First, central banks under fixed exchange rates have sterilised 26.5 per cent of any change in net foreign assets compared with 3.2 per cent for floaters and 10.4 per cent for managed exchange rate central banks; the finding that floaters do not sterilise simply confirms their classification. Second, fixed-rate central banks neutralised 26.2 per cent of any increase in net domestic credit to the government by reducing domestic credit to the private sector compared with –12.5 per cent for managed-rate and 6.8 per cent for floaters. Central banks under fixed exchange rates increased domestic credit after improvements in terms of trade by less than the other groups. Finally, their reaction to foreign debt buildup has been substantially greater than the reactions of the other two sub-groups.

NOTES

1 Most of the information in Table 4.1 is taken from the International Monetary Fund's *Exchange Arrangements and Exchange Restrictions: Annual Report 1994* and refers to the situation at the end of 1993; this publication does not cover Brunei.
2 US dollar for Argentina (since 1991), Bahamas, Barbados, Belize, Hong Kong, St Lucia, Saudi Arabia and the United Arab Emirates, South African rand for Lesotho, Namibia and Swaziland, and the ECU for Cyprus.
3 Argentina adopted a fixed exchange rate *vis-à-vis* the US dollar in 1991, while Mexico has floated since December 1994.
4 For example, Lesotho and Swaziland have their exchange rate regimes determined by South Africa.
5 Presumably in comparison with a floating exchange rate regime.
6 All the differences and associations mentioned in this and the next paragraph are significant at the 95 per cent confidence level.
7 Ratios of bank reserves to their deposits are also lowest in the fixed exchange rate group and highest in the floating exchange rate country group.
8 That many countries reacted in the opposite way, with inflationary and growth-inhibiting consequences, to the first oil price increase in 1973 is documented in Fry and David Lilien (1986).

5

THE CENTRAL BANK AND THE PRIVATE SECTOR

From examining central bank–government relations in Chapter 3 and central bank external activities in Chapter 4, we now turn to various aspects of the central bank's role *vis-à-vis* the private sector of the economy. There is a large literature on the relationship between the growth and development of the real economy and of the financial system, with two-way causation (e.g., Cameron 1972; Cameron *et al.* 1967; Fry 1995; Gerschenkron 1962; Goldsmith 1969; McKinnon 1973; Shaw 1973; World Bank 1989). Central banks in all countries have great concern for the health, development and stability of their payments, banking and financial systems more broadly, including the development of appropriate financial markets in their countries. But the responsibility of central banks in developing countries for the evolution and improvement of such systems in their own countries is even stronger because of their more predominant role within their own country's financial system, as noted in Chapter 1.

We shall proceed by examining what roles the central banks in the BoE group have played in the development of each of these main systems – the payments system, the banking system, and the non-bank financial system – in turn, concentrating in the latter case on the development of financial markets for equities, bonds and money market instruments.

THE PAYMENTS SYSTEM

We devoted a sub-section of our questionnaire, questions B1–B6, to this subject. Every country in the BoE group that responded to the questionnaire has some form of organised payments system (100 per cent response to B1). In the lesser-developed countries this took the form of a clearing house for paper-based cheque clearing. In the more developed members of the BoE group, e.g., Israel, Hong Kong, Malaysia, Singapore, South Africa and Sri Lanka, this is augmented by automated and electronic inter-bank transfer systems. In almost all of our countries the net payments are finally settled by transfers between commercial bank deposits held with the central bank (B4).[1]

We tried to get some measure of the scale of the clearing operation by asking for data on average daily turnover (B2). We scale this, where the answers to B2 allow, by the GDP in each country, so the histogram below expresses the daily turnover at the clearing as a per cent of annual GDP:

Daily turnover/GDP (per cent)	0–0.5	0.5–1	1–3	3–8	>8
Number of central banks	14	7	4	5	4

This shows a remarkably skewed distribution. Four central banks in countries with highly developed financial markets had turnover rates far above the norm for this group (Hong Kong 30.2 per cent, Mexico 25 per cent, Malaysia 21 per cent, Singapore 17.5 per cent). Then there was a gap to the next group of countries with turnover in the range of 3–8 per cent, headed by South Africa (7.9 per cent) and including Barbados, Chile, St Lucia and Zimbabwe. The ratio of turnover to GDP is mildly positively correlated with real income (+0.33 on a PPP basis, +0.24 on a market exchange rate basis), but several relatively high real income countries, notably some in the Middle East (Israel, Kuwait and United Arab Emirates), had much lower turnover rates (in each of these cases less than 0.5 per cent) than one might have expected. Our conjecture is that turnover is more closely related to the use made in each country of financial asset markets than to real incomes and expenditures. We tested this by regressing turnover as a percentage of GDP against per capita real income (on a PPP basis), the average ranking of the three financial markets reported subsequently in Table 5.7 (QFMI), and a dummy for the Middle East countries.[2] This gave the equation reported in Table 5.1 (*t* values in parentheses).

In most countries in the BoE group, the central bank directly runs the clearing system. Even when it does not, it is almost always

Table 5.1 Daily turnover of payments system

Dependent variable	Per capita real income (logs)	QFMI	Middle East	$\bar{R}^2$	Number of countries
Turnover/ GDP (logs)	0.552 (2.38)	0.293 (3.74)	−1.294 (−2.00)	0.46	33

intimately involved as a participant and supervisor. Table 5.2 records the answers to B3, including notes on the nature of the relationship. On the whole the speed of clearing payments in the countries in the BoE group has become reasonably fast, with a few exceptions mostly among African countries, though one very small, non-African, country replied that its delay was 'dismal'. In the larger African countries, e.g., Nigeria and Uganda, and in some other countries, e.g., Chile, Jordan, Sri Lanka, the delay in clearing country cheques remains, however, a sizeable multiple of the time required to clear cheques in the capital, and represents an unsatisfactory delay. A histogram of those reporting the time elapse for their capital is shown in Figure 5.1.

What we found impressive is that 24 out of the 40 central banks completing our questionnaire stated that there had been major reforms to the payments system since 1975, and that in these 24 countries reporting major reforms, 16 stated that they had initiated them. Of the others, only in Chile was the initiator clearly reported as *not* being the central bank; in Jamaica 'some' of the reforms were initiated by the central bank, and in the other cases (Argentina, India, Pakistan, East Caribbean, Solomon Islands and United Arab Emirates) this part of question B6 was not answered, or not usably so. In Table 5.3 we show the nature of the reforms to the payments system where these were specified by the central bank in its response.

Thus the central banks in the BoE group have generally taken the initiative in improving their payments systems, a somewhat mundane but nevertheless vital aspect both of their functions and of the proper working of the monetary system.

THE BANKING SYSTEM

We did not ask about the number of banking institutions and branches extant and/or recently established in our questionnaire,

Table 5.2 Payments system

Country	CB runs payments system	Nature of relationship between central bank and payments system
Argentina	Yes	
Bahamas	Yes	Clearing house
Bangladesh	Partially	CB runs clearing houses in cities; elsewhere, Sonali Bank
Barbados	Yes	Clearing house
Belize	Yes	Supervisor and manager
Brunei	No	Run by the Brunei Association of Banks
Botswana		Settlement through transfer between CB accounts
Chile	No	'Rules' and participates
Cyprus	Yes	Chairs the clearing house meetings, houses the meetings
Fiji	No	Settlement through transfer between CB accounts
Gambia, The	Yes	Chairs clearing sessions
Ghana		
Guyana	No	Hosts clearing operations and has a clearing relationship with commercial banks
Hong Kong	No	Advises on regulation
India	Partially	Runs clearing houses where it has banking offices
Israel	No	Member of Clearing House Committee, supervises paper-based clearing
Jamaica	Yes	Coordinates, provides facilities
Jordan	Yes	
Kenya		
Kuwait	Yes	Clearing house
Lesotho	Yes	Clearing house, supervisor
Malawi	Yes	Clearing house
Malaysia	Yes	Administers clearing house and electronic transfer system
Malta	Yes	Clearing house
Mauritius	Yes	Clearing house
Mexico	Yes	Regulator
Namibia	Yes	Provides clearing house and settlement facilities
Nigeria	Yes	Clearing house, supervisor
Pakistan	Partially	Runs clearing houses where it has banking offices
Papua New Guinea		
St Lucia	Yes	Clearing house

Table 5.2 Continued

Country	CB runs payments system	Nature of relationship between central bank and payments system
Saudi Arabia	Yes	Operates and controls
Sierra Leone	Yes	Clearing house
Singapore	No	Chairman of the Singapore Clearing House Association
Solomon Islands		Settlement through transfer between CB accounts
South Africa	No	Participates and runs settlement
Sri Lanka	Yes	Clearing house
Swaziland	Yes	Clearing house
Tanzania		
Trinidad and Tobago	Yes	Clearing house
Uganda	No	Provides logistical support and ensures adherence to regulations
United Arab Emirates	Yes	Clearing house
Zambia	Yes	Paid for services by participating institutions
Zimbabwe	Yes	Chairs clearing committee, supervisor

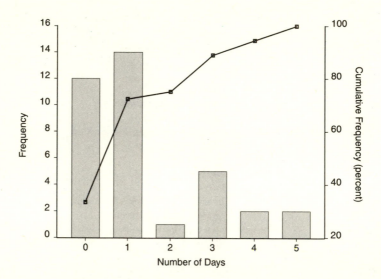

Figure 5.1 Average settlement delay (capital)

Table 5.3 Reforms to payments system since 1975

Country	Reforms	CB initiated reforms	Nature of reform
Argentina	Yes		Deregulation
Bahamas	No		
Bangladesh	No		
Barbados	No		
Belize⁻	Yes	Yes	Facilitate and expedite presentation and settlement of financial instruments
Brunei	No		
Botswana	No		SWIFT system is in use as of 1993
Chile	Yes	No	Electronic transfer of funds system
Cyprus	Yes	Yes	Automation of clearing
Fiji	No		
Gambia, The	No		
Ghana			
Guyana	No		
Hong Kong	Yes	Yes	Reforms of payments system under way
India	Yes		Automatic clearing, MICR technology
Israel	Yes	Yes	Encoding of cheques, automated clearing house
Jamaica	Yes	Some	
Jordan	Yes	Yes	Automation of settlement system
Kenya			
Kuwait	Yes	Yes	Occasional procedural changes
Lesotho	No		
Malawi	No		
Malaysia	Yes		Electronic transfer system, automated clearing
Malta	Yes	Yes	SWIFT, Direct Credit, automated clearing
Mauritius	No		Automated Clearing and Payments System under consideration
Mexico	Yes	Yes	
Namibia	No		
Nigeria	Yes	Yes	Automated system for sorting cheques in 1990
Pakistan	Yes		
Papua New Guinea			
St Lucia	Yes		Clearing system
Saudi Arabia	Yes	Yes	
Sierra Leone	No		
Singapore	Yes	Yes	Automated Clearing System, Interbank GIRO, SWIFT
Solomon Islands	Yes		Current system started 1992
South Africa	Yes	Yes	National Payment System Strategy

Table 5.3 Continued

Country	Reforms	CB initiated reforms	Nature of reform
Sri Lanka	Yes	Yes	Automated cheque clearing, interbank funds transfer
Swaziland	No		
Tanzania			
Trinidad and Tobago	Yes	Yes	Special clearing items
Uganda	Yes	Yes	Automated clearing, local settlement, inter-town clearing
United Arab Emirates	Yes		
Zambia	No		
Zimbabwe	Yes		Plans to introduce automated clearing

thinking mistakenly that we could get such data on a consistent basis for each of the countries from other sources. We were wrong about this. While in most, if not all, cases such data do exist, it would have taken longer than we had available to collect them ourselves from the individual countries. So, partly also in view of the large amount of other data that we already had to examine, we did not attempt to collect such institutional data. Consequently we cannot report anything on the institutional development of commercial banking activities in the BoE group.

Among such institutional issues, which we would have liked, but are not able, to discuss here, is the question of how far it is justifiable to restrict competition in the domestic financial system – for example, from international banks and securities houses headquartered abroad – in order to support and develop indigenous financial institutions. And, if done at all, how can this discrimination best be undertaken without resulting in feather-bedding, inefficiency and a loss of welfare to clients of the financial system?

What we can do, however, is to examine the comparative development of bank intermediation via increased holdings of bank deposits. Commercial banks are usually the first, and often remain the most important, financial intermediaries. Channelling saving through such intermediaries, with their specialised ability to assess the value of loan projects, should allow both larger and better projects to be financed (than when investment is done directly through family and friends). The development of the banking habit can encourage both saving and investment, and there is an association between a higher bank deposit/income ratio and both the level and rate of growth of output. There is a sizeable literature on the relationship between the development of banking and the growth of output (e.g., De Gregorio and Guidotti 1993; King and Levine 1993a, 1993b; Pagano 1993; World Bank 1989).

As an illustration of this, albeit in an exceedingly simple format, we examined the relationship between a number of variables relating to growth, i.e., the level of per capita incomes, the growth rate of real GDP, the saving/income and investment/income ratios over the *whole* period (taken as the average of the 15 years, 1979–93) and the deposit/income ratio at the *beginning* of our period (taken as the average of the first five years). In the case of two countries, the saving ratio over this period was reported as negative. If these outliers are removed, the fit of the relationship with the saving ratio improves considerably; so this equation is reported with and without these outliers in Table 5.4.

In all these regressions the relationship is positive, and with the investment ratio and saving ratio, excluding outliers, it is significantly so. Of course, the relationship between the increasing use of banks and growth is two-way, which is why we regressed the dependent variable over the whole period on the deposit/income ratio at the start of the period. If we run the relationship the other way around, in this instance by examining the relationship between the deposit income ratio at the *end* of the period (1989–93) and the growth variables over the whole period (1979–93), the fit improves for the saving ratio and per capita GDP, but not for the investment ratio, as shown in Table 5.5. It is perhaps

Table 5.4 Growth and monetisation

Dependent variable	t value of M/GDP coefficient, 1979–83	$\bar{R}^2$	Number of countries
GDP per capita	1.77	0.052	40
Growth in real GDP	1.06	0.003	36
I/Y	3.75	0.277	35
S/Y	1.45	0.046	24
S/Y (without outliers)	4.96	0.530	22

plausible to surmise that the main causal forces run from saving to greater use of bank deposits, and from an expansion of financial intermediation through banks to investment.

We examine the development of the banking habit by applying demand for money functions for M1, M2, and M2 minus currency. We examined several specifications of this function to see which fitted best, an exercise which we confess involves a degree of 'data-mining'. In all cases real income (in log form) was a major determinant of the demand for real (i.e., deflated by the CPI price level) money balances in log form. With narrow money, demand for money seemed homogeneous of degree 1, i.e., with a coefficient of unity on the real income term. Moreover, we were concerned about the sometimes wide disparities between countries' assessed real incomes in US dollars when measured at 1992 market exchange rates and on an estimated 1993 PPP basis (Appendix 3). So, in order to minimise the errors in data from the conversion into US dollars, we took as our dependent variable in each case the log of the average over the period of the ratio of money balances to GDP.[3] Given data availability, we used the log of the average per capita real income measured at market exchange rates in the M2 and in the M2 minus currency equations.

The next problem was that the standard cost/substitution variables that enter such functions, inflation and nominal interest rates, and the volatility (variance) of these variables, were all highly multicollinear. Entering any two of these together (and also real interest rates and their variability) tended to result in extremely unstable coefficient estimates with varying signs and significance. Again after some experimentation (data-mining), we took the log of the concurrent rate of CPI inflation (i.e., for 1991 in the estimates

Table 5.5 Monetisation and growth

Explanatory variable	t value of explanatory variable coefficient, 1989–93	$\bar{R}^2$	Number of countries
GDP per capita	2.93	0.156	42
Growth in real GDP	1.44	0.028	38
I/Y	2.32	0.093	37
S/Y	1.76	0.080	25
S/Y without outliers	5.56	0.576	23

for 1991 and the 15-year average 1979–93 in the estimates averaged over that same period) as the 'best' variable to measure the relative cost of holding money balances.

As noted in Chapter 3, financial repression can have a variety of effects on the growth of the banking habit. On the one hand, such repression can reduce competition between banks in the services that they provide, not only via reduced interest rates but more generally in worse customer services. On the other hand, governments may favour the banking system relative to other potential channels for financial flows, in part because the banks represent an easier target for extorting quasi-fiscal revenues.

Again we examined a wide range of potential measures of repression, based mostly on the answers given to section B of the questionnaire, as potential explanatory variables. We also examined a variable attempting to measure the efficiency of the payments system (the cheque clearing delay). Nothing worked very strongly. From this set of variables, the ones that worked 'best' were:

- the answer to B16 (QB16), which indicated that when the central bank used open-market techniques (rather than direct controls) money holdings would rise. We assume that this is a proxy to indicate whether the banking system has been liberalised, or not. As noted earlier, the potential effect of repression on the demand for money is ambiguous.

- the ranking of the three financial markets as reported in Table 5.7 (QFMI), which indicated that narrow money holdings are smaller if the financial markets are more developed. We would have expected a negative effect on the demand for *broad* money, on account of the availability of alternative savings instruments, but not on *narrow* money.

- a measure of the concentration of the population (LDENS, the log of Population/Area), which indicated that broad money holdings are higher in countries with higher population concentration. Perhaps this is a measure of ease of access to bank branches.

- the answer to C1 on exchange rate regime (QC1D2), which indicated that with pegged exchange rates, people held relatively higher domestic narrow money balances. We have no explanation at all why this regime, rather than fixed or floating regimes, appeared to affect money holdings.

65

Although on the usual statistical criteria all these variables should be included in their respective equations, the theoretical basis for expecting these to be significant is generally rather weak. Moreover, we did run numerous experimental (data-mining) regressions, and the likelihood of obtaining spuriously significant results in a small sample in such cases is high.

So, in Table 5.6 we present a selection of our results, both those just with real income and inflation as explanatory variables, and some of the 'better' equations from our data-mining. The results for the M2 minus currency equations were similar to the results for the M2 equations, so we do not include them in Table 5.6 to save space.

OTHER FINANCIAL MARKETS

In common with most other economists studying the relationship between financial and real development (e.g., Caprio *et al.*, 1994; McKinnon 1973; Patrick and Park 1994; Shaw 1973; World Bank 1989), we are critical of financial repression. We do want to emphasise, however, that governments and central banks have now in most cases come to recognise the advantages of relying on indirect open-market mechanisms rather than direct controls whenever possible. Of the 40 countries in the BoE group who responded to question B16 about the use of indirect open-market operations, 28 (70 per cent) stated that they were already used (and of these, two – Malta and Mauritius – referred to new financial instruments and liberalisation being introduced). In some cases, however, as reported below, the use of such market mechanisms did not extend much further than the introduction of (primary) auctions in treasury bills, or other money market instruments, with little secondary market activity. Of the remainder, two, Cyprus and Trinidad and Tobago, reported reforms (e.g., removal of interest rate ceilings) that should enable them to introduce such techniques within the next year or two; Israel only uses open-market operations on a limited basis, since the volume of treasury bills is too small for monetary management purposes; beginning in 1995, however, the Central Bank of Israel is also purchasing government bonds to inject liquidity. Of the nine further countries reporting that they did *not* use open-market operations, two, Bahamas and Barbados, both noted specifically their participation in other respects in financial markets (Bahamas in the government securities

Table 5.6 Demand for money functions

Dependent variable	Period	Real income	Inflation	QB16	QFMI	LDENS	QC1D2	$\bar{R}^2$	Number of countries
M2	1979–93	0.234 (4.19)	−0.186 (−3.02)					0.483	41
M2	1979–93	0.213 (3.92)	−0.174 (−2.94)			0.076 (2.11)		0.526	41
M2	1989–93	0.250 (3.77)	−0.250 (−3.38)					0.473	40
M2	1989–93	0.271 (4.00)	−0.293 (−3.97)	0.409 (2.13)				0.546	36
M2	1991	0.295 (3.68)	−0.358 (−3.27)					0.484	36
M2	1991	0.284 (3.68)	−0.452 (−4.16)	0.625 (2.67)				0.565	33
M1	1979–93		−0.221 (−3.86)					0.258	41
M1	1979–93		−0.238 (−4.03)	0.279 (1.59)	−0.047 (−1.65)			0.328	36
M1	1989–93		−0.210 (−3.56)					0.226	41
M1	1989–93		−0.207 (−3.30)	0.362 (1.98)	−0.036 (−1.27)		0.349 (1.99)	0.379	36
M1	1991		−0.259 (−3.02)					0.189	36
M1	1991		−0.227 (−2.31)	0.334 (1.37)	−0.036 (−1.09)		0.514 (2.33)	0.357	32

67

market and Barbados in the treasury bill tender), and Namibia replied 'Not yet'. The other negative replies came from the smallest countries, Belize, Brunei, Guyana, East Caribbean, Solomon Islands and Swaziland.

We obtained the impression, from the answers to questions B13 and B14 on financial markets and interest rates, that there was now some considerable momentum, at least among the BoE group of developing countries, towards financial liberalisation and the use of indirect open-market techniques. Despite the advantages of this, the transition to a more liberalised financial system does have its own dangers.

Experience indicates that interest rate liberalisation typically raises at least two major questions. The first is how to curb or counter an explosion in consumer lending after financial liberalisation, particularly when it takes the form of the abolition of credit ceilings. The second is how to cope with the capital inflow and real exchange rate appreciation that can attend a process of stabilisation and liberalisation.

International evidence suggests that easier access to consumer credit lowers private saving ratios in the medium term (Jappelli and Pagano 1994; Liu and Woo 1994; Patrick 1994). A burst of consumer lending following financial liberalisation may also jeopardise monetary control or squeeze out investment lending. Perhaps the pragmatic answer lies in imposing high downpayment requirements for mortgages and loans for durable consumer goods at the outset of the liberalisation programme. Subsequently such requirements can be gradually reduced, particularly when the economy is in no danger of overheating.

Many newly liberalised banking systems have become overly enthusiastic about property development, housing and credit card lending only to find that expected returns failed to materialise. Loan officers have an incentive to follow the herd when it comes to sectoral lending decisions. To be wrong in the company of most other loan officers is excusable. To be wrong in isolation may not be forgiven so readily.

One specific way of containing systemic risk inherent in over-exuberant financial sector growth, and a possible herd instinct,[4] involves deterring excessive lending concentration to (a) a single sector of the economy, such as construction or real estate, (b) a single region of the country, such as the coastal areas, or (c) a single borrower, through the application of risk-weighted capital-adequacy requirements. These would be aimed at gradually raising the marginal cost of excessive growth in loans of such particular types. Thus, a bank that increased risk through rapid expansion of any loan category by either changing the composition of its portfolio or increasing its total portfolio size would incur increased risk weighting on all loans in its high-growth categories. Hong Kong imposes an informal deterrent to portfolio concentration along these lines.

Such a system could start with an increased risk weighting on all loans in any category whose growth exceeded, say, 25 per cent in real terms by the actual percentage growth of this loan category. For example, a 30 per cent growth of loans in any specific category would involve an increase in risk weighting of 30 percentage points on each loan. In this way the price mechanism can be used, for example, to increase the financial institutions' marginal cost of property lending, so raising interest rates on such loans and deterring speculative real estate booms. A more sophisticated version of this proposal would be to assess a bank's portfolio in terms of the covariance of individual loan default probabilities. The score in this exercise would then produce an adjusted capital adequacy requirement. The main problem is that the internationally agreed system of risk-weighted capital adequacy assessment is already too complicated for most developing economies to implement effectively. Adding yet more complexity may have to wait.

A second problem that the transition to a liberalised financial system may bring, especially if it is accompanied by a credible financial stabilisation package, is that it may make short-term international capital inflows into the country's bank deposits and other money market instruments suddenly more attractive. Such inflows can put undesirable downwards pressure on real interest rates and/or cause unwanted appreciation of real exchange rates (Schadler *et al.* 1993). The sequencing of liberalisation in internal and in external financial arrangements is an important and complex issue but is too large a subject for us to pursue further here (see, e.g., Bisat *et al.* 1992; Blejer and Sagari 1987; Johnston 1991; McKinnon 1993; Sundararajan 1992).

Be that as it may, financial liberalisation not only includes the removal of direct controls and excessive taxes and other impediments on financial institutions and markets, but also involves positive encouragement, by the central bank and other relevant authorities, of financial markets, such as the money market, bond and equity markets.[5] In order to assess progress on this front, we asked two specific questions: B12 on the current conditions in such markets, and B13 on the difficulties being faced in establishing them, in our questionnaire.

These questions covered a large field, and it is not easy to summarise the responses in any simple or tabular form. Nevertheless one can, perhaps, divide the markets into four groups in each case. In the money market, the ladder might be:

1 No market, or informal market between banks.
2 Primary treasury bill market, very limited and thin secondary market.
3 Secondary market in treasury bills developing; introduction of some other instruments.
4 Fully developed money market.

In the bond market, it would be:

1 No market.
2 Primary market in government, government guaranteed and parastatal bonds. Very limited and thin secondary market.
3 Secondary market in government bonds developing. Some limited primary issues of private sector bonds.
4 Fully developed bond market.

And in the equity market, it would be:

1 No formal market; no legislation; only deals OTC.
2 Formally organised stock exchange, but few placements and low capitalisation and turnover.
3 Moderate capitalisation and turnover relative to GDP.
4 Fully developed stock market.

Somewhat arbitrarily we have used the data from B12 to divide the BoE group into the following categories shown in Table 5.7.[6]

In both the money market and the bond market, but especially in the latter, there appears to be a need for a market, initially primary and then secondary, to be established in government debt, both to provide a benchmark for pricing, an infrastructure of market making, a culture of investing and portfolio management, and a pool of liquidity, before there is much chance of developing an active market in private sector corporate debentures. Thus in Hong Kong, despite the advanced nature of its money and equity markets, its bond market was relatively dormant until the recent

Table 5.7 Market classification

1 *Money*	*Bond*	*Equity*
Bahamas	Bahamas	Bahamas
Belize	Belize	Belize
Brunei	Brunei	East Caribbean
East Caribbean	East Caribbean	Gambia
Gambia	Gambia	Guyana
Guyana	Guyana	Lesotho
Namibia	Lesotho	Sierra Leone
Sierra Leone	Namibia	Solomon Islands
	Sierra Leone	Uganda
	Uganda	United Arab Emirates
	United Arab Emirates	

2 *Money*	*Bond*	*Equity*
Bangladesh	Bangladesh	Bangladesh
Botswana	Barbados	Botswana
Cyprus	Botswana	Brunei
Fiji	Cyprus	Cyprus
Jamaica	Fiji	Fiji
Jordan	Jamaica	Jordan
Kuwait	Jordan	Kuwait
Lesotho	Kuwait	Malawi
Malawi	Malawi	Malta
Malta	Mauritius	Mauritius
Mauritius	Saudi Arabia	Namibia
Saudi Arabia	Solomon Islands	Swaziland
Solomon Islands	Swaziland	Zambia
Swaziland	Zambia	Zimbabwe
Trinidad and Tobago	Zimbabwe	
Uganda		
United Arab Emirates		
Zambia		
Zimbabwe		

3 *Money*	*Bond*	*Equity*
Argentina	Argentina	Argentina
Barbados	Hong Kong	Barbados
Israel	India	Jamaica
Malaysia	Israel	Nigeria
Nigeria	Malaysia	Pakistan
Pakistan	Malta	Saudi Arabia
Sri Lanka	Nigeria	Sri Lanka
	Singapore	
	South Africa	
	Sri Lanka	

Table 5.7 Continued

4 Money	Bond	Equity
Chile	Chile	Chile
Hong Kong	Mexico	Hong Kong
India		India
Mexico		Israel
Singapore		Malaysia
South Africa		Mexico
		Singapore
		South Africa

initiative to issue Exchange Fund Bills and Notes.[7] On the other hand, the public sector can have such a large appetite for longer-term borrowing that it may seem to crowd out private sector debentures, as in South Africa, and over some periods Israel. In some countries and at some times, moreover, institutional investors have been required to take up government bonds (at unfavourable prices, as discussed in Chapter 3), thereby further weakening the private sector bond market. The relationship between the roles of the public sector and the private sector in the development of the bond market is more complex than in the case of the money and equity markets. This may well account for the fact that we have classified many fewer countries as having a fully developed bond market than in the other two cases.

Again, however, we noted the number of responses that reported developments in progress, and that indicated that these were being initiated by the central bank. We did not ask specifically for the central bank to indicate its own involvement in such developments, so the references both to reforms and developments that are underway and the role of the central bank in them, as shown in note 8 (see p. 77), are surely an underestimate of activity on this front. Again, however, we obtained the impression that progress in developing the money and equity markets was rather more rapid than in bond/debenture markets.

What we *did* ask specifically was what were the three biggest difficulties in establishing these domestic financial markets in question B13. This was an open-ended question, so classification is again somewhat difficult and arbitrary. We have, however, sought to divide the answers into three main categories: (1) problems of *size* (small market) and *underdevelopment* of legislation (including regulation and supervision), lack of skilled personnel and poor market infrastructure; (2) structural problems in markets such as lack of institutional investors prepared to buy and trade paper, unwillingness of entrepreneurs to go public, unhelpful role of public sector in bond market, other problems of market structure; (3) problems from the macro economy, government tax and repressive control systems. Using this categorisation, the responses divided up as shown in Table 5.8. A number of smaller countries without formal markets did not respond, presumably since, without such markets, they had faced no problems. In addition, India, Mexico and Singapore did not mention that they had had any problems.

What are we to make of this? The problems reported in the first section of Table 5.8 are mostly self-explanatory and obvious. Given the sizeable number of countries reporting problems of a lack of appropriate securities legislation, it is good that the IMF makes available technical legal assistance and a standardised legal blueprint which could be adjusted to suit local idiosyncrasies, but a pity that, for various reasons, more countries have not made use of these services. Where countries are physically too small to sustain satisfactory financial markets on their own there must be at least a case for contemplating currency union with a larger neighbour (if politically feasible) in order to establish a sufficient *masse de manoeuvre*.

Relatively few countries reported that the general macroeconomic context, or explicit taxes on financial markets, were a major problem; and few also reported that the costs and expenses of actually running the market were a deterrent. A considerably larger number complained about factors under the general heading of market repression, e.g., administered interest rates, exchange controls, statutory requirements to hold bonds, but most of these complaints were backwards looking, relating to controls and requirements that either had been, or were in the process of being, phased out. The problems caused by market repression would seem to be passing into history.

Instead, many complaints related to the activities, or rather lack of activity, of private sector participants. You can take the private sector to a liberalised financial sector but you cannot necessarily expect it to develop an investment 'culture' immediately. Entrepreneurs do not want to go public; investors sometimes seem to prefer a world of fixed and administered interest rates to one in

Table 5.8 Market impediments

1 *Small market*	*Legislative and regulation problems*	*Limited personnel*	*Poor infrastructure*
Belize	Bahamas	Belize	Lesotho
East Caribbean	Bangladesh	East Caribbean	Nigeria
Jordan	Belize	Guyana	Pakistan
Kuwait	Chile[2]	Sierra Leone	Sierra Leone
Lesotho	East Caribbean		Uganda
Malawi[1]	Fiji		
Malta	Jordan		
Namibia			
Swaziland			
Uganda			

2 *Market structure*	*Weakness of institutional investors*	*Entrepreneurs not going public*	*Public sector inappropriate bond issue*
Argentina[3]	Bahamas[11]	Bahamas[24]	Hong Kong[30]
Bangladesh[4]	Barbados[12]	Cyprus[25]	Israel[31]
Malawi[5]	Chile[13]	Guyana[26]	Malta[32]
Malaysia[6]	Cyprus[14]	Malaysia[27]	Mauritius[33]
Saudi Arabia[7]	Fiji[15]	Malta[28]	South Africa[34]
South Africa[8]	Kuwait[16]	Nigeria[29]	
Sri Lanka[9]	Malaysia[17]		
Zambia[10]	Malta[18]		
	Mauritius[19]		
	Pakistan[20]		
	Saudi Arabia[21]		
	Sri Lanka[22]		
	Uganda[23]		

3 *Macroeconomic problems*	*Repression of markets*	*Tax on markets*
Argentina[35]	Barbados[40]	Argentina[48]
Chile[36]	Cyprus[41]	Barbados[49]
Nigeria[37]	Fiji[42]	South Africa[50]
Pakistan[38]	Israel[43]	
Zimbabwe[39]	Malta[44]	
	Mauritius[45]	
	South Africa[46]	
	Zimbabwe[47]	

Notes to Table 5.8:

1 'For a long time the financial system has been monopolised by two commercial banks. The result has been that the system was not operating on principles of market forces. For example bank credit to the private sector was allocated based on non-economic factors and interest rates did not fully reflect economic fundamentals.'

2 'Other problems . . . were the lack of a good financial supervision and regulation.'

3 'In the case of the OTC bond market, settlement arrangements are very poor. Settlement of bonds and money transactions take place at different institutions – Caja de Valores and BCRA, respectively. Because both operations are not simultaneous and centralised a high counterpart risk is involved.'

4 'The money market is yet to be fully developed. Money market is not yet adequately responsive to indirect controls of the Bangladesh Bank.'

5 'Oligopoly is the state of affairs in this [financial] market and an interbank money market has not fully developed.'

6 'to establish a one-stop agency, which will expedite and streamline the cumbersome issuing process involving various government agencies'.

7 Poor bond pricing mechanism. No tender or auction mechanism.

8 'Lack of Liquidity due to a scarcity of scrip, the absence of market-making and a limited number of participants.'

9 'Limited number of financial instruments.'

10 'The markets fragmented or segmented or polarised/imperfect . . . The Bond market (auction) is relatively new as well as the equity market.'

11 'The inability for public corporations with substantial liquidity to partake in financial markets.'

12 'Lack of market information . . . and a lack of familiarity with investment trading in a market environment . . . Traditional rigidity in investment patterns.'

13 'low activity of institutional investors'.

14 'institutional investors though significant in number and size are not active players in the financial markets'.

15 'Lack of public awareness on the usage of the financial markets . . . institutional investors . . . invariably hold these [securities] to maturity.'

16 'non-trading of a significant part of government ownership of some companies' shares'.

17 need 'to develop a large domestic institutional base' and to promote unit trust funds as a savings vehicle.

18 'limited number of market participants'.

19 'Players, apart from banks, do not seem to be willing to hold long-term debt instruments'.

20 'Inherited deep-rooted informal financial sector; lack of awareness of general public'.

21 'investment culture of the end investor is short-term oriented. Banks' preferences to hold GDBs . . . to avoid having to mark to market and hence price volatility in their portfolio.'

22 'the financial system in Sri Lanka is inadequately equipped with specialised financial institutions'.

23 'absence of a "securities" culture. There is a limited demand for securities, a limited supply of securities and no skilled financial intermediaries.'

24 'Companies' reluctant to release performance information or to go public.'

25 'The majority of Cypriot firms are small, family-owned units. As a result only a small proportion of them have gone public.'

26 'Closed ownership, high project risks, limited information on companies and reluctance on information disclosure.'

27 'At present, issuers prefer to offer bonds by way of private placement, [. . .] in order to avoid the requirement for the accompaniment of the prospectus.'

28 'reluctance of private entrepreneurs to reduce extent of their control . . . and to disclose sensitive information . . . The actual/perceived expense of listing . . . is an additional problem.'

29 'Paucity of shares available for trading coupled with Nigerian aversion to ownership dilution.'

30 'absence of a government debt market' prior to 'launch of the Exchange Fund Bills and Notes Programme.'

31 'Government deficits have reduced notably, . . . so . . . the supply of bonds has not always kept up with the demands generated, mostly, by household savings.'

32 'irregularity of primary market issues'.

33 'long-dated Government papers issued to rather meet fiscal needs than for monetary management'.

34 'Crowding-out effect resulting from relatively large public-sector borrowing requirement.'

35 Inflation and associated macroeconomic instability.

36 'high and extreme volatility . . . of inflation'.

37 'low savings'.

38 'low income and low savings'.

39 Macroeconomic instability, and supply shocks, via weather effects on agriculture.

40 'rigidity in investment patterns influenced by the ready accessibility to the Central Bank both for buying and selling securities and for providing liquidity at the discount window'.

41 'exchange controls'.

42 'institutional investors hold these securities to meet statutory requirements'.

43 Prior to 1987 'nearly all of the long term contractual savings in Israel was deposited in non-tradable, earmarked government "bonds", by force of government decree'. Since then the market has developed well, but a problem is that 'The Ministry of Finance requires that contractual savings institutions mark their assets to market so returns fluctuate . . . the public has not yet resigned itself to this feature of the liberalised regime.'

44 'regulated interest rate structure'.

45 'as interest rates were administered until recently, holders of long-dated Government papers have yet to develop a culture to trade'.

46 'exchange controls'.

47 Exchange control regulations.

48 'the existence of regulations that prevented market forces from working efficiently; e.g. fixed commissions for market makers. Taxes on transactions, punitive tax withholding for non-domestic and domestic investors on capital and earning taxes, etc. punished heavily investment in domestic markets.'

49 '12½ percent withholding tax on income from Government securities.'

50 'marketable securities tax is also constraining liquidity'.

which they have to make portfolio choices, which can go wrong. One question is whether such attitudes will naturally adjust over time; and, if not, what, if anything, the central bank can usefully do to improve the investment 'culture' among potential private sector participants?[9]

NOTES

1 This was not so in Brunei and Hong Kong, where settlement was over the books of a commercial bank. In Bangladesh and India settlement is only partially over the central bank's accounts.
2 Israel, Jordan, Kuwait, Saudi Arabia and United Arab Emirates.
3 This, of course, also greatly reduces the reported fit, R^2, of the regression equations.
4 The extent to which commercial bankers suffer from a herd instinct, or do so more than central bankers and/or economists, remains a contentious issue, which we shall not pursue further here.
5 We have already discussed the development of the foreign exchange market in Chapter 4.
6 The reply from Trinidad and Tobago related only to the treasury bill and money market; and there were no data on the bond market from Pakistan.
7 In Singapore, in contrast, 'the domestic corporate bond market . . . is still small because generally Singapore companies have surplus cash'. In Malaysia, open market techniques have become less important, 'due to the limitations in the holdings of Government papers since 1991'.

8

Bahamas	Work in progress on a Securities Act.
Cyprus	Removal of interest rate ceilings; liberalisation of financial markets (initiated by Central Bank); an act to establish a Stock Exchange passed in 1993, now being implemented.
East Caribbean	Central Bank has a Money and Capital Markets Development Plan.
Fiji	Studies being taken to reactivate Suva Stock Exchange, with support of ADB.
Guyana	Call exchange launched at Bank of Guyana in January 1994.
Hong Kong	Issue of Exchange Fund Bills and Notes programme by HKMA.
India	'In the recent years, several measures have been taken to widen and deepen the money markets . . . setting up specialised institutions . . . introduction of new instruments . . . new participants.' These are detailed at length in their reply. In the domestic bond market an auction system and repos for government bonds introduced in 1992; zero coupon bonds in 1994; DVP system for government securities at an advanced stage. For equities Capital Issues (Control) Act repealed 1992; National Stock Exchange of India (NSE) started operations in 1994. Bombay Stock Exchange started on-line computerised trading in 1995. This is only a selection of the many innovations reported.
Kuwait	Restoration of markets following liberation in 1991.

Malawi	Malawi Stock Exchange and Stockbrokers Malawi Limited established in December 1994. Stock Exchange Committee which runs MSE answerable to Reserve Bank which has overall regulating powers. First listing of securities expected before end 1995. Also financial sector has recently been liberalised.
Malaysia	Major reform in financial markets 'took place in January 1989 when Bank Negara introduced the Principal Dealers network for the purpose of developing the domestic money and bond market. Following this, Bank Negara had also introduced in 1990 the electronic payment and securities trading system known as the Interbank Fund Transfer and Scripless Securities Trading System'.
Malta	Weekly auctions of term deposits initiated by Central Bank in July 1994. Central Bank also developing repos.
Mauritius	Central Bank established a Secondary Market Cell.
Saudi Arabia	Money market developed by SAMA, which is also closely involved in ongoing developments in equity markets.
Sri Lanka	Primary dealers in treasury bills appointed. Central Bank starts repos 'with a view to developing the short end of the market'. Several recent developments in equity market.
Uganda	'Efforts are being made to develop a formal interbank money market.'
Zambia	Activities of formal money market enhanced in last two years; starting this year bonds are being auctioned, previously rate was administratively set; Lusaka Stock Exchange set up in 1994.

9 We suspect, however, that if we had questioned such private sector participants we would have received rather a different slant on the nature of the problems.

6

REGULATION AND
SUPERVISION

Central banks have two main interrelated functions, first the macro-function of maintaining nominal price stability and second the micro-function of ensuring the healthy development of the payments, banking and financial systems. The functions are interrelated because the stability of the banking system will be threatened by high and volatile inflation, while the price mechanism in turn is likely to be disturbed by booms and busts, especially systemic crises, in the payments and banking systems, and perhaps within the wider financial system as well.

In Chapter 5 we described certain aspects of the role of central banks within the BoE group in the development of these systems. Here we discuss their role in the ongoing function of maintaining the continuing health of these systems by acting as their regulator and supervisor. There is much debate about the proper scale and scope of the conduct of this function by central banks, perhaps especially now that the dividing lines between banks and non-bank financial intermediaries have become blurred. But this is not the right place to enter that debate. Instead, our concern here is primarily to describe what the central banks in the BoE group have been doing in this area.

Out of 40 central banks in the BoE group responding to our questionnaire, all of them, except Chile, *supervised* their domestic banks, though the Banco de Mexico did so in conjunction with the Comisión Nacional Bancaria.[1] *Regulation*, unlike supervision, involves making laws and decrees, and here responsibility has, perforce, to be shared with the government; so several respondents emphasised that they were the *supervisory* authority,[2] which we took to imply that *regulation* was a more widespread responsibility including a major role for the three arms of government, executive, legislative and judicial.

Among the 39 respondents undertaking such supervision, eight countries[3] reported that their supervisory functions were limited to the banking system only. By contrast, in five countries, Brunei, Lesotho, Malawi, Malaysia and Singapore, the central bank was asked to supervise virtually all financial institutions. In the remaining 26 countries the central banks were responsible for the supervision of a variety of near-bank deposit-taking and credit-giving institutions, building societies, etc. In part because of the fuzziness of the dividing line between banks and non-bank financial intermediaries, there is no standardised remit for the ambit of the central bank's supervisory function. That fuzziness, and the resulting uncertainty about the scale and scope of a central bank's supervisory responsibilities, is unlikely to diminish over time.

Of these 39 countries undertaking supervisory functions, all (with the exception of Zimbabwe, and the possible exception of the Solomon Islands which did not respond to this question) maintained specialist staff for this purpose. The actual number of such staff will obviously depend on the size of the country, so we scaled the number of specialised staff by two scale variables, the overall size of the central bank and the volume of bank deposits (M2 less currency) in 1991 transformed into US$ bn.[4] The number of such staff as a percentage of total staff varied from a low of 1.5 per cent to a high of 50 per cent. The two central banks with the highest proportion of such specialised staff were Singapore (50 per cent) and Hong Kong (34.5 per cent), both with very large and sophisticated financial markets. Apart from these two outliers, the highest percentage was 19 per cent. We reproduce in Figure 6.1 a histogram recording the number of central banks with their percentage falling in each 3 per cent range between 2 per cent and 20 per cent.[5]

This showed a concentration of central banks with a relatively small proportion of their staff, 2–5 per cent and 5–8 per cent, engaged in the specialist work of supervision. This surprised us, since supervision would be, we thought, quite labour intensive, and, if done at all, would require a minimum number of skilled staff.

Perhaps a better, though still unsatisfactory, metric would be the number of specialised supervisory staff per US$ bn of bank deposits, M2-currency. The results of this varied between 0.78 and 571.3. A histogram of the results, Figure 6.2, showed a massively skewed distribution. This is primarily due to the (unsurprising) fact

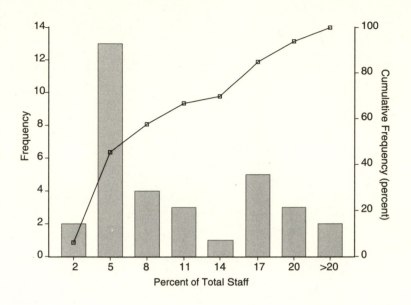

Figure 6.1 Supervision staff (relative to total staff)

that there are large economies of scale in supervision, i.e., it takes just about as long to monitor a bank with a balance sheet of $10 million as for a bank with footings of $10 billion. Thus almost all the countries with high ratios of staff to deposits have comparatively low totals of deposits (in comparative US$ form) and vice versa (indeed the lowest *ratios* were posted by Hong Kong and South Africa, and the highest by Uganda, Sierra Leone and Gambia). We formalise this by regressing (the log of) supervisory staff numbers SN on (the log of) deposits (in US$ bn). The results for 32 countries are (t values in parentheses):

$$\text{Ln } SN = -6.41 + 0.475 \text{ Ln US\$ deposits}$$
$$(-4.45) \ (7.20) \qquad\qquad \bar{R}^2 = 0.621$$

One question is whether the number of specialised staff required (per $ bn of deposits) might be a function of the supervisory methodology involved. We asked in question D3 whether the supervision of commercial banks was conducted on the basis of

(a) ordinary audited accounts

81

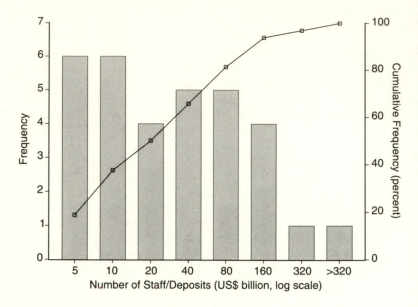

Figure 6.2 Supervision staff (relative to deposits)

(b) special audits done by accountants
(c) on-site examinations
(d) regular returns
(e) other

Presumably method (c) would be more labour intensive than (a) or (b). In any case the answers may be of some interest in themselves.

Of the 39 banks undertaking supervision, the number using each method was as follows (D3):

(a) ordinary audited accounts   24
(b) special audits done by accountants   13[6]
(c) on-site examinations   34
(d) regular returns   25
(e) other   2[7]

As is obvious from the above, the banks undertaking this function undertook multiple methods; only Malawi used one method only. The distribution of number of methods reported being used was:

82

Number of methods used	1	2	3	4
Number of central banks using	1	21	13	4

We ran a regression to see if the ratio of staff to bank deposits was significantly related either to the use of any particular supervisory technique, e.g., on-site examinations, or to the number of different techniques used. We also added an additional dummy variable taking a value of 2 or 1 for the countries where the central bank reported supervisory responsibilities outside the banking system, whether such additional responsibilities included insurance companies or not, respectively, and 0 where the supervisory activity was restricted to the banking system. Since there were large economies of scale in supervision, as shown in the previous equation, we also included the log of deposits (measured in comparable US$s) in the equation. This gave the equation (t values in parentheses) reported in Table 6.1.

This regression indicates that having special audits by accountants (D3b) and on-site examinations (D3c) use specialised staff intensively. The extra duties dummy was wrong-signed. We explored removing some of the insignificant, or wrong-signed variables, but this did not improve the results. Instead, one country had a much smaller ratio of supervisory staff than predicted, and we ran the same equation, reported in Table 6.2, without this outlier (Mauritius), obtaining a considerably better fit.

To be able to explain 80 per cent of the variability in the ratio of supervisory staff to deposits is encouraging, especially since two of the significant explanatory variables, D3b and D3c, relate to supervisory methods that may reasonably – especially D3c, on-site examinations – be held to require more specialised staff. The negative, and significant, coefficient on D3e (other methods) is unreliable, since only two countries reported that these were used.

Whether or not banks (and other financial entities) are supervised, some will make large losses and fail. One of the commonest cause of such failure is fraud, which will certainly entail trying to dupe the external supervisor (e.g., BCCI), and may often involve subverting internal risk-management controls as well (as may have been the case in Barings). Once a bank has prospectively failed, and become potentially insolvent, the question of whether it should be rescued or not is contentious and depends, *inter alia*, on the likelihood of any systemic effect if it is not rescued; on the culpability of the management and owners; and on the relative size

Table 6.1 Ratio of staff to deposits

Dependent variable	Constant	Ln deposits (US$)	D3a	D3b	D3c	D3d	D3e	Extra duties dummy	$\bar{R}^2$	Number of countries
Ratio staff/deposits	12.0 (7.65)	−0.466 (−6.26)	−0.302 (−0.85)	0.843 (2.28)	1.036 (2.28)	0.443 (1.22)	−1.230 (−1.91)	−0.218 (−0.63)	0.713	32

Table 6.2 Staff/deposits ratio excluding outlier

Dependent variable	Constant	Ln deposits (US$)	D3a	D3b	D3c	D3d	D3e	Extra duties dummy	$\bar{R}^2$	Number of countries
Ratio staff/deposits	12.1 (9.06)	−0.472 (−7.45)	−0.221 (−0.73)	0.991 (3.12)	1.146 (2.95)	0.295 (0.94)	−1.277 (−2.32)	−0.187 (−0.64)	0.792	31

of loss that would need to be shouldered by the depositors, if the bank was to fail, and by the central bank, by other commercial banks (if there was to be a 'lifeboat' rescue party), or taxpayers if a rescue was to be mounted.

Consequently the event and size of bank failure is not a measure of the success, or otherwise, of bank supervision. Nevertheless the incidence, resolution and problems involved in such crisis occasions may be of interest in themselves. There was a wide range of experience. Within the BoE group, 14 central banks[8] (about one-third of the group) reported no failures, or occasions for central bank restructuring, or other reported involvement during our chosen period, 1985–93, and in six other countries the one problem needing resolution had arisen as part of the BCCI débâcle, in Bangladesh, Barbados, Botswana, Mauritius, Pakistan and Sri Lanka, where in most cases the local business of BCCI was merged with another local financial institution (a finance company in Barbados, and a bank in Mauritius, Pakistan and Sri Lanka; it was restructured as a commercial bank in Bangladesh).

At the other end of the spectrum, in Kuwait, following the Iraqi invasion, the whole banking system had to be reorganised and recapitalised at considerable expense to the government. In the remaining 17 cases, where we had data, the number of banks (or supported financial institutions) involved in each country were as follows:

Number of financial institutions	1	2	3	4	7	8
Number of countries[9]	7	4	1	3	1	1

In terms of the percentage of deposits involved, the distribution was as follows:

Percentage of deposits	Negligible	<1	2–5	5–10	10–15
Number of countries[10]	3	4	4	2	2

Of the methods of dealing with failing banks, nationalisation (or a version of it) was used in three countries (in two of these temporarily prior to sale to private sector), mergers with another bank (including the BCCI cases) in 11 countries, liquidation in 13 countries and other measures (mostly recapitalisation and re-structuring with central bank assistance) in seven countries. Ten countries used two or more methods generally involving the liquidation of some banks, and merging or restructuring others.

Seventeen central banks reported that the support operations had involved them in some expense. In those cases where such costs were heavy, e.g., in Chile (largely before 1985) and Kuwait, the cost of the exercise was predominantly borne by the government. In another case it was reported that there was a public outcry at state funds being used to 'bail out' a private bank. The central bank bore administrative and audit costs, and in several cases, especially of smaller banks, was prepared to give loan guarantees in order to facilitate a merger between the bank in difficulties and another domestic bank. In addition, the central bank in some cases was prepared to make liquidity available on concessionary terms. In Malaysia, although the central bank had to apply a significant amount of funds in the initial restructuring process, most of the cost was recouped when the shares were subsequently resold to the private sector.

What was, however, noticeable was that there were *no cases* mentioned among this group where the support costs were shared and divided up among other private sector (banking) institutions, as was done in the 'lifeboat' format so often used historically in the UK. It is easiest to use this latter method of cost sharing when there is a tightly knit cartel of domestically headquartered banks. The breakdown of this cartel, and greater competition from overseas banks, made it harder to organise a lifeboat for Johnson-Matthey Bankers in 1984, and may preclude its further use, even in the UK. In most of the countries in the BoE group, the important role played by international or by government-owned commercial banks may have made loss-sharing (lifeboat) arrangements among private sector banks impractical.

With the small sample that we had (both in terms of number of countries and in number of years covered) and the outliers involved (Kuwait, and the international ramifications of BCCI), we did not think that any econometric investigation, e.g., of the relationship between supervisory mode and the probability and extent of failures, would have been illuminating. So we did not try any.

Our final questions in this area related to deposit insurance. What surprised us here was how *few* of the BoE group had adopted any form of explicit deposit insurance, given both the US example and the recent enthusiasm of European countries for the introduction of some (partial) deposit insurance. Even counting Barbados (with a bill to introduce such insurance) as already having it, 30 out of the BoE group of 40, three-quarters of them, did not. However, four countries, notably two close to the European Union, Cyprus and Malta, stated that they are 'considering' its introduction, as are Jordan and Pakistan. Hong Kong, however, had already considered and rejected the idea. South Africa noted that, although there was no explicit insurance scheme, all depositors in failing banks had been made whole by a combination of central bank and government pay-outs. Of the remaining ten countries with such schemes, Kuwait is again an outlier with 100 per cent government-financed insurance (instituted in 1986 to counteract the collapse of the unofficial stock market) and there is a small, voluntary, private-sector scheme among some rural banks in Sri Lanka. In the other eight cases, Bahamas (bill under consideration), Bangladesh, Chile, India, Mexico, Nigeria, Trinidad and Tobago, and Uganda, there is an explicit deposit insurance scheme. In each case the commercial banks contribute to the financing of the fund, usually as a straight percentage of liabilities, ranging from 0.2 per cent in Trinidad and Tobago and Uganda to 0.94 per cent in Nigeria. In two cases, Chile and Uganda, the government provides some additional funding, and in two countries, Trinidad and Tobago and Bahamas, the central bank also participates in the financing. In Trinidad and Tobago, unusually, the deposit insurance scheme is reported to be compulsory for *non-bank* financial institutions. The US example would appear to have influenced the design of the schemes in Chile and Mexico, since there is 100 per cent insurance in these cases (though only for demand deposits in Chile; savings deposits there are 90 per cent insured up to a maximum of the US$ equivalent of $3,400). In the other six countries (Bahamas, Bangladesh, India, Nigeria, Trinidad and Tobago and Uganda), the European approach, with a maximum level for insured deposits, has been adopted.

Nevertheless, the conclusion of this aspect of the questionnaire is that the current fashion for deposit insurance among many OECD, especially European countries, has *not* been transmitted to developing countries. Whether this is because of the potential expense of such schemes, or because they are seen as unnecessary and/or undesirable in such a context, we do not know.[11]

In contrast, the BoE group of developing countries has included a larger proportion of central banks with supervisory authority over banks, and in many cases other financial institutions as well. If the BCCI related problems are ignored, almost half of the group had no reported difficulties with failing banks. Apart from the special case of Kuwait, and of Chile – though at an earlier date – and perhaps Malaysia and Zambia, the problems of failures in these countries were relatively mild in comparison with those in the OECD countries. Whereas this BoE group of countries compares poorly with the OECD countries in terms of inflation control, they compare well in terms of maintaining systemic stability. Nor is there any evidence that the inflation problems have been systematically caused by measures, e.g., expansionary monetary policy, aimed at propping up a fragile banking system, though it may be argued that the financial fragility of Chile in the early 1980s may have had macro-monetary consequences.

NOTES

1 The Comisión Nacional Bancaria is the supervisory authority; the central bank monitors transactions and carries out analysis of risk management and efficiency to prevent excessive risk taking.
2 In the Bahamas, however, the central bank described itself as the regulatory agency. In Zimbabwe, the Reserve Bank is not the supervisory agent although it is the supervisory authority.
3 Belize, Gambia, Guyana, Mauritius, Saudi Arabia, Sierra Leone, Solomon Islands and South Africa. Moreover, in one of these, Guyana, financial legislation has just been enacted giving, in future, the central bank responsibility for supervising all institutions engaged in banking and/or financial business.
4 We would have liked also to scale the number of staff by the number of separate institutions which they have to supervise, but, as noted earlier at various points, we did not ask for, and have not been able to obtain, such data.
5 The Reserve Bank of Zimbabwe does not maintain specialist supervisory staff, so we excluded it from our set of banks for the exercises relating to supervisory staff.
6 In one country this was only done if the central bank requested it.
7 In one country these constituted a tripartite discussion with bank and auditor, and in another interviews with management. We would guess that most other countries also held such interviews, but that these were subsumed under other headings, e.g., on-site examination.
8 These were Belize, Cyprus, Fiji, Guyana, India, Lesotho, Malawi, Malta, Mexico, Namibia, Saudi Arabia, Singapore, Solomon Islands and Zimbabwe. Whether there were cases, in these and other countries, of commercial bank 'difficulties' requiring some remedial action by the central bank, e.g., loans at concessionary rates, capital adequacy forbearance, etc. (which did not involve failure or require

restructuring), we did not ask and do not know. In any case the definition of 'difficulties' and of 'remedial action' would be amorphous, so it would not be easy to be confident that one was comparing like with like.

9 One country (Jordan) reported the percentage of deposits involved, but not the number of banks.

10 In two countries where there was no bank failure as such, but a commercial bank needed some support, no detail of the percentage of deposits in that bank was given.

11 See, however, Fry (1995, pp. 365–368) and Samuel Talley and Ignacio Mas (1992) for discussions of deposit insurance schemes in other developing countries.

7

THE STATUS OF THE CENTRAL BANK

So far in Chapters 2–6 we have been describing what the central banks in the BoE group have been doing, their operations and functions. Here we look at certain internal aspects of how they are run in order to carry out these functions.

THE USE OF SKILLED STAFF BY THE CENTRAL BANK

Central banking requires certain professional skills, a high level of human capital. Our first set of questions, on the status of this group of central banks, in section E of the questionnaire, sought to discover how well central banks were placed to obtain the skilled staff that they required and how assiduously they had recruited staff who had already received training in some of these skills.

The central bank in almost all countries, with a few exceptions, is part of the wider public sector, a public corporation. We therefore asked whether the central bank was able to recruit separately for its own purposes, or did so as part of the wider civil service. The unanimous answer was that it could, and did, recruit independently, with one exception, Brunei, and another country, which noted that it was still constrained by public corporation rules. Similarly, in very few of the countries of the BoE group did the central bank need to abide by civil service pay scales. Only in Brunei and Mexico did the central banks use such scales, though in Hong Kong, where the Monetary Authority is adjusting its role from being a part of the civil service to becoming a central bank, the longer-serving employees remained on civil service pay scales, whereas the newer recruits were not. In almost all cases, the central banks with separate pay scales reported that these were higher than those of the civil service, in several cases being based both on market forces *and* on comparable civil service pay scales. A number of central banks reported, however, that their pay scales were 'close' or 'similar' to those in the civil service (Bangladesh, Botswana, Chile, Saudi Arabia, Swaziland) and two central banks just stated that their pay scales were 'different' (Kuwait and Namibia). Otherwise they were uniformly reported as higher, except for Pakistan, which stated that its central bank pay scale was 'lower'.

Given the higher pay scales (than the civil service) and the relatively high esteem, status and public service role of the central bank (combined with the low market risk), the central bank should be relatively well placed to recruit those young job seekers which it sought, with at least one exception; the central bank of Sierra Leone has been subject to a freeze on new employment for three years, so we excluded it from our set of banks for these exercises. For the remainder, we began by comparing their intake of both graduates and undergraduates together (over the last three years) as a proportion of their total staff, as reported under question A4. This immediately opened up two problems. First, many central banks, including the Bank of England, improve the professional skills of their existing young staff by sending some of these back to university for further training. Of the BoE group of central banks, five (Gambia, Jamaica, Malaysia, Malta and Singapore) made special reference to their sponsoring programmes for putting existing staff through further university training, although they had not been actually asked about this.[1] It is reasonable to conjecture that these central banks rely particularly heavily on such training mechanisms. Hence to exclude their staff graduate training would bias the results in one way. Yet it is also likely that other central banks in the BoE group may also have made some use of such procedures. So to include staff trainees for the four central banks who mentioned it but not for the others will bias the results another way. Hence, we ran the distributions both including and excluding the reported sponsored staff trainees.

Our second problem was that Israel only reported the total of existing staff with degrees, not the number of new recruits in the last three years. Rather than drop Israel from the group, we have applied a somewhat arbitrary ratio of new recruits to total skilled staff of one to five. Sri Lanka reported both new recruits (143) and the total staff with degrees (707), giving a ratio of about one to five. This also gives an average career length in the central bank of graduates of about 15 years, which seems plausible.

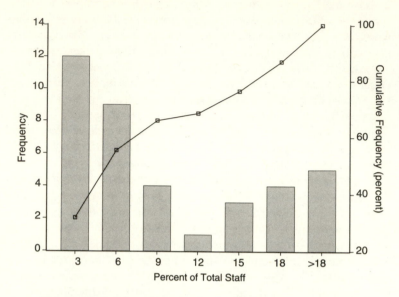

Figure 7.1 Total graduate intake (excluding sponsored staff)

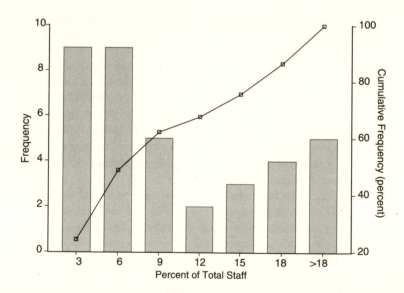

Figure 7.2 Total graduate intake (including sponsored staff)

Clearly the number of graduates hired will depend on the size of central bank, so we scaled by total staff. Histograms of the distribution of the ratio (with and without sponsored staff graduates) are shown in Figures 7.1 and 7.2. These show a rather wider disparity in graduate recruitment than we had expected. This disparity is, however, somewhat reduced if we include sponsored staff (where mentioned). But even in this latter case the intake (over the last three years) varies between a low level of below 3 per cent of staff in nine central banks to a very high ratio of 'over 18 per cent in five central banks. We examined whether the distribution of this ratio could be explained by a number of variables, including real income, measures of the indigenous *supply* of university graduates, inflation and the central bank's assessment of its own independence (the answer to F9).

The variables measuring the indigenous supply of university graduates had the wrong sign (negative). When this was dropped, we obtained the estimated equation (*t* values in parentheses) shown in Table 7.1. The fit of this equation is reasonably good, and we note the positive correlation between the recruitment of skilled staff and self-assessment of independence. The positive relationship with inflation is, perhaps, counter-intuitive, but this is largely, though not entirely, due to the inclusion of Argentina, which has hired a vast number of university graduates in the last three years, was recovering from hyperinflation in 1991, but has since reconstituted its central bank as a highly independent entity.

If we exclude Argentina, the basic equation is that reported in Table 7.2. Now the fit worsens sharply, and inflation is no longer significant. However, the positive relationship between independence and the recruitment of skilled staff remains significant.

We have already noted, but not been able fully to document, that central banks differ between recruiting graduates, or sending their existing staff off for graduate training. Similarly, central banks can differ in their policies of hiring postgraduates (those who have a Masters, an M.Phil. or a Ph.D.) as contrasted with graduates. We were also interested in whether the central banks concentrated their hiring of postgraduates among those who had specialised in relevant disciplines (we specified accounting, economics, finance and statistics; with hindsight we should have added business and law to our list).

The results showed more diversity than we had expected. Because in some cases there was no, or very limited, hiring of one

Table 7.1 Ratio of graduates to total staff

Dependent variable	Constant	Relative real income (logs)	F9: Central bank independence	Inflation in 1991	$\bar{R}^2$	Number of countries
Ratio of graduates/ total staff	−30.9 (−2.84)	2.613 (1.79)	4.613 (2.86)	0.141 (3.76)	0.548	29

Table 7.2 Graduates/total staff ratio excluding outlier

Dependent variable	Constant	Relative real income (logs)	F9: Central bank independence	Inflation in 1991	$\bar{R}^2$	Number of countries
Ratio of graduates/ total staff	−27.47 (−1.85)	2.474 (1.59)	3.546 (2.09)	1.353 (0.73)	0.228	28

category, usually postgraduate, we took as our metric $(n - N)/(N + n)$, where N is the number of postgraduates hired and n the number of graduate recruits. We had expected the results to be bunched around +0.6 (four undergraduates to every graduate, $(4 - 1)/5 = +0.6$). In fact, as shown by the histogram in Figure 7.3 (without sponsored staff), the distribution was far wider ranging from +1 (Belize, Brunei and Malawi) to –0.75 (Cyprus). Again we examined whether we could explain the distribution of this ratio by the same set of variables as we used to explain total graduate hiring. The results of this exercise were of no use. None of the above variables approached significance, and the explanatory power, $\bar{R}^2$, was zero.[2]

Next we looked at how closely the BoE group of central banks stuck in their recruitment of postgraduates to the four specified skill areas mentioned above, as measured by the simple ratio of specified skill to total postgraduates. Again the distribution was much wider than we had anticipated, ranging from 100 per cent in countries such as Chile, Jordan, Lesotho and East Caribbean, down to 20 per cent in Botswana; the histogram is shown in Figure 7.4.

Our questionnaire enquired about the hiring of skilled staff, not

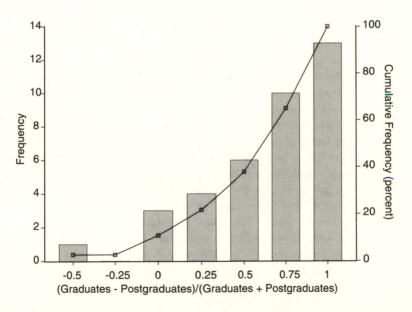

Figure 7.3 Graduates/postgraduates ratio

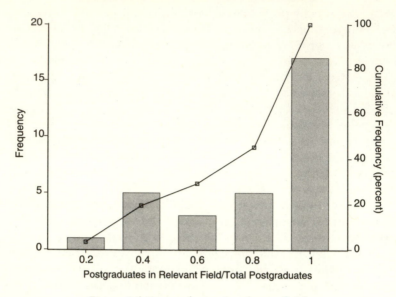

Figure 7.4 Postgraduates in relevant fields

about the use made of them once in the central bank. One such use, which was emphasised by our discussant, Professor Fischer, and supported by other central bankers, is to establish a research department to prepare, *inter alia*, macroeconomic models and forecasts for the economy. In less-developed countries the central bank's macroeconomic model is often the only one extant in the country; and even where there are others, either in the public or private sectors, the model and the calibre of the research staff at the central bank is again often the best in the country. That gives the central bank both status and an advantage in setting the agenda, e.g., in discussions with the Ministry of Finance.

But we failed to take the opportunity of this questionnaire to investigate this and other uses of such skilled staff. All that we could do was to see if the ratio of graduates to total staff was correlated with current inflation and central banks' self-assessment of independence, though in both cases, probably more so with independence, there may be some considerable simultaneity. Be that as it may, the simple correlations were 0.163 and –0.06, respectively, neither of them significant at the 95 per cent level.

To conclude, there appear to be quite large differences in the policies of the various central banks on how best to obtain the skilled staff that they need, and what skill pool to tap. Our attempts to explain some of these differences have, however, not been notably successful.

THE DETERMINANTS OF TOTAL STAFF NUMBERS

But what determines the overall size of the labour force in each central bank? We have already sought to explain the number of staff specialised in dealing with regulatory and supervisory issues in Chapter 6. So here we seek to explain total staff numbers less the specialised supervisory staff. Obviously the size of the country is relevant, so we scale our staff number by the total population in that country. Then we use as possible explanatory variables: population; real income per head in US$; the amount of money outstanding, both M1 and M2 in US$ per capita; the average inflation rate; the exchange regime; the use of exchange controls;[3] the answers to B16 and B17 (as a measure of the use of market vs direct control mechanisms and also of the need for staff to operate in the government bond market); the concentration of the population (population divided by size); the ratio of graduate intake to total staff; the number of branches; and the self-assessed degree of independence. We enter the variables in log form, where these are not dummies of various kinds.

Our prior expectations about the signs of the coefficients were as follows:

- Population: (−) economies of scale.
- Real income: (+) central banking is a luxury, but some economies of scale.
- Money balances: (+) more to do, but some economies of scale.
- Average inflation: (?) simultaneity.
- Exchange rate regime: (?) pegged > float > fixed?
- Exchange controls: (+) a heavy administrative duty.
- Answer to B16: (−) direct controls more labour intensive.
- Answer to B17: (+) managing debt market requires staff.
- Ratio of graduates: (−) skilled labour is more productive.
- Number of branches: (+) branches need officials.
- Concentration of population: (−) requires less branches and less work.
- Independence: (+) for obvious reasons.

In the event our cynical expectation that central banks which assessed themselves as more independent would also take advantage of that independence to build small empires turned out to be wrong. While the coefficient was not always significant, it was invariably negative. With so many potential explanatory variables, relative to sample size, multicollinearity and simultaneity, the coefficients often varied considerably between equations, and it was not easy to distinguish between such equations.

The number of branches and the need to operate exchange controls both appeared, quite stably and sensibly, related to a larger staff. Besides these, either real income or real money balances generally had a positive effect. So, on grounds of simplicity, goodness of fit, significance of all coefficients, and, apart from the effect of independence, concordance with our priors, we took as our best equation that shown in Table 7.3 (*t* values in parentheses).

To explain the larger part of the ratio of central bank (non-supervisory) staff to population is encouraging. While there was some considerable experimentation, data-mining, done here, the positive effects on central bank staff numbers of exchange controls and branches are surely clear. We are quite pleased that our cynicism about the effect of independence on staff numbers was found to be incorrect. Overall, the extent to which this equation explained relative staff numbers did rather better than we had expected.

CENTRAL BANK INDEPENDENCE

As we have found when we ran the various equations that formed the basis for the previous section, there is only a tenuous relationship at best between the size of the central bank (exclusive of supervisory staff and as a ratio to total population) and inflation experience. The simple correlations between the logs of the size variable and average inflation in 1991, over the last five and 15 years are all negative at -0.53, -0.51, and -0.44, respectively. While these are relatively moderate values in absolute terms, a relatively larger central bank does seem to be associated with a lower level of inflation.

Research on OECD countries has shown a negative relationship between inflation and central bank independence, with the latter measured in a variety of ways, but usually including various measures of the central bank's statutory status. Cukierman's research

Table 7.3 Ratio of nonsupervisory staff to population

Dependent variable	Constant	Population	Real per capita income	Number of branches	Exchange controls used	F9: independence	$\bar{R}^2$	Number of countries
Staff minus super./ population	10.24 (9.34)	−0.484 (−12.01)	0.214 (2.62)	0.094 (5.31)	0.736 (3.27)	−0.165 (−2.04)	0.887	30

among his set of developing countries, however, suggested that such statutory variables were less effective in explaining inflationary differences than a variable measuring the turnover rate among central bank governors; the lower the turnover rate, the lower inflation.

We sought to explore the same general issues by asking not only for data on the turnover rate on governors, from question A3, but also a variety of questions in section F of the questionnaire, which might help to elucidate how subservient to the government, or alternatively independent, the central bank in each country was, together with a question about how independent each central bank assessed itself as being. In such exercises there is always a problem of getting the periodicity right. The status and independence of a central bank can change, as can its inflation experience (Chile and New Zealand represent two good examples). Moreover it may take time for any changes in the position of a central bank to become apparent in (average) inflation figures. Ideally perhaps we should have sought data for the central bank's status in 1989, and examined whether and how this influenced inflation in 1991 and over the average of the last five years. In practice, we are running the regressions the other way around, comparing the role of the central bank in 1995, with *prior* inflationary experience in 1991 and over the average of 1989–93. In particular, this caused severe problems in the case of Argentina. During our data period Argentina was the most inflationary country in our group. But in October 1992 its central bank, the Banco Central de la Republica Argentina (BCRA), was given a new Charter, as part of the country's sweeping currency and financial reform process. Following this reform BCRA now assesses itself as one of the most independent central banks in our group. To relate its current status, *vis-à-vis* independence, to inflation in 1991 or the average of 1989–93 makes no sense at all. Consequently, where relevant, we exclude Argentina as an outlier.

Let us turn now to the answers to the final set of questions F1–F5. The first of these, on who appoints the Governor, showed very little differentiation. It was in all cases done within the public sector, by the head of state, or government, or head of state on the advice of the government. With the benefit of hindsight, the question that we *should* have asked is whether the advice of those connected with the central bank, e.g., the outgoing governor or the bank's directors, is solicited and, if so, is usually followed. Not having asked that question, we could make no use of question F1.

Question F2, on the period of appointment, again showed little diversity, less than we had expected. There was a great concentration on five-year appointments (usually renewable), with 29 out of 38 central banks falling into this category.[4] (Two central banks did not answer this section.) Given Cukierman's prior finding on his set of developing countries that the actual, *ex post*, turnover rate of governors in each central bank was positively associated with inflation, we also worked with that statistic, obtained from question A3, rather than the *ex ante* term of appointment. Histograms showing the actual number of central bank governors, first actually and second after correction for the age of the central bank, if founded since 1975, in each country since 1975 are shown in Figures 7.5 and 7.6.

We replicated Cukierman's exercise regressing the log of the inflation experience over our 15-year period 1979–93 against the (corrected) number of governors in each central bank; the result was positive, and significant at the 95 per cent level, but this was largely due to the influence of Argentina:

Log of 15-year average inflation = 1.61 + 0.185 (number of governors)
$$(4.06)$$
$\bar{R}^2 = 0.307$ Number of central banks: 36

The same result held, with a higher *t* ratio (4.99), over the final five-year average. Without Argentina, the results were considerably weaker. The *t* ratio over the final five-year average fell to 2.37, and the equation for the 15-year period became:

Log of 15-year average inflation = 1.89 + 0.122 (number of governors)
$$(1.99)$$
$\bar{R}^2 = 0.080$ Number of central banks: 35

Reverting to the questionnaire, the government, or the head of state with the government, or some public sector body, was also responsible for appointing the directors of the central bank in almost all cases (34 out of 38) (question F3). Only in four cases did the central bank itself (Bahamas, Hong Kong, Solomon Islands) or private sector shareholders (South Africa) play a role.

There was, however, a much greater diversity of experience on whether a member of the Ministry of Finance (minister or permanent secretary) or other member of the government was, *ex officio*, a director (question F4). The results from our 37 responses are shown in Table 7.4.

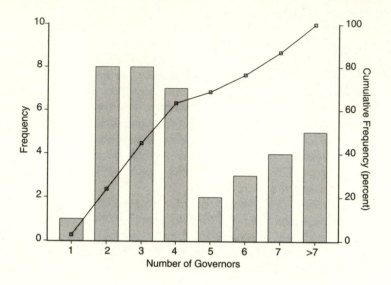

Figure 7.5 Number of governors since 1975

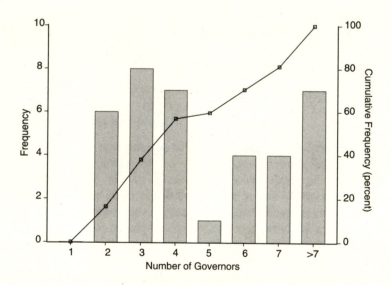

Figure 7.6 Number of governors since 1975, corrected for the age of the central bank

102

Table 7.4 Government representation on the central bank's Board

	No	No but may attend	Yes		
Number of government officials			1	2	3+
Number of central banks	11	3	15	5	3

In question F5, we asked for the statutory objectives of the central bank. We wanted to assess the degree of primacy being given to the achievement of price stability in the statutes. This proved exceedingly difficult to do. Five central banks did not answer and four do not have statutory objectives. Four now gave primacy to the achievement of price stability (Argentina, Chile, Cyprus and Mexico). In Belize the statutes relate to functions rather than objectives and do not mention nominal stability. In the other 26 cases, nominal stability (external, internal or both) was an objective among others; an attempt at a finer gradation of these 26 cases was attempted, but abandoned as futile.

We then asked who decided on (a) interest rate changes, (b) changes to administered bank ceilings, ratios, etc., (c) new issues of government debt. Decision (b) was almost always done solely by the central bank (28 out of 38 cases) and jointly with another governmental body in seven more cases. Decision (c) was most usually (22 out of 38 cases) done solely by the government. Decision (a) was most frequently shared between the two. Giving a value 1 when the central bank either took the decision itself, or took the lead in a joint decision, and ½ where it was consulted or the junior partner, provided an index of central bank powers over decision-making,[5] with the histogram shown below:

	0	1	1½	2	2½	3
Number of central banks	2	9	3	16	3	5

Again there was a wide range of answers in response to question F7, whether the government can require the central bank to finance its deficit. In four cases this was not answered; of the remaining 36, 26 stated yes that it could, subject to a variety of limitations, and ten that it could not.

There was again a wide range of responses to question F8: what happens if government bond sales fail to cover the deficit? Out of the 38 central banks responding to this question, six stated that the question was not applicable, in most of these cases and certainly in three (Hong Kong, Singapore and United Arab Emirates) because there was no deficit to finance. Of the remaining 32, three stated that such financing was now prohibited (Argentina, Chile and Saudi Arabia), 12 that it would normally be provided but *not* automatically, and 13 that it would be provided automatically.[6] Out of the 29 cases where such financing would (normally) be provided, in 25 cases statutory limits on such borrowing, almost always in the form of a percentage on government revenue, were in place but the penalty for transgressing these was rarely more than the need to report it to Parliament, and to regularise the position quite soon.

Finally we asked central banks, F9, how independent they viewed themselves as being on a scale of 1 (least) to 5 (most). The distribution of answers was as follows:

	2	2½	3	3½	4	5
Number of central banks[7]	5	1	12	4	7	3

We then regressed the central banks' self-assessment of independence against inflation, in 1991 and over the last five years (but not over the longer average for the reason earlier stated). The results, omitting Argentina for the reasons specified, are given in Table 7.5. The independence variable, F9, is significant (at the 95

Table 7.5 Inflation and central bank independence

Inflation	1991	1989–93
Coefficient on F9	−9.979	−14.272
t value	(−1.94)	(−2.45)
R^2	[0.09]	[0.15]
Number of countries	30	30

per cent level for the five-year average and at the 90 per cent level for 1991) and with the 'correct' sign.

Our next step was to examine the simple (Pearson) correlations between the F questions, F3–F9 (F1 and F2 being dropped, since the answers were too similar), and both inflation over the last five years and also the self-assessment of independence (omitting Argentina in the correlations with inflation). The indices we used, where not already reported or 1/0, were:

F4: Public sector directors:
     0 if No; ½ if may attend; otherwise number participating.
F8: What happens if deficit uncovered:
     0 if financing prohibited or not required;
     1 if financing normally provided but *not* automatic;
     2 if financing automatically provided.

We also indicate our expectation of the sign of the relationship in parentheses, and emphasise when the correlation is significant in Table 7.6.

In these simple correlations only the relationships between F7 and F8 (which in any case overlap) and independence are correctly signed *and* significant; the same variables have the correctly signed relationship with inflation, but are not significant. Otherwise all the other F variables have an insignificant relationship with inflation or perceived independence, and only the relationships between perceived independence and F5A and F5B have the correct sign. This suggests that it is the relationship with government financing that is the key to the role and status of the central bank.

It may, however, be that these simple correlations obscure some more complex multiple relationship, so we looked at multiple regressions, using the log of inflation (1989–93) and independence (F9) as alternative dependent variables, incorporating all the F variables (F3–F8), the (corrected) number of governors (since 1975) (A3), and the total graduate intake as explanatory variables. We began with this full set of variables, and then progressively eliminated the most insignificant until we reached our preferred equation. The results are shown in Table 7.7. Finally we added the independence variable (F9) back into the best inflation equation. We omitted Argentina throughout this exercise, due to the unusually high level of inflation and turnover of governors before 1992. In addition, the results are shown exclusive of two other outliers in the inflation equations (Belize and Zambia).

Table 7.6 F question correlations

Correlation of	With (log of) inflation	Independence
F3: Private appointment of directors	+0.006 (–)	–0.151 (+)
F4: Government officials on the central bank's Board	–0.163 (+)	+0.061 (–)
F5A: Statutory objective for price stability	+0.070 (–)	+0.212 (+)
F5B: Statutory objective for growth	–0.110 (+)	–0.216 (–)
F6: Powers of central bank	+0.092 (–)	–0.188 (+)
F7: Government can force central bank to monetise deficit	0.151 (+)	*–0.595 (–)*
F8: Automatic finance if bond sales fail	0.186 (+)	*–0.640 (–)*

Our ability to explain a central bank's self-assessment of independence using this set of variables is reasonably good. Two of these variables are straightforward. The *most* important is the primacy given to price stability in the statutes (F5A), and the second most important is the rate of turnover of central bank governors (A3) (though this relationship may involve simultaneous causation, and we are unsure how we could instrument for this). Although not very significantly, the role of the central bank regarding government financing also affects the self-assessment of independence: this is higher when central banks do not finance the government (F7), and if they do finance it, when such financing is not automatic (F8). We also found a *positive* and marginally significant relationship between the self-assessment of independence and the number of ex officio government participants on the Board of Directors (F4). This was in contrast to our prior expectations. It may, of course, be a spurious small sample result. Nevertheless in conjunction with the similar, a priori anomalous, result obtained in Chapter 3, it made us want to reconsider whether having government directors on the Board is as harmful of independence as might have been thought. We report how our views on this have changed in the next section.

Our ability to explain inflation using this set of variables is also reasonably good,[8] although we had to exclude two outliers to achieve this result.[9] The results for A3, F4 and F8 are consistent

Table 7.7 Inflation and the status of the central bank

Dependent variable	Explanatory variables							$\bar{R}^2$	Number of countries
	A3	F4	F5A	F5B	F7	F8	F9		
Inflation 1989–93	0.134 (2.30)	−0.263 (−2.04)		−1.008 (−2.17)		0.381 (1.85)		0.350	25
Inflation 1989–93	0.160 (2.51)	−0.310 (−2.45)		−1.028 (−1.84)		0.247 (0.85)	−0.142 (−0.56)	0.400	21
Independence assessment	−0.117 (−2.02)	0.178 (1.46)	1.191 (2.36)		−0.623 (−1.46)	−0.297 (−1.20)		0.477	23

with the results for the independence equation. Once again a major conclusion is that the relationship between the central bank and its government is an important determinant of its role and status in the economy. The *negative* and significant relationship between inflation and F5B (explicit requirement in the central banks' statutes to pursue growth) is hard to believe. It is probably a small sample result, but at least suggests that being statutorily constrained to pursue growth does not induce the central banks to follow inflationary policies. With independence F9 included in the set, the results do not change much, only F8 loses explanatory power.

CENTRAL BANK AND GOVERNMENT COOPERATION

Two anomalous results thrown up by this study are the greater conservatism in their monetary policy reactions and self-assessment of greater independence of central banks with government officials on their Boards. Two possible explanations suggest themselves. The first is that no useful purpose would be served in placing senior government officials on the Board of a completely subservient central bank. Hence, they are only placed on Boards of central banks with some degree of independence.

The second possible explanation, the one to which we would be more inclined to subscribe, is that government representation on the central bank's Board signals a cooperative rather than noncooperative strategy for macroeconomic policy-making. Since cooperation in such activities is likely to prove more efficient than noncooperation, both the government and its central bank may feel greater satisfaction with the outcomes of cooperative policy-making than they would otherwise. This feeling of satisfaction over the results would, we conjecture, increase the central bank's self-esteem and so its feeling of independence.

In addition to this game theoretic explanation, closer and more regular contact with government can provide the central bank with the means to educate its government in what can and cannot be achieved by the central bank. Specifically, the establishment of a monetary policy committee consisting of, among others, the minister of finance and the central bank governor may enable the central bank to achieve greater influence over the thrust of monetary policy.

The Mauritian experiment with such an arrangement since June 1994 appears to have increased central bank independence quite considerably, despite the fact that no other change in personalities or legal powers has occurred. The monthly monetary policy committee meetings enable the Bank of Mauritius not only to set the agenda of the debate between it and the government on possible conflicting objectives of monetary policy but also to explain to the government in analytical fashion matters pertaining to monetary policy. The results have been considerably more harmonious relations between government and central bank as well as, more importantly, more effective and successful monetary policy implementation.

This experiment also demonstrates the value of a well-staffed central bank research department. In the Mauritian case, it now has the opportunity to communicate on a regular basis with the minister of finance and other government officials through a briefing paper modelled along the lines of the Bank of England's *Inflation Report*. Given that briefing papers for these meetings are prepared by the research staff of the central bank, this provides the central bank with a forum for explaining what it believes to be appropriate policy and what consequences would follow from pursuing alternative policies. In this light, expertise within the central bank may well be the key to independence, regardless of any statutory provisions. Cukierman makes the point that

> A governor who is backed by an absolutely and relatively strong research department carries more weight vis-à-vis the Treasury and other branches of government. The reason is probably that the governor is perceived as a relatively impartial provider of reliable information about the economy. A possible indicator of the quality of bank's research department is the quality of the annual report it produces.
>
> (Cukierman 1992, pp. 393–394)

A second key ingredient of central bank independence lies in the acceptance by the government of the benefits to the economy of playing on a level playing field with all other borrowers. This is the first step to producing marketable government debt, which in turn is essential for central bank open market operations. Perhaps more important is the fact that once the government accepts the case against financial repression for raising funds at below-market interest rates the central bank can assume the responsibility of funding the government by auctioning treasury bills.

Again, Mauritius provides an example. After the government

accepted the level playing field principle, the Bank of Mauritius was able to divorce monetary policy from fiscal policy using its primary instrument of treasury bill auctions. By ensuring that the government was not directly affected financially by how its deficit was financed, the Bank of Mauritius could offer the appropriate volume of treasury bills for auction each week without regard to the precise weekly or monthly financing requirements of the government. When sales exceed the government financing require-ment, the balance is placed in a special treasury bill management account at the Bank of Mauritius that earns interest equal to the auction yield. When sales fall short of the government financial requirement, the Bank of Mauritius lends to the government at a rate equal to the auction yield. In this way, the Bank of Mauritius can determine the appropriate volume of treasury bills to offer without consulting the Ministry of Finance over the financing implications (Fry and Basant Roi, 1995).

Again Cukierman (1992, p. 395) makes a related point in a situation in which the government has not accepted the benefits of marketable debt which necessitates level playing field government borrowing: 'The ability of the Bank of Israel to conduct open market operations is seriously restricted despite the fact that it holds a large amount of government securities. The reason is that these securities are not tradable and the Israeli Treasury has consistently refused to make them tradable.'

NOTES

1 Malaysia stated that it placed its staff on postgraduate courses, but gave no numbers for that.
2 One reader suggested that the difference in hiring postgraduates may be due to the behaviour of trade unions. It is possible that such trade unions may try to hinder the hiring of new employees other than at relatively low levels in the rank scale.
3 Information on this variable came from IMF data sources.
4 Of the remainder, Nigeria specified that the five-year term represented a non-renewable maximum; in India the government fixed the dur-ation on appointment with a maximum of five years; Pakistan and Singapore had a renewable three-year term, United Arab Emirates a four-year term, Fiji a three- to five-year term, Argentina and Mexico six years, and Hong Kong was not fixed.
5 In quite a number of cases the central bank did not answer, or stated that the question was not applicable to itself. So the alternative to a central bank decision should not automatically be assumed to be a government decision.

6 Malaysia also noted that its 'Government has never taken advantage of this credit facility, since it has been able for most years, to generate sufficient revenue'.

7 Seven central banks declined to classify themselves.

8 We also tried entering some variables measuring the extent of the government deficit to be financed, i.e., both the deficit and the debt ratio as percentages of GDP, but the number of usable countries (and particularly the degrees of freedom) fell so drastically that we could not pursue this line of enquiry on this data set.

9 If we include Belize and Zambia in the regressions, the $\bar{R}^2$ falls to 17 per cent and 18 per cent, in the equations with and without F9, respectively.

8

CONCLUSION

Twenty-five years ago, the central bank in a typical developing country was subservient to its government and used, in the main, to fill a large gap between government expenditure and conventional tax revenue. It was also called upon to finance the Plan, in the same way as central banks in communist countries, through selective credit programmes implemented through various measures of financial repression. Governments pre-empted the supply of domestic saving by preserving a sheltered market for their own bills and bonds. *Dirigism* was the order of the day.

Since then, however, theoretical and empirical advances in economics have improved our understanding of the effects of alternative monetary and financial regimes in developing countries. The main intellectual basis for financial sector analysis in developing countries over the past 23 years lies in the work of Ronald McKinnon (1973) and Edward Shaw (1973). McKinnon and Shaw analyse developing economies that are financially repressed. Their central argument is that financial repression – indiscriminate 'distortions of financial prices including interest rates and foreign-exchange rates' – reduces 'the real rate of growth and the real size of the financial system relative to nonfinancial magnitudes. In all cases this strategy has stopped or gravely retarded the development process' (Shaw 1973, pp. 3–4). Their prescription is the removal of these distortions imposed by so many governments in developing countries.

These advances have changed the thinking of central bankers, finance ministry officials and politicians about the way a central bank should operate. As the answers to C12 attest, central bankers have shared views on these and many other issues at a large number of international gatherings. The meeting for which this book was written provides just one such example. We hope it proves as useful in this respect as others apparently have been in providing mutual reinforcement for continuing the reforms that most of the BoE group central banks are still undertaking as they move towards indirect market-based techniques of monetary policy implementation to achieve price stability.

With this turn of the tide, the role of central banks in the BoE group has distinctly changed, albeit gradually and moderately. We detect a general acceptance of the benefits of price stability as the primary central bank objective to be achieved increasingly through indirect market-based instruments of monetary policy. While change in the role of central banks in the BoE group has inevitably met some resistance from certain quarters, it has also faced exogenous difficulties, such as underdeveloped and uncompetitive financial systems, the lack of a skilled labour force, a preponderance of state-owned financial institutions and the endemic problem of government finance. Despite all the difficulties and setbacks, we believe that reforms now occurring in the way central banks operate in developing countries are irresistible as well as irreversible, in large part because we all understand much better now than we did 25 years ago that inflationary finance is inimical to economic growth.

APPENDIX 1

Central Bank Questionnaire

Basic details

A1 Name of central bank:
A2 Date when founded:
A3 Number of governors since 1975 (or from foundation if later):
A4 Number of staff (current):
A5 Number of branches (outside headquarters):

Latest balance sheet (preferably 1993)

A6 If published, please send copy.
A7 We would also be grateful if you would send us a balance sheet in the format set out in Appendix A.

Latest profit and loss account (preferably 1993)

A8 If published, please send copy.
A9 We would also be grateful if you would send us a profit and loss account in the format set out in Appendix A.
A10 On what basis are profits distributed between retentions, government and any other shareholders?
A11 (a) Is interest paid to banks on the reserves they hold at the central bank? (b) If so, is interest paid on required or excess reserves? (c) What are the current rates of interest? (d) Please give total amount of interest paid on bank reserves for the years 1990, 1991 and 1992.

Domestic role

(1) Payments system

B1 Is there a domestic system(s) for settling payments?
B2 What is its/their daily average turnover?
B3 Is it run by the central bank? Please specify relationship of central bank to the payments system(s).
B4 Are payments settled by transfers of commercial bank deposits held with the central bank? If not, please specify the alternative mechanism?
B5 What is the average delay between initiation and final settlement?
B6 Have there been any major reforms to the payments system since 1975? If so, did the central bank initiate these reforms?

(2) Control over banking system

B7 What balance sheet ratios are imposed on banks (capital, reserves, liquidity, other)? Please give percentages.
B8 What direct controls are imposed on bank loans to the private sector at present?
B9 Do such controls involve selective policies between sectors? If so, please specify.
B10 Are there different central bank rediscount facilities for separate sectors? If so, please specify.
B11 Does the central bank guarantee any category of domestic loans? If so, which?

(3) Financial markets

B12 Please specify the dates of development, the form and turnover of the following: (a) formal money market; (b) domestic bond market; (c) domestic equity market.
B13 Please list and explain the three biggest difficulties in establishing all or any of these domestic financial markets.

(4) Interest rates

B14 Please specify the current interest rate on: (a) central bank (discount window) loans to banks; (b) commercial bank lending (please state type of loan and whether the rate is average or prime); (c) government bonds; (d) commercial bills; (e) treasury bills; (f) priority loans under directed credit schemes.

B15 Which of these rates are either administratively set or have administratively set ceilings?

B16 Does the central bank employ indirect (open) market techniques? If so, in which market(s) and how?

B17 Does the central bank act as the government's agent in the issue and management of any of these financial markets? If so, what techniques are used?

External role

C1   What is the type of exchange rate regime?

C2   Is the exchange rate regime decided by the government, the central bank, jointly, or other?

C3   On what basis was the current exchange rate regime chosen (if known)?

C4   Is intervention on the foreign exchange market decided by the government, the central bank, jointly, or other?

C5   What are the techniques and modalities of intervention on the foreign exchange market?

C6   Are foreign exchange controls decided by the government, the central bank, jointly, or other?

C7   Who administers foreign exchange controls?

C8   Who decides foreign borrowing?

C9   Who arranges foreign borrowing?

C10 Does the central bank implement any foreign exchange rate guarantee schemes? If so, what kind?

C11 Have your external operations, e.g., foreign exchange rate guarantees, caused serious financial loss at any time? If so, how was the problem met?

C12 Which international meetings (excluding those hosted by the Bank of England) does your central bank attend and which are the most useful (and why)?

Supervision and regulation

D1   For which financial markets and financial institutions, e.g., banks, mortgage houses, insurance companies, etc., is the central bank the supervisory authority?

D2   If the central bank is a supervisory agent, are specialised staff used for supervision purposes? If so, what is the percentage of total staff?

D3   Is the supervision of commercial banks conducted on the basis of: (a) ordinary audited accounts; (b) special audits done by accountants; (c) on-site examinations.; (d) regular returns; (e) other?

D4   Please specify the extent of bank failure, 1985–1993, in terms of the percentage of total deposits.

D5   Have bank failures been resolved by: (a) nationalisation; (b) merger with another bank; (c) liquidation; (d) other (please specify)? [We would be grateful for the numbers of banks and total deposits involved in each case.]

D6   Has the resolution/restructuring of problem banks involved a cost to the central bank? If so, did this cause a problem and how was that resolved?

D7   Is deposit insurance used? If so, please specify the nature of the scheme (e.g., limits, percentage insured, etc.).

D8   How is deposit insurance financed?

Professional status of the central bank

E1   Please specify the number of University postgraduates (i.e., with Masters and Ph.D. degrees) hired by the central bank during the past three years (of which, how many in economics, finance, accounting or statistics?).

E2   Please specify the number of University graduates hired by the central bank during the past three years (not counting those listed in the previous question).

E3   Does the central bank use Civil Service pay scales? If not, does it use a higher scale?

E4   Does the central bank recruit independently or as part of the wider Civil Service?

Central bank independence

F1   Who appoints the Governor?

F2   What is the period of the Governor's appointment?

F3   Who appoints other directors of the central bank?

F4   Are any directors members of the government or Ministry of Finance? If so, please specify.

F5 Does the central bank have statutory objective(s)? If so, please specify.

F6 Who decides on: (a) adjustments of administered interest rates; (b) adjustments of administered bank ceilings, balance sheet ratios, etc.; (c) the issue of additional public sector debt?

F7 Can the government require the central bank to finance its deficit?

F8 What happens if government bond sales fail to cover the government's deficit? Is central bank financing automatic? Are there any limits? If so, what happens if the limits are exceeded?

F9 On a scale 1–5 (1 is least, 5 most), how independent would you rate your central bank?

APPENDIX A

Central bank balance sheet

Assets, claims on:	*Liabilities, owing to:*
	Currency
Commercial banks	Commercial banks
Other private sector	Other private sector
Public sector	Public sector
External	External
Other	Other
	Net capital

Central bank profit and loss account

Interest paid to:	*Interest received from:*
Commercial banks	Commercial banks
Other private sector	Other private sector
Public sector	Public sector
External	External
Other costs	Other income
Net profits	

APPENDIX 2

**Some macroeconomic and monetary characteristics of the
Bank of England group, 1979–93 (per cent)**

Country	YG	INF	M/Y	H/M	R/D
Argentina	0.3	555.8	11.3	44.4	29.8
Bahamas	3.0	6.1	41.7	14.6	7.9
Bangladesh	4.3	9.8	18.3	26.5	12.7
Barbados	1.5	6.6	43.3	20.3	9.7
Belize	5.3	4.0	36.2	25.4	13.0
Botswana	10.2	11.6	27.0	29.1	22.1
Chile	4.5	21.5	31.6	18.3	10.3
Cyprus	6.1	5.9 ·	67.3	33.3	24.3
Fiji	1.6	7.1	38.5	19.9	9.7
Gambia	3.2	14.5	22.3	47.6	22.3
Ghana	2.9	41.8	13.0	67.3	43.8
Guyana	−2.3	15.7	84.3	47.3	35.4
Hong Kong	6.8	9.2	83.7	7.2	0.7
India	5.5	9.2	40.3	33.6	14.6
Israel	4.0	95.6	53.1	57.0	57.0
Jamaica	1.5	23.8	45.0	36.5	27.7
Jordan	0.8	7.8	97.8	44.6	21.0
Kenya	4.0	15.7	38.5	27.0	10.6
Kuwait	−2.6	4.7	66.5	12.7	5.4
Lesotho	4.1	14.3	44.8	32.9	27.1
Malawi	2.5	16.8	22.5	38.7	25.4
Malaysia	5.9	3.7	94.9	20.2	7.0
Malta	3.9	3.6	127.7	51.7	22.2
Mauritius	5.8	10.8	49.5	25.3	12.5
Mexico	1.7	52.2	23.2	40.1	29.0
Namibia	1.9	12.9	n.a.	n.a.	n.a.
Nigeria	1.9	24.3	25.1	32.8	11.2
Pakistan	6.4	8.0	38.5	40.7	12.4
Papua New Guinea	2.1	6.2	29.7	16.6	5.6
St Lucia	7.3	5.6	n.a.	20.9	10.8
Saudi Arabia	0.5	0.7	40.2	32.9	11.3
Sierra Leone	1.2	63.6	18.3	73.7	55.5
Singapore	6.8	2.9	98.4	22.5	8.5
Solomon Islands	6.0	11.8	28.5	32.2	17.8
South Africa	1.3	14.2	52.3	12.6	4.9
Sri Lanka	4.3	13.1	35.2	33.0	14.8
Swaziland	5.2	13.7	33.2	36.3	31.2
Tanzania	3.6	26.7	32.2	37.1	6.2
Trinidad and Tobago	−1.5	10.9	50.0	24.9	17.9
Uganda	3.2	86.2	9.1	54.8	27.0
United Arab Emirates	−1.1	n.a.	22.7	18.2	11.5
Zambia	0.9	66.6	31.7	56.5	41.7
Zimbabwe	3.0	17.1	46.4	24.8	12.0

Key: See Table 1.2 (p. 4)

Country	CBCG	CGDC	GS/Y	GR/Y	DT/Y
Argentina	116.7	33.6	−4.1	13.0	42.3
Bahamas	23.8	16.7	−0.8	19.6	n.a.
Bangladesh	44.1	17.2	0.0	13.3	45.4
Barbados	25.1	20.4	−3.5	29.6	36.7
Belize	51.1	15.4	−0.5	25.3	43.7
Botswana	−441.2	−87.1	10.7	52.8	20.8
Chile	53.6	21.8	0.6	27.4	75.5
Cyprus	22.3	17.2	−4.8	25.5	n.a.
Fiji	−9.9	7.4	−3.4	24.4	31.3
Gambia	−25.4	−0.4	−5.2	21.6	116.4
Ghana	154.2	67.1	−2.8	9.6	37.1
Guyana	413.2	79.6	−36.3	44.8	342.7
Hong Kong	0.0	0.0	2.0	16.7	n.a.
India	99.4	45.0	−7.2	13.4	19.6
Israel	27.2	46.4	−11.2	59.8	n.a.
Jamaica	123.1	22.4	−8.6	29.6	122.0
Jordan	33.6	21.1	−7.1	31.9	104.2
Kenya	90.9	31.7	−5.3	22.5	64.1
Kuwait	−100.2	−5.9	−2.9	57.6	n.a.
Lesotho	6.7	41.3	−7.5	47.7	51.4
Malawi	121.0	41.5	−7.9	23.4	83.4
Malaysia	−1.3	5.4	−6.1	26.7	48.0
Malta	−5.3	−4.6	−2.2	39.1	17.2
Mauritius	113.3	45.8	−5.0	22.2	44.1
Mexico	92.0	43.3	−7.7	16.1	49.2
Namibia	10.5	−1.3	−0.4	41.1	n.a.
Nigeria	104.6	49.3	−7.4	14.3	57.2
Pakistan	79.5	46.2	−7.0	17.6	44.6
Papua New Guinea	−15.5	10.2	−2.8	30.1	65.2
St Lucia	34.9	5.4	−0.6	36.4	17.7
Saudi Arabia	−373.5	−14.4	n.a.	n.a.	n.a.
Sierra Leone	137.3	75.3	−8.7	10.9	85.9
Singapore	−119.6	−31.6	4.0	27.4	n.a.
Solomon Islands	15.2	15.5	−6.8	28.4	41.9
South Africa	−18.5	6.9	−4.2	25.5	n.a.
Sri Lanka	158.1	39.6	−10.9	23.0	61.2
Swaziland	−76.3	−16.1	−0.8	31.8	42.5
Tanzania	138.1	54.9	−9.3	19.6	115.6
Trinidad and Tobago	−47.7	11.3	−4.6	34.8	30.0
Uganda	98.0	55.7	−2.9	5.6	40.8
United Arab Emirates	−43.5	−10.2	0.4	14.6	n.a.
Zambia	250.4	60.7	−12.8	22.4	177.8
Zimbabwe	41.5	27.3	−8.6	30.2	41.9

Key: See Table 1.2 (p. 4)

Country	YG			INF		
	1979–83	1984–88	1989–93	1979–83	1984–88	1989–93
Argentina	−1.7	1.1	6.4	174.7	372.6	1120.2
Bahamas	1.0	2.1	−0.7	8.5	4.8	5.1
Bangladesh	3.2	3.9	4.5	13.2	10.2	5.9
Barbados	−1.5	4.6	−3.9	11.5	3.6	4.5
Belize	2.9	6.8	6.2	7.7	3.1	2.6
Botswana	11.1	9.4	7.2	12.7	9.0	13.0
Chile	−1.6	5.6	6.7	25.1	20.9	18.6
Cyprus	5.0	5.9	5.2	9.0	3.7	4.9
Fiji	−0.7	2.1	3.1	9.4	5.8	6.2
Gambia	3.4	3.1	2.8	8.1	26.4	9.0
Ghana	−2.6	5.1	4.3	73.2	29.1	23.1
Guyana	−4.9	−0.0	4.7	18.0	23.4	3.1
Hong Kong	6.9	9.3	4.1	12.2	5.6	9.8
India	5.9	6.0	3.2	10.1	8.2	9.4
Israel	2.9	4.5	5.6	118.4	152.5	15.9
Jamaica	0.4	2.4	1.9	17.5	16.7	37.3
Jordan	8.5	3.5	6.5	9.1	2.6	11.8
Kenya	3.1	6.0	1.3	13.1	9.4	24.7
Kuwait	−12.3	1.1	−5.9	6.8	1.1	7.4
Lesotho	−1.0	5.2	2.1	14.7	13.1	15.0
Malawi	−0.2	2.5	2.8	11.7	20.7	15.8
Malaysia	6.6	3.5	8.6	5.9	1.6	3.6
Malta	2.9	4.6	5.7	7.9	0.5	2.4
Mauritius	1.3	8.7	5.6	17.6	5.1	9.7
Mexico	2.9	0.2	3.6	46.6	91.1	18.9
Namibia	n.a.	4.6	3.3	14.1	12.0	13.1
Nigeria	−2.8	4.6	4.4	14.7	23.7	34.5
Pakistan	7.1	6.6	5.4	8.9	5.7	9.5
Papua New Guinea	0.8	3.8	6.3	7.9	5.1	5.5
St Lucia	1.9	7.5	3.8	10.0	2.6	4.1
Saudi Arabia	−1.4	1.9	7.3	1.9	−1.7	1.8
Sierra Leone	2.6	0.8	0.5	30.6	87.4	72.8
Singapore	8.5	5.2	7.5	5.2	0.7	2.8
Solomon Islands	2.7	−1.0	4.2	11.4	12.4	11.8
South Africa	2.4	1.2	−0.8	13.8	15.1	13.6
Sri Lanka	−1.4	3.3	5.0	15.9	9.6	13.7
Swaziland	1.7	14.7	5.9	15.5	14.6	11.1
Tanzania	0.1	3.9	4.1	25.0	32.6	22.7
Trinidad and Tobago	2.6	−3.8	1.8	14.7	9.4	8.7
Uganda	3.8	4.4	4.3	60.7	151.5	36.2
United Arab Emirates	2.4	−6.4	6.1	n.a.	n.a.	n.a.
Zambia	1.1	2.6	−1.1	13.5	41.5	144.9
Zimbabwe	6.9	3.6	0.8	14.1	12.6	24.6

Key: See Table 1.2 (p. 4)

Country	M/Y			H/M		
	1979–83	1984–88	1989–93	1979–83	1984–88	1989–93
Argentina	16.0	10.7	6.2	49.7	40.4	42.9
Bahamas	38.9	41.5	46.8	15.1	15.3	13.5
Bangladesh	18.3	n.a.	n.a.	27.6	25.9	26.1
Barbados	36.5	42.5	52.7	22.1	20.1	18.8
Belize	32.0	38.4	38.8	25.6	25.2	25.3
Botswana	27.0	n.a.	n.a.	30.2	29.7	27.0
Chile	26.1	34.1	35.3	24.9	15.4	14.7
Cyprus	63.3	64.9	75.1	34.5	35.5	30.0
Fiji	33.0	38.0	45.8	20.7	21.7	17.3
Gambia	21.9	22.8	22.2	67.5	35.8	39.6
Ghana	14.8	11.1	13.1	70.2	70.6	61.1
Guyana	72.7	113.6	62.0	41.2	61.3	39.5
Hong Kong	75.9	85.5	91.2	7.7	6.9	6.9
India	36.7	42.0	43.5	34.3	34.3	32.2
Israel	36.0	62.4	62.7	110.2	37.8	23.1
Jamaica	40.5	48.7	45.9	25.1	40.7	43.7
Jordan	76.8	96.4	125.7	44.7	36.9	52.3
Kenya	37.2	38.1	40.7	25.1	26.9	29.1
Kuwait	49.1	76.8	84.3	17.5	12.2	8.4
Lesotho	45.4	49.6	38.4	29.9	37.5	30.8
Malawi	22.3	23.6	21.4	27.5	49.8	38.8
Malaysia	78.1	111.8	n.a.	22.2	18.7	19.7
Malta	117.7	133.4	133.1	61.3	56.9	36.9
Mauritius	40.2	48.2	62.7	28.9	21.0	26.0
Mexico	27.1	20.6	21.5	58.2	44.1	18.0
Namibia	n.a.	n.a.	n.a.	n.a.	n.a.	n.a.
Nigeria	26.9	28.2	19.1	34.1	28.2	38.4
Pakistan	38.4	39.8	37.0	38.1	39.5	44.4
Papua New Guinea	29.7	n.a.	n.a.	22.1	14.5	13.1
St Lucia	n.a.	n.a.	n.a.	17.7	23.0	22.0
Saudi Arabia	21.8	52.7	49.9	41.1	31.6	26.2
Sierra Leone	21.3	18.7	14.1	83.6	75.4	62.1
Singapore	80.4	101.4	117.3	26.1	23.1	18.3
Solomon Islands	27.8	26.8	33.8	44.1	31.9	20.7
South Africa	52.6	51.6	53.2	14.3	11.7	10.7
Sri Lanka	34.6	36.2	34.8	30.2	34.4	34.4
Swaziland	33.1	33.3	n.a.	37.3	44.5	27.2
Tanzania	36.8	27.7	n.a.	32.7	39.4	42.1
Trinidad and Tobago	37.2	59.0	54.6	31.5	22.8	20.6
Uganda	9.9	7.7	n.a.	52.1	64.4	47.4
United Arab Emirates	22.7	n.a.	n.a.	20.3	16.8	17.5
Zambia	33.6	29.4	n.a.	57.5	61.4	46.6
Zimbabwe	n.a.	45.9	46.9	21.7	23.8	28.1

Key: See Table 1.2 (p. 4)

Country	R/D			DT/Y		
	1979–83	1984–88	1989–93	1979–83	1984–88	1989–93
Argentina	39.7	26.8	22.9	29.9	49.8	48.3
Bahamas	8.0	7.8	7.8	n.a.	n.a.	n.a.
Bangladesh	9.9	12.8	15.3	34.7	48.9	54.3
Barbados	10.0	9.7	9.3	31.1	40.4	39.0
Belize	11.3	13.6	14.1	41.9	49.8	38.2
Botswana	21.7	23.3	21.1	17.7	27.4	16.3
Chile	15.4	8.0	7.4	59.8	106.2	56.9
Cyprus	23.1	26.5	23.2	n.a.	n.a.	n.a.
Fiji	7.9	11.7	9.6	28.0	38.0	27.0
Gambia	44.7	6.3	15.9	76.6	148.2	126.6
Ghana	44.2	44.1	43.0	8.0	46.9	61.4
Guyana	27.2	51.9	27.1	172.1	373.2	517.7
Hong Kong	0.9	0.7	0.6	n.a.	n.a.	n.a.
India	13.1	15.4	15.1	13.6	20.1	26.6
Israel	114.7	36.2	20.2	n.a.	n.a.	n.a.
Jamaica	14.0	33.3	35.8	85.5	160.0	119.9
Jordan	15.8	11.6	35.6	55.0	87.9	185.9
Kenya	8.5	10.1	13.0	50.9	65.1	79.2
Kuwait	10.0	5.4	0.9	n.a.	n.a.	n.a.
Lesotho	23.4	31.5	25.6	26.6	63.4	67.3
Malawi	11.8	40.2	24.3	67.9	95.8	87.5
Malaysia	7.0	5.7	8.4	39.0	65.0	38.1
Malta	28.9	27.9	9.9	11.1	18.1	23.5
Mauritius	11.8	9.2	16.6	45.1	48.6	37.3
Mexico	50.7	32.1	4.2	40.9	64.0	40.9
Namibia	n.a.	n.a.	n.a.	n.a.	n.a.	n.a.
Nigeria	12.7	7.4	14.8	14.7	62.7	103.4
Pakistan	9.8	11.5	15.9	40.9	44.5	49.2
Papua New Guinea	10.8	3.5	2.5	46.0	75.3	76.6
St Lucia	4.5	14.0	13.9	14.5	16.5	23.2
Saudi Arabia	15.9	11.0	7.2	n.a.	n.a.	n.a.
Sierra Leone	75.5	59.6	31.5	42.7	85.2	140.6
Singapore	9.0	8.7	7.8	n.a.	n.a.	n.a.
Solomon Islands	32.1	16.5	5.0	16.7	49.7	63.5
South Africa	6.1	3.9	4.3	n.a.	n.a.	n.a.
Sri Lanka	13.1	16.1	15.3	50.7	63.6	71.4
Swaziland	31.1	40.5	22.0	40.5	53.7	30.9
Tanzania	3.4	6.5	12.3	47.0	101.7	218.7
Trinidad and Tobago	23.7	15.8	14.2	15.4	31.9	45.9
Uganda	25.1	36.2	17.8	13.9	36.6	79.6
United Arab Emirates	12.2	11.2	11.1	n.a.	n.a.	n.a.
Zambia	39.5	47.5	35.7	94.9	238.2	206.0
Zimbabwe	9.4	10.7	15.3	22.1	48.7	58.1

Key: See Table 1.2 (p. 4)

Country	CBCG			CGDC		
	1979–83	1984–88	1989–93	1979–83	1984–88	1989–93
Argentina	57.2	196.5	96.4	29.7	38.5	37.2
Bahamas	14.3	4.4	52.5	16.8	14.4	18.9
Bangladesh	92.2	35.6	14.1	28.0	14.4	9.1
Barbados	34.5	6.9	33.8	16.4	18.0	26.7
Belize	72.5	74.4	6.4	22.8	30.5	−7.0
Botswana	−144.0	−538.7	−690.7	−87.1	n.a.	n.a.
Chile	42.7	61.6	56.5	4.8	34.7	25.9
Cyprus	27.2	20.3	19.5	15.3	18.3	18.1
Fiji	−13.5	−1.6	−14.7	10.0	8.2	3.9
Gambia	44.8	−10.9	−110.1	19.2	−4.6	−25.9
Ghana	106.8	164.8	191.1	69.8	71.0	60.5
Guyana	239.2	276.0	724.4	69.0	79.9	89.7
Hong Kong	0.0	0.0	0.0	0.0	0.0	0.0
India	88.9	106.3	103.1	42.1	45.1	47.9
Israel	31.2	46.2	4.1	49.0	54.5	35.6
Jamaica	343.8	88.0	−62.4	58.0	41.8	−32.5
Jordan	19.5	39.1	42.2	13.3	22.4	27.7
Kenya	96.4	117.6	58.8	31.6	35.8	27.7
Kuwait	−102.2	−98.5	−99.9	−32.4	−8.8	23.4
Lesotho	40.3	33.5	−47.0	52.0	53.2	15.6
Malawi	189.4	114.1	59.4	36.4	53.6	34.5
Malaysia	−7.2	15.6	−12.2	5.8	6.3	4.1
Malta	−9.1	−9.5	2.7	−24.9	−4.9	15.8
Mauritius	212.5	134.2	−6.8	60.9	48.3	28.3
Mexico	91.4	110.1	74.6	50.9	56.3	22.8
Namibia	n.a.	n.a.	10.5	n.a.	n.a.	−1.3
Nigeria	75.4	144.5	86.7	43.9	55.7	47.7
Pakistan	83.9	79.5	75.2	47.9	42.3	48.3
Papua New Guinea	−18.8	−53.8	26.1	8.5	2.9	19.3
St Lucia	52.8	40.2	11.7	14.0	14.6	−12.5
Saudi Arabia	−614.0	−326.7	−50.5	n.a.	n.a.	−14.4
Sierra Leone	211.1	146.3	54.6	80.6	86.8	58.4
Singapore	−115.6	−74.2	−169.2	−45.0	−13.2	−36.5
Solomon Islands	−6.5	−20.4	72.4	−13.5	12.8	47.4
South Africa	−1.3	−19.1	−35.2	12.8	3.0	1.7
Sri Lanka	199.2	151.6	123.5	43.0	39.5	36.4
Swaziland	−49.9	−8.0	−170.9	−28.5	−8.8	n.a.
Tanzania	113.4	135.7	165.1	61.4	54.1	49.2
Trinidad and Tobago	−247.2	16.9	87.2	−31.8	8.1	23.0
Uganda	138.2	86.4	34.9	67.9	57.4	22.9
United Arab Emirates	−58.1	−16.4	−46.3	−15.4	−1.2	−14.0
Zambia	405.5	204.3	68.8	68.6	63.4	43.2
Zimbabwe	42.7	24.8	57.1	43.8	21.9	19.3

Key: See Table 1.2 (p. 4)

Country	GS/Y			GR/Y		
	1979–83	1984–88	1989–93	1979–83	1984–88	1989–93
Argentina	−6.2	−3.1	−0.4	13.8	12.8	9.7
Bahamas	−1.2	0.1	n.a.	20.3	18.4	n.a.
Bangladesh	0.8	−0.7	−0.4	14.4	12.1	14.5
Barbados	−3.4	−4.0	−1.0	28.3	30.3	32.7
Belize	−1.7	0.8	−1.1	24.9	24.2	27.1
Botswana	1.6	19.4	11.4	41.6	62.2	55.9
Chile	1.8	−1.2	1.4	31.0	27.2	21.5
Cyprus	−6.6	−4.2	−2.7	23.5	26.3	27.7
Fiji	−4.1	−3.3	−2.5	24.0	24.5	24.8
Gambia	−7.4	−4.3	−1.8	22.6	19.7	23.8
Ghana	−5.1	−0.6	n.a.	6.4	12.8	n.a.
Guyana	−33.6	−43.0	n.a.	40.9	54.4	n.a.
Hong Kong	1.7	2.1	2.2	17.9	15.7	16.4
India	−6.0	−8.4	−7.3	12.4	13.9	14.2
Israel	−19.4	−6.7	−5.0	65.3	64.4	42.9
Jamaica	−15.4	−3.6	−0.3	28.6	32.0	n.a.
Jordan	−7.9	−8.2	−4.0	35.3	27.5	33.4
Kenya	−6.1	−5.2	−4.3	22.2	21.2	25.1
Kuwait	28.9	5.4	−69.8	73.8	56.2	32.7
Lesotho	−6.2	−10.5	−3.2	40.2	47.0	54.0
Malawi	−10.4	−7.6	−2.2	22.9	23.5	24.5
Malaysia	−9.9	−5.3	−1.0	25.8	27.3	27.1
Malta	0.6	−2.8	−5.0	40.5	38.7	38.1
Mauritius	−10.8	−1.8	−0.6	20.5	22.9	23.8
Mexico	−7.0	−10.5	−2.2	15.5	16.7	16.2
Namibia	n.a.	0.7	−1.6	n.a.	43.8	38.5
Nigeria	−13.5	−5.5	−4.5	n.a.	14.3	n.a.
Pakistan	−6.5	−7.5	−7.0	16.5	17.8	18.9
Papua New Guinea	−4.1	−1.7	−2.2	29.0	29.5	33.0
St Lucia	−1.2	−1.0	1.2	42.4	33.6	31.3
Saudi Arabia	n.a.	n.a.	n.a.	n.a.	n.a.	n.a.
Sierra Leone	−11.7	−8.2	−4.7	15.0	8.4	8.2
Singapore	2.1	2.4	10.0	26.6	28.3	27.2
Solomon Islands	−6.0	−7.6	n.a.	27.5	29.3	n.a.
South Africa	−3.9	−5.4	−2.3	23.5	26.1	29.0
Sri Lanka	−13.5	−9.6	−8.7	22.5	23.4	23.2
Swaziland	−2.3	−0.7	1.7	33.7	29.2	33.0
Tanzania	−10.4	−8.1	n.a.	20.5	16.7	n.a.
Trinidad and Tobago	−3.0	−6.3	−3.9	38.7	32.6	26.8
Uganda	−3.2	−2.6	n.a.	4.5	7.4	n.a.
United Arab Emirates	1.4	−0.5	−0.6	15.2	14.6	12.5
Zambia	−13.4	−13.9	−5.0	24.5	22.0	14.3
Zimbabwe	−8.8	−8.9	−7.7	26.1	32.2	33.7

Key: See Table 1.2 (p. 4)

APPENDIX 3

Alternative measures of per capita income in US dollars

Key: *WB*: World Bank, *Socio-Economic Time-Series Access and Retrieval System (July 1994)*.

SH: Summers, Robert and Alan Heston (1991), 'The Penn World Table (Mark 5): An Expanded Set of International Comparisons, 1950–1988', *Quarterly Journal of Economics*, 106(2), May, pp. 327–368.

PPP: *World Bank Atlas 1995* (figures for Belize, Kuwait, St Lucia, Saudi Arabia, Solomon Islands, South Africa and Tanzania in italics are per capita incomes converted at market exchange rates, as they are in columns 2 and 5; hence, they are not used in columns 7 and 8).

(1) Country	(2) WB 1985	(3) SH 1985	(4) (3)/(2)	(5) WB 1992	(6) PPP 1993	(7) (6)/(5)	(8) (7)/(4)
Argentina	3,150	3,982	1.26	6,050	9,130	1.51	1.19
Bahamas	9,010	10,294	1.14	12,070	16,820	1.39	1.22
Bangladesh	150	700	4.67	220	1,290	5.86	1.26
Barbados	4,670	6,152	1.32	6,540	10,940	1.67	1.27
Belize	1,220	n.a.	n.a.	2,220	2,440	n.a.	n.a.
Botswana	1,040	2,555	2.46	2,790	4,650	1.67	0.68
Chile	1,430	3,763	2.63	2,730	8,380	3.07	1.17
Cyprus	n.a.	6,905	n.a.	9,820	15,470	1.58	n.a.
Fiji	1,650	3,517	2.13	2,010	5,220	2.60	1.22
Gambia	240	725	3.02	370	1,280	3.46	1.15
Ghana	370	852	2.30	450	2,160	4.80	2.08
Guyana	510	1,265	2.48	330	1,710	5.18	2.09
Hong Kong	6,120	10,183	1.66	15,360	21,670	1.41	0.85
India	290	696	2.40	310	1,250	4.03	1.68
Israel	6,630	9,293	1.40	13,220	14,890	1.13	0.80
Jamaica	920	2,381	2.59	1,340	3,000	2.24	0.87
Jordan	1,970	2,731	1.39	1,120	4,010	3.58	2.58
Kenya	310	845	2.73	310	1,310	4.23	1.55
Kuwait	15,620	12,684	0.81	n.a.	23,350	n.a.	n.a.
Lesotho	390	1,236	3.17	590	1,800	3.05	0.96
Malawi	170	575	3.38	210	780	3.71	1.10
Malaysia	1,980	4,751	2.40	2,790	8,630	3.09	1.29
Malta	3,410	5,766	1.69	7,300	n.a.	n.a.	n.a.
Mauritius	1,110	3,756	3.38	2,700	12,450	4.61	1.36
Mexico	2,300	5,332	2.32	3,470	7,100	2.05	0.88
Namibia	1,070	n.a.	n.a.	1,610	3,930	2.44	n.a.
Nigeria	990	1,066	1.08	320	1,480	4.62	4.30
Pakistan	370	1,452	3.92	420	2,110	5.02	1.28
Papua New Guinea	750	1,669	2.23	950	2,470	2.60	1.17
St Lucia	n.a.	2,892	n.a.	2,920	3,040	n.a.	n.a.
Saudi Arabia	8,700	9,541	1.10	7,510	7,780	n.a.	n.a.
Sierra Leone	340	1,017	2.99	160	770	4.81	1.61
Singapore	7,880	10,417	1.32	15,730	20,470	1.30	0.98
Solomon Islands	530	1,865	3.52	710	750	n.a.	n.a.
South Africa	2,010	4,407	2.19	2,670	2,900	n.a.	n.a.
Sri Lanka	390	1,962	5.03	540	3,030	5.61	1.12
Swaziland	810	2,113	2.61	1,090	1,690	1.55	0.59
Tanzania	290	480	1.66	110	100	n.a.	n.a.
Trinidad and Tobago	7,120	7,478	1.05	3,940	8,850	2.25	2.14
Uganda	170	430	2.53	170	840	4.94	1.95
United Arab Emirates	21,620	20,529	0.95	22,020	23,390	1.06	1.12
Zambia	350	762	2.18	450	1,170	2.60	1.19
Zimbabwe	640	1,434	2.24	570	1,900	3.33	1.49

APPENDIX 4

Estimated seigniorage revenue in the Bank of England group, 1979–93 (per cent)

Estimated seigniorage revenue/GDP in the Bank of England group, 1979–93 (per cent)

Estimated seigniorage revenue/government revenue in the Bank of England group, 1979–93 (per cent)

Estimated seigniorage revenue in the Bank of England group, 1979–93 (per cent)

Country	Inflation tax/GDP 1979–93	Inflation tax/government revenue	Government revenue/ GDP	Inflation tax/GDP 1989–93	Central bank profit 1993/GDP
Argentina	4.0	43.7	13.0	2.4	0.37
Bahamas	0.3	1.7	19.6	0.3	0.47
Bangladesh	0.6	5.4	13.3	0.4	0.55
Barbados	0.6	2.1	29.6	0.5	0.47
Belize	0.4	1.3	25.3	0.3	0.29
Botswana	0.8	1.4	52.8	1.0	0.01
Chile	5.5	22.3	27.4	5.1	–0.02
Cyprus	1.3	5.4	25.5	1.2	0.23
Fiji	0.6	2.3	24.4	0.5	0.00
Gambia	1.4	7.2	21.6	0.8	1.32
Ghana	1.9	29.1	9.6	1.2	n.a.
Guyana	2.0	3.0	44.8	1.2	–9.04
Hong Kong	0.6	2.9	16.7	0.7	2.82
India	1.2	8.8	13.4	1.3	0.21
Israel	1.2	2.2	59.8	0.5	0.69
Jamaica	2.2	4.8	29.6	3.7	–3.28
Jordan	2.7	8.6	31.9	4.3	0.85
Kenya	1.2	4.2	22.5	1.8	n.a.
Kuwait	0.5	1.6	57.6	0.5	0.78
Lesotho	1.9	4.3	47.7	1.5	0.58
Malawi	1.4	6.0	23.4	1.0	0.38
Malaysia	0.5	1.7	26.7	0.5	–0.43
Malta	2.4	4.6	39.1	1.2	3.43
Mauritius	1.1	4.8	22.2	1.2	0.82
Mexico	3.3	23.6	16.1	0.7	0.01
Namibia	0.2	n.a.	41.1	0.2	0.34
Nigeria	1.9	8.7	14.3	1.6	1.41
Pakistan	1.2	6.7	17.6	1.5	0.32
Papua New Guinea	0.3	1.0	30.1	0.2	n.a.
St Lucia	0.6	1.8	36.4	0.7	4.48
Saudi Arabia	0.0	n.a.	n.a.	0.3	0.04
Sierra Leone	4.4	66.7	10.9	3.9	–0.08
Singapore	0.4	1.7	27.4	0.5	1.27
Solomon Islands	1.0	3.8	28.4	0.7	0.30
South Africa	0.6	2.2	25.5	0.6	0.04
Sri Lanka	1.1	4.7	23.0	1.2	0.56
Swaziland	1.9	6.3	31.8	0.7	0.01
Tanzania	2.6	14.8	19.6	2.0	n.a.
Trinidad and Tobago	1.3	4.2	34.8	0.6	0.38
Uganda	1.7	30.6	5.6	0.8	–0.10
United Arab Emirates	0.1	1.9	14.6	0.1	0.62
Zambia	3.1	14.5	22.4	4.2	0.09
Zimbabwe	1.1	3.6	30.2	1.6	0.43

Estimated seigniorage revenue/GDP in the Bank of England group, 1979–93 (per cent)

Country	1979–93	1979–83	1984–88	1989–93
Argentina	4.0	5.3	4.3	2.4
Bahamas	0.3	0.4	0.3	0.3
Bangladesh	0.6	0.7	0.7	0.4
Barbados	0.6	0.9	0.3	0.5
Belize	0.4	0.4	0.5	0.3
Botswana	0.8	0.7	0.6	1.0
Chile	5.5	2.7	8.7	5.1
Cyprus	1.3	1.8	1.0	1.2
Fiji	0.6	0.7	0.5	0.5
Gambia	1.4	1.6	1.7	0.8
Ghana	1.9	2.8	1.5	1.2
Guyana	2.0	1.2	3.5	1.2
Hong Kong	0.6	0.8	0.4	0.7
India	1.2	1.2	1.0	1.3
Israel	1.2	1.6	1.6	0.5
Jamaica	2.2	0.9	1.9	3.7
Jordan	2.7	2.3	1.4	4.3
Kenya	1.2	1.0	0.8	1.8
Kuwait	0.5	0.8	0.1	0.5
Lesotho	1.9	1.6	2.5	1.5
Malawi	1.4	0.8	2.0	1.0
Malaysia	0.5	0.7	0.2	0.5
Malta	2.4	5.0	0.7	1.2
Mauritius	1.1	1.5	0.6	1.2
Mexico	3.3	5.2	3.5	0.7
Namibia	0.2	n.a.	n.a.	0.2
Nigeria	1.9	2.3	1.7	1.6
Pakistan	1.2	1.3	0.9	1.5
Papua New Guinea	0.3	0.4	0.2	0.2
St Lucia	0.6	0.7	0.4	0.7
Saudi Arabia	0.0	0.0	−0.2	0.3
Sierra Leone	4.4	n.a.	5.9	3.9
Singapore	0.4	0.7	0.1	0.5
Solomon Islands	1.0	1.1	1.1	0.7
South Africa	0.6	0.6	0.5	0.6
Sri Lanka	1.1	1.2	0.9	1.2
Swaziland	1.9	2.5	2.3	0.7
Tanzania	2.6	3.2	2.6	2.0
Trinidad and Tobago	1.3	2.0	1.1	0.6
Uganda	1.7	0.8	3.0	0.8
United Arab Emirates	0.1	0.1	0.1	0.1
Zambia	3.1	1.4	4.1	4.2
Zimbabwe	1.1	1.1	0.8	1.6

Estimated seigniorage revenue/government revenue in the Bank of England group, 1979–93 (per cent)

Country	1979–93	1979–83	1984–88	1989–93
Argentina	43.7	47.0	35.6	67.7
Bahamas	1.7	1.8	1.4	n.a.
Bangladesh	5.4	4.9	6.0	4.7
Barbados	2.1	3.1	1.2	1.6
Belize	1.3	1.5	1.2	1.0
Botswana	1.4	1.8	1.0	1.6
Chile	22.3	8.9	31.8	28.6
Cyprus	5.4	7.6	3.8	4.4
Fiji	2.3	2.8	2.3	1.8
Gambia	7.2	7.4	8.8	3.2
Ghana	29.1	47.4	10.7	n.a.
Guyana	3.0	3.0	3.2	n.a.
Hong Kong	2.9	3.6	1.8	3.4
India	8.8	9.7	7.3	9.7
Israel	2.2	2.5	2.3	1.5
Jamaica	4.8	3.3	8.5	n.a.
Jordan	8.6	6.3	5.3	18.1
Kenya	4.2	4.7	3.6	4.5
Kuwait	1.6	1.0	0.2	4.8
Lesotho	4.3	3.7	5.4	3.0
Malawi	6.0	3.8	8.6	2.5
Malaysia	1.7	2.8	0.7	1.7
Malta	4.6	9.2	1.9	2.9
Mauritius	4.8	7.5	2.6	4.0
Mexico	23.6	33.3	21.4	5.2
Namibia	n.a.	n.a.	n.a.	n.a.
Nigeria	8.7	n.a.	8.7	n.a.
Pakistan	6.7	7.8	4.9	7.7
Papua New Guinea	1.0	1.5	0.7	0.5
St Lucia	1.8	1.8	1.3	2.8
Saudi Arabia	n.a.	n.a.	n.a.	n.a.
Sierra Leone	66.7	n.a.	64.2	68.3
Singapore	1.7	2.9	0.3	2.0
Solomon Islands	3.8	4.0	3.6	n.a.
South Africa	2.2	2.4	2.0	2.2
Sri Lanka	4.7	5.1	3.8	5.4
Swaziland	6.3	7.3	7.8	2.3
Tanzania	14.8	15.3	13.6	n.a.
Trinidad and Tobago	4.2	5.2	3.4	3.0
Uganda	30.6	10.3	44.1	n.a.
United Arab Emirates	1.9	2.2	1.5	1.7
Zambia	14.5	5.7	19.0	36.0
Zimbabwe	3.6	4.3	2.5	4.1

APPENDIX 5

**Estimated revenue from financial repression in the Bank of
England group, 1979–93 (per cent)**

Note: Government debt/GDP and private sector domestic credit/GDP are
calculated using geometric means of beginning- and end-of-year data for the stock
variables. Each column gives the simple period average of the annual estimates.
Hence, the average subsidy columns do not equal average subsidy rates times
average subsidy bases.

Country	Exchange rate depreciation	Government bond/bill yield	Bank loan rate to private sector	US minus ex. rate-adjusted gov. yield	US minus ex. rate-adjusted loan rate
Argentina	583.5	n.a.	n.a.	n.a.	n.a.
Bahamas	0.0	5.8	9.6	2.1	1.2
Bangladesh	6.8	n.a.	13.8	n.a.	4.0
Barbados	0.0	6.7	10.9	1.2	−0.6
Belize	0.0	8.8	14.6	−0.9	−4.2
Botswana	8.2	n.a.	11.7	n.a.	6.7
Chile	19.6	n.a.	39.3	n.a.	−7.4
Cyprus	2.3	n.a.	9.0	n.a.	3.4
Fiji	4.2	5.3	13.2	6.6	2.0
Gambia	12.0	n.a.	22.3	n.a.	−1.3
Ghana	62.5	18.5	20.8	22.5	29.9
Guyana	40.0	15.7	18.4	14.3	15.1
Hong Kong	3.6	n.a.	10.5	n.a.	3.9
India	9.4	n.a.	16.6	n.a.	3.7
Israel	88.9	54.8	158.3	9.8	−17.6
Jamaica	25.0	18.3	25.6	8.1	4.8
Jordan	6.4	n.a.	9.7	n.a.	2.8
Kenya	15.7	14.9	14.2	7.4	7.2
Kuwait	0.7	6.0	6.9	3.3	5.1
Lesotho	10.2	13.9	16.2	4.7	4.4
Malawi	12.0	13.4	20.2	7.6	3.8
Malaysia	0.8	n.a.	8.8	n.a.	4.1
Malta	0.4	4.4	8.2	0.4	2.1
Mauritius	7.7	n.a.	15.1	n.a.	1.8
Mexico	47.0	42.0	43.6	1.4	6.4
Namibia	10.2	13.0	20.5	−0.8	−4.8
Nigeria	31.5	n.a.	15.1	n.a.	17.4
Pakistan	7.3	n.a.	8.0	n.a.	9.9
Papua New Guinea	2.4	10.0	12.8	0.1	0.2
St Lucia	0.0	6.8	11.5	0.9	−0.7
Saudi Arabia	0.7	n.a.	n.a.	n.a.	n.a.
Sierra Leone	62.9	21.2	24.8	23.2	25.5
Singapore	−2.2	n.a.	8.1	n.a.	0.1
Solomon Islands	9.2	10.5	15.3	7.7	6.2
South Africa	10.2	13.0	16.8	3.8	3.2
Sri Lanka	7.9	13.3	14.5	3.0	4.6
Swaziland	10.2	11.1	14.7	5.6	5.1
Tanzania	32.9	n.a.	18.6	n.a.	19.7
Trinidad and Tobago	6.2	5.1	12.6	7.7	3.8
Uganda	115.9	23.4	26.3	42.1	48.2
United Arab Emirates	−0.4	n.a.	n.a.	n.a.	n.a.
Zambia	63.6	21.0	26.6	22.5	24.4
Zimbabwe	17.2	9.7	18.4	12.2	7.3

Country	Government domestic debt/GDP	Subsidy on government debt/GDP	Private sector domestic credit/GDP	Subsidy on private sector borrowing/GDP
Argentina	7.4	n.a.	11.8	n.a.
Bahamas	6.1	0.15	28.7	0.48
Bangladesh	4.7	n.a.	15.0	0.29
Barbados	8.3	0.02	31.1	−0.18
Belize	10.0	−0.21	28.2	−1.31
Botswana	n.a.	n.a.	11.0	0.81
Chile	20.2	n.a.	49.3	−2.24
Cyprus	10.6	n.a.	53.6	1.40
Fiji	2.2	0.16	24.0	0.60
Gambia	9.9	n.a.	17.1	0.63
Ghana	11.7	2.83	2.6	0.60
Guyana	146.9	21.07	19.8	2.90
Hong Kong	n.a.	n.a.	118.8	−1.28
India	20.6	n.a.	23.9	0.83
Israel	46.8	5.40	46.5	−7.51
Jamaica	30.0	3.18	22.4	1.16
Jordan	19.2	n.a.	55.8	1.83
Kenya	10.0	0.67	18.7	1.38
Kuwait	47.1	n.a.	66.7	2.63
Lesotho	15.8	0.76	12.1	0.51
Malawi	11.7	1.16	12.2	0.58
Malaysia	3.9	n.a.	54.9	1.96
Malta	8.9	−0.04	42.1	−0.17
Mauritius	24.1	n.a.	26.5	0.10
Mexico	13.3	0.62	12.6	0.44
Namibia	6.0	0.31	25.7	−1.12
Nigeria	14.9	n.a.	12.5	2.45
Pakistan	21.9	n.a.	25.7	2.53
Papua New Guinea	2.7	−0.02	22.3	−0.04
St Lucia	10.5	0.25	55.5	−0.21
Saudi Arabia	n.a.	n.a.	15.7	n.a.
Sierra Leone	20.1	5.71	4.5	1.01
Singapore	n.a.	n.a.	78.7	0.10
Solomon Islands	3.5	0.29	15.5	1.38
South Africa	2.3	0.14	31.7	1.52
Sri Lanka	15.5	0.60	18.7	0.81
Swaziland	1.6	−0.01	20.3	1.34
Tanzania	21.9	n.a.	3.4	0.46
Trinidad and Tobago	10.8	0.37	29.7	1.14
Uganda	5.9	2.98	2.3	1.08
United Arab Emirates	3.3	n.a.	35.0	n.a.
Zambia	27.9	6.78	14.9	3.51
Zimbabwe	6.8	0.86	7.7	0.61

SYMPOSIUM PROCEEDINGS

MINUTES OF SYMPOSIUM ON CENTRAL BANKING IN DEVELOPING COUNTRIES HELD AT THE BANK OF ENGLAND, 9 JUNE 1995

1 **Mr Eddie George**, Governor of the Bank of England welcomed the participants (see list at Annex A). He said their discussions would be stimulated by a paper entitled 'Central Banking in Developing Countries', to be introduced by its authors, Professors Charles Goodhart and Maxwell Fry and then commented on by three discussants: Dr Rangarajan, Governor of the Reserve Bank of India, Dr Chikaonda, Governor of the Reserve Bank of Malawi and Dr Stanley Fischer, First Deputy Managing Director of the IMF.

2 Mr George explained that Dr Courtney Blackman, who originally suggested the theme of the Symposium, had unfortunately been detained by urgent government business. Before handing over to Professor Maxwell Fry, Mr George asked for any errors of fact in the paper to be raised outside the Symposium, for inclusion in the revised paper.

3 **Professor Maxwell Fry** thanked the Governors for the care and effort taken in responding to the questionnaire that he and Professor Goodhart had sent to 44 central banks in developing countries. Their responses formed the basis of the paper before them. He expressed some diffidence in presenting the result to such a knowledgeable audience and stressed that the paper was more akin to a Monet than a Rembrandt! He said he would introduce the first four chapters of the paper and Professor Goodhart the last four chapters.

4 They found that central banks in developing countries dominated their financial systems more than central banks in OECD countries.

137

5 To their surprise respondents to the questionnaire ('the BoE group'), were representative of developing countries as a whole. For example, in both the BoE group and all other developing countries inflation had averaged 20 per cent over the past 15 years, government deficits averaged 5 per cent of GDP and foreign debt averaged 70 per cent of GDP.

6 They detected a shift over the past 15 years away from a *dirigiste* environment of administratively fixed interest rates, credit rationing and directed credit policies towards financial liberalisation and the use of indirect market-based techniques of monetary control.

7 The data exhibited some simple statistical associations for the BoE group: for example inflation was positively related to the proportion of government borrowing met by the central bank and to the proportion of government borrowing in total domestic credit.

8 He then turned to the relationship between price stability, monetary expansion and growth. Their first finding was that inflation was negatively related to growth. This had not been the accepted position in the past. In the 1960s, the economics profession had misunderstood or had been misled by Professor Phillips into thinking that a trade-off existed between inflation and growth. In the 1970s, more sophisticated expectations-augmented Phillips curves became popular. In fact, simple bivariate regressions, cross-section and pooled time-series indicate negative relationship between inflation and growth for the BoE group in both the long and short runs. There were similar findings for many other countries, particularly developing countries.

9 What explained this negative relationship? Two possible reasons: high inflation was volatile inflation and volatility led to uncertainty. Secondly, key prices might be fixed – specifically interest and exchange rates. As inflation rose, lower real interest rates resulting from fixed nominal rates reduced credit availability and distorted resource allocation, while a fixed exchange rate priced exports out of world markets. Both effects were growth-reducing.

10 Following from all this evidence and given that the great majority of central banks were given a statutory obligation to maintain the value of their currencies, they asked why central banks failed to maintain price stability? The answer, they thought, lay in 'the fiscal connection'. So they then turned to the relationship between the central bank and its government.

11 First, they noted that governments in the BoE group had

received considerable revenue from the inflation tax. (Estimated inflation tax revenue averaged 1.5 per cent of GDP and 9.2 per cent of government current revenue for the BoE group over the period 1979–93.) They believed that this explained the positive relationship between the reserve/deposit ratio and the inflation rate presented earlier. Governments rationally increased both the tax base, in the form of required reserves, and the tax rate, in the form of inflation, when they needed more revenue from the inflation tax.

12 Secondly, governments in the BoE group had reduced their own interest costs through financial repression. The disadvantages of this financial repression were too well-known to require elaboration.

13 They then estimated a monetary policy reaction function to address the question: do central banks pursue monetary policy in a way that reduces credit to the private sector when the public sector's borrowing requirements rise? The answers were: not across the group as a whole; generally where government officials were on their Boards and only where they lend automatically to their governments.

14 Given that quite a number of central banks reported losses, the authors wondered whether some governments were confused as to what they could get out of their central banks. Perhaps this confusion was one of distinguishing stock and flow variables.

15 In *flow* terms, Professor Fry said we could think of the central bank as the government's golden goose. There were three types of goose:

- The free-range goose, to which he felt sure everyone in this room aspired, conducted conservative monetary policy with a fair degree of independence and produced golden eggs in the form of seigniorage worth 0.5 to 1 per cent of GDP.
- The battery farm goose, bred specially for intensive egg-laying, could produce golden eggs in the form of an inflation tax yielding 5 to 10 per cent of GDP.
- The force-fed goose could produce revenue of up to 25 per cent of GDP for a limited period before both it and the economy expired.

16 In *stock* terms, the central bank was an asset whose value derived from its monopoly over legal tender. With an unimpaired balance sheet and an obligation to maintain price stability, governments could in principle privatise their central banks expecting to achieve a price in the region of 50 per cent of GDP.

17 However, he said many central banks were no longer in the pristine textbook condition in which they held assets earning market-determined interest rates and had liabilities on which they paid no interest. In part as a response to IMF pressures to reduce fiscal deficits, a number of governments had required their central banks to undertake various *quasi-fiscal activities*, such as operating directed credit policies at subsidised rates, bailing out insolvent financial institutions and providing exchange-rate guarantees. If the government burdened it with additional liabilities in these ways, the central bank's present value fell and so did its ability to lay golden eggs. Not only could and did central banks make losses, they could go bust if their governments burdened them with too many quasi-fiscal activities. Then the government had killed the goose that laid the golden eggs.

18 They concluded from all this a simple lesson for governments: as Milton Friedman would undoubtedly have liked to say 'There's no such thing as a free lunch,' even when it comes to the central bank's monopoly over legal tender.

19 Professor Fry then turned to central banks' external activities. He started by looking at the exchange rate regimes adopted in the BoE group. They divided into fixed (11 countries), managed (19) and floating (13) exchange-rate regimes. Apart from historical accident, reasons for choice of regime included:

Fixed:	optimum currency area;
	nominal anchor;
	oil priced in US dollars.
Managed:	greater flexibility;
	balance-of-payments equilibrium;
	export competitiveness;
	exchange rate stability.
Floating:	balance-of-payments equilibrium;
	avoidance of speculative attack;
	consistency with market-based economic policy.

20 In fact, they found that over the period 1979–93 fixed exchange-rate countries devalued by 21 per cent, managed exchange-rate countries by 56 per cent and floaters by 92 per cent against the US dollar. They also found that fixed and managed exchange-rate regimes produced substantially less volatility in real exchange rates than did floating exchange-rate regimes.

21 They then estimated their monetary policy reaction function

again to examine the question of sterilisation, i.e., changing domestic credit to offset the effects of changes in foreign assets on the money supply. The results indicated that floaters did not sterilise, but fixed exchange-rate central banks not only sterilised but also neutralised government borrowing requirements.

22 Was there a causal interpretation? Did conservative central banks enable the adoption of a fixed exchange rate or did a fixed exchange rate force central banks to be conservative? Both might be correct because the choice of exchange-rate regime and the ability of a central bank to pursue conservative monetary policy are interdependent and both are determined by the government's fiscal stance.

23 **Professor Goodhart** took over, saying Professor Fry had mostly concentrated on the relationship between central banks and government, whereas he would primarily be concerned with the interaction between the central bank and the private sector. If only because the central bank played a larger role within the financial system in developing countries that in OECD countries, it had an even greater responsibility for shaping and encouraging the structural development of the financial system.

24 In this latter respect, they had concentrated on three main aspects. First, the crucial function of ensuring the efficient functioning of the payment system. In the BoE group the majority of payments systems had been reformed since 1975, and the central bank initiated most of these reforms.

25 Secondly, they explored the extent to which central banks had encouraged the banking habit. He said that there was evidence of two-way causation between the spread of the banking habit and the investment and saving ratio.

26 They had expected that the demand for money, mainly bank deposits, would have responded quite strongly and positively to the removal of restrictions on interest rates and to the adoption of a more liberal regime. In the event their demand-for-money functions showed the standard strong response to real incomes and a negative relationship to inflation. But when they looked at evidence relating money holdings to the regime, whether liberal or restrictive, they found only some rather weak results, whereby the use of open-market techniques (rather than direct controls) were weakly but positively related to the extent of monetisation in an economy.

27 The third aspect of the structural development of the

financial system that they explored was the increasing efforts of central banks to strengthen and improve their financial markets. They had asked an open-ended question on the three main difficulties faced by central banks in this area.

28 One issue that they did not discuss in the paper, but which had been raised in one of the several welcome comments on their paper, was how far it was justifiable to restrict competition – for example from international banks and securities houses head-quarters abroad – in order to support and develop indigenous financial institutions. And if done at all, how could this discrimin-ation best be achieved without resulting in inefficiency and a loss of welfare to clients of the financial system?

29 He said virtually all economists supported the shift to a market-based system, and Professor Fry and he were no exception, but it was still necessary to observe that such transitions had their dangers and costs. They noted in particular two problems arising from deregulation, and not only in developing countries. These were, first, that deregulation could lead to an inopportune lending surge, especially to those sectors such as housing and property which had previously both appeared relatively safe *and* had been discriminated against in the prior direct control regime. Secondly, there was, of course, the problem of handling the potentially large international monetary flows once exchange controls were relaxed. But the latter was very widely discussed elsewhere and they did not dwell on it.

30 Next he turned to the role of the central bank in maintaining the continuing health of the financial system.

31 Here he was struck by several findings from the questionnaire which he had not expected. First, the problems of widespread fragility in banking systems which, though quite common in OECD countries, had *not* been nearly so prevalent in developing countries. Secondly, where rescue actions had been undertaken which involved any significant outlay of funds, they were almost always directly financed by government and not by private sector contributions from other banks – unlike, for example, the previous tradition in the UK.

32 Thirdly, the current fashionable enthusiasm for deposit in-surance in OECD countries had not infected developing countries to anything like the same degree. Whereas central bankers in developing countries had had continuing serious problems in containing inflation, they seemed to have had generally an easier

ride in maintaining systemic stability than the OECD countries. He asked if anyone would like to conjecture why.

33 One topic that they had sought to explore, which was not commonly analysed, is what determined the size of a central bank's staff, first in the supervisory part of the central bank and second in the rest. On the supervisory front, the relative size of the supervisory staff could be quite easily explained in most cases by strong economies of scale, but there was also some evidence that the choice of supervisory technique, for example on-site examinations, would influence the size of staff needed.

34 The main factor input into central banks *must* be human capital. He was, therefore, somewhat surprised by the wide variations that there appeared to be in their policies towards hiring skilled staff, which the study had generally not been able to explain.

35 Central bankers at various levels met to exchange notes on many operational and functional questions. He wondered whether there had been enough meetings on the question of personnel policies. In contrast, however, to their inability to explain the widely differing policies on hiring graduates, they were able to explain the cross-country variations in total non-supervisory staff quite well as a positive function of the extent of monetisation and the use of exchange controls, and a negative function of maintaining a pegged exchange rate regime and of inflation. He hoped his audience would be relieved to find that a larger central bank was associated with lower inflation!

36 The status of a central bank was related to its size, the skills of its staff and its constitutional position, especially in relation to government. However, he said that some of the enthusiasm for legislating for central bank independence which had been engendered by the apparent negative statistical relationship between constitutional independence and inflation among OECD countries, had been dissipated by the absence of a similar relationship among developing countries, as both Cukierman and Barro had recently shown. What appeared important in developing countries was not so much the formal constitutional position as the practical appreciation of the importance of price stability, and that may not be related so much to the *constitutional* interrelationships between government and central bank, as to the size of the fiscal gap that the government had allowed to develop.

37 They had asked finally a rather delicate question, which was

how independent each central bank saw itself as being. They found such self-assessment was negatively, but rather weakly associated with inflation.

38 In conclusion he said that their findings indicated a continuing trend from *dirigisme*, subservience to government, and a role for the central bank as a fiscal stop-gap, towards market liberalisation and development and acceptance of the primary need to achieve price stability. But while there were clear successes to point towards on the structural front, the record in combating endemic inflation had been generally less impressive.

39 Mr George then asked for **Dr Rangarajan's (India)** comments. Dr Rangarajan welcomed the wholesome conclusion drawn by the paper and welcomed its wide scope. He said with such a large group of countries it was hard always to capture the degree of variation between them. Whilst controlling inflation was important to developing countries, their major concern was economic growth. He saw no conflict between the two in the long term, but said in the short term this was not always so for developing countries, where structural rigidities made them more vulnerable to supply shocks. A sharp monetary brake in face of, for example, a sharp decrease in output, might make matters worse. So inflation was not always a monetary phenomenon in developing countries, although variations in the money supply were important. If the demand-for-money function was unstable, it could cause problems for policy makers. In India they had found 3–4 year averages a better guide to policy than annual changes in the money stock.

40 Dr Rangarajan argued that because of structural rigidities and the urge to grow faster, developing countries can tolerate higher inflation than OECD countries. In India they regarded inflation above 7–8 per cent as requiring action, before inflationary expectations became too damaging.

41 He said it was true that government borrowing from the central bank could impede the implementation of monetary policy. In India they had recently limited such government borrowing, with the result that government was now paying higher interest rates. The government securities market had also developed, which enabled the central bank to undertake open market operations as a means of monetary control. Whilst these were an important technique, he believed reserve requirements were also needed as an instrument of monetary control, in addition to their dual function of providing prudential norms.

42 On the question of government borrowing crowding out private sector borrowing, he said it was important not only to consider the relative sizes of government and private sector borrowing, but also to look at the relative growth rates and public sector activities in relation to the growth of savings in the economy. Many developing countries were adopting the conditions of the IMF's Article VIII and had experienced a very favourable response from their economies.

43 He noted that the constitutional position of central banks varied greatly, even in democracies, but urged central banks to speak out, whatever their constitutional position. He disagreed with those who said that central bank intervention risked the possibility of adverse selection and moral hazard: developing country central banks needed to monitor their developing markets *more* than OECD central banks.

44 **Dr Chikaonda (Malawi)** was the second discussant. He said the authors implied that inflation in developing countries implied a failure on the part of their central banks. Yet many were legally answerable to their ministries of finance and so could not be held responsible for the inflation in their countries. Such was the situation in Malawi until 1989, when the central bank was separated from the Ministry of Finance. Yet legal independence did not guarantee independence in reality. He likened a central bank to a dog who could bark but not bite, as government had removed its teeth. Yet government continued to look in the dog's mouth in the hope that new teeth had emerged! In Malawi they dealt with a loophole that enabled restrictions on government borrowing from the central bank to be evaded, by moving all government accounts to the commercial banks.

45 He said *The Economist* had published a study showing that central bank independence was correlated with growth. He said that the end goal of a central bank had to be growth. The question was how best to reach it.

46 **Stanley Fischer** was the third discussant. He said the paper not only displayed the authors' wide range of knowledge but also would be used as a rich source of data for mining in future years. It was impossible to discuss the paper in full, so he concentrated on five key points. Firstly, the relationship between inflation and growth: there was absolutely no question that annual inflation over 40 per cent was negatively correlated with growth. Slower growth might indeed encourage inflation, as authorities dependent on seigniorage for revenue would need to print more money than the

economy required. But what about the relationship between lower inflation and growth? Robert Barro's recent work suggested there was no relationship between the two below 10 per cent inflation. Fischer himself had expected to find this result in his own work, but did not, possibly because the correlations were very sensitive to additional variables. But although there was some unevenness in the evidence, Fischer said he would be surprised if there was a big causal relationship between inflation and growth below 5 per cent inflation. Above 5 per cent inflation, he believed that the negative association between growth and inflation does obtain.

47 Secondly he turned to the measurement of seigniorage, which he said the paper overestimated. There were two methods of measurement in the literature – how much people pay (the higher of the two methods) and how much government receives (rarely above 3–4 per cent of GDP). He said the paper had got absolutely right the fiscal reason why inflation was higher in developing countries and had provided much detailed evidence to demonstrate it.

48 Thirdly, the only function of a central bank that had been neglected in this paper was its ability to provide independent economic analysis as a public good.

49 Fourthly, there seemed to be two vital elements behind effective central bank independence: first and most important was the freedom from obligation to finance the government's deficit; second was the freedom to set interest rates.

50 Fifthly, in what direction were central banks and developing country financial systems heading? Liberalisation was growing at a rate inconceivable 25 years ago, and there had been a remarkable growth in the convertibility of the capital account. This would increasingly lead to convergence of financial standards around the world, which in turn would reduce governments' fiscal incentive for withholding central bank independence. At the same time governments would find it less attractive to try to vary domestic prices from world prices by changing the exchange rate. So it might be that financial liberalisation would eventually lead to a trend towards greater exchange rate fixity than seen in the past.

51 **Mr George** recalled the reason for this meeting was that similar discussions on developed countries last year had posed the question whether central banking was different in developing countries. Without wishing to constrain discussion he suggested the Symposium might wish to consider several questions:

- could developing countries tolerate different levels of inflation?
- was the 'fiscal' connection different: the extent to which government deficits are financed by monetary means?
- the relationship of these questions to the independence of a central bank.

52 The following discussion focused on several main themes, principally how the environment in which developing country central banks operate differs from that in OECD countries; the relationship between inflation and growth in developing countries; and the 'fiscal connection', including the independence of central banks from government.

53 Discussing how developing countries differed from OECD countries **Professor Frenkel (Israel)** said they were more vulnerable to supply shocks than more diversified economies, they had less budgetary control and less access to capital markets. These factors had consequences both for central bank independence and inflation.

54 **Mr Venner (East Caribbean)** said the monetarists had won the debate with structuralists in Latin America and price stability was now being pursued. But developing countries needed growth, which was elusive when capital markets were being liberalised across the world. He believed, unlike Stanley Fischer, that developing countries needed to retain some controls on the capital account for protection until they were fully integrated into the international economy. But they also needed to liberalise their domestic financial sectors, both to attract domestic and foreign savings and foreign financial institutions.

55 With Fischer he argued for the importance of developing country central banks having a research function, to provide reputable studies of the local economy. This point was also echoed by **Mr Alam (Bangladesh), Dr Maruping (Lesotho)** and **Professor Fry**, who believed that a research function could increase the independence of developing country central banks by gaining them greater respect from their financial communities.

56 **HE Sheikh Al-Sayari (Saudi Arabia)** said another difference from OECD countries was that the quality of public expenditure was not as high in developing countries. This point was taken up by **Mr Hermans (Botswana)**, who said it was not enough to look at fiscal deficits as a percentage of GDP without analysing the quality of the public spending that had caused them. In many developing countries there was excessive defence ex-

penditure, unnecessary travel abroad by senior officials, spiralling agricultural subsidies and superfluous regulation. The study should cover this and also examine what other prices were regulated: it was not enough to liberalise exchange and interest rates as the economy could not respond to them if other key prices – such as transport, school fees, housing and land – were controlled.

57 **Dr Stals (South Africa)** said that it was a luxury for developing countries to talk of achieving price stability through macroeconomic policies. If this study led to further research it should cover:

- the role of a central bank in developing countries, the source of its profits and losses, who were its clients and what services it should provide;
- how to encourage the establishment of private sector banks and financial institutions;
- how to develop money, foreign exchange and capital markets; and finally
- how to achieve price stability through the operation of macro-economic policy.

58 The second major theme, the relationship between inflation and growth in developing countries, was explored by many governors. **Mr Thiessen (Canada)** said there are surely large errors in measuring inflation in a rapidly changing developing economy. If the goods and services available to consumers are changing rapidly, the basket of goods used to measure consumer prices is probably always out of date and misleading. In these circumstances the central bank perhaps ought to have objectives for controlling inflation that reflect this uncertainty. **Dr Mwanza (Zambia)** denied that inflation was inimical to growth asking, 'Is regression analysis so dependable? Is there no evidence that inflation is consistent with growth, for example Brazil? Is all we have proved to be sensible (i.e., inflationary financing) now not sensible?' But his was something of a lone voice, most governors accepting that inflation was inimical to growth in the long term.

59 **Professor Frenkel (Israel)** said governments unconsciously operated on a Phillips curve, in that they would set interest and exchange rates lower than would central banks, in the belief that the resulting higher inflation would stimulate growth. Central banks had largely freed themselves from the Phillips curve and as a result should be entrusted with controlling inflation. Regular

inflation reports helped to focus responsibility for inflation on the central bank, although if inflation rose, this could be a double-edged sword.

60 **Mr Hermans (Botswana)** and **Mr Alam (Bangladesh)** agreed with the first discussant that some inflation was good for growth in the short term in developing countries, as a transitional phase. Mr Hermans said this was so, provided that public expenditure enlarged the capital base on which to build future growth, for example by investing in schools, roads and hospitals. This was echoed by **Mr Kikonyogo (Uganda)**, who said inflation was not always a monetary phenomenon. **Mr Alam** argued that each central bank needed to study the relationship between inflation and growth in its own country, as it would differ across countries.

61 **Professor Frenkel (Israel)** and **Dr Maruping (Lesotho)** both commented that the rate of inflation in small open economies would be greatly influenced by rates in their larger trading partners and it would be hard for such economies to deviate from externally set inflation norms. **Dr Maruping** suggested common monetary areas should be considered.

62 The theme of most interest to governors was the relationship between inflation and central bank financing to fiscal deficits – the 'fiscal connection'. Most recognised the connection, the history of which was set out by **Dr Rashidi (Tanzania)**.

63 He said most Commonwealth central banks were now about 40 years old. When they had emerged from currency boards on independence, they had considered as beneficial to growth the low inflation caused by the central bank financing the government deficit. A culture of financing government then set in, particularly as the population was unaware of the problems caused by inflation, and as inflation figures were published selectively. The result over time was little foreign exchange, shortages of everything and public insistence on corrective action. He believed that public support for anti-inflation policies could only be generated by the public first experiencing inflation. But even then it was hard for central banks in the British tradition to gain independence of government. (**Mr George** interjected here that the British were very much in this 'British tradition'!)

64 **Dr Rashidi (Tanzania)** said that politicians in Tanzania were reluctant to accept that inflation was a monetary phenomenon; they argued that it is imported from foreigners who raise their prices. Dr Rashidi noted that the central bank's task in

containing inflation could be facilitated by the IMF putting pressure on the government to reduce its deficit.

65 **Professor Frenkel (Israel)** said that the law now forbade the central bank to finance government deficits and this had forced more fiscal responsibility. Several other delegates mentioned that such legal stipulations were not always observed in reality in their countries. **HE Sheikh Al-Sayari (Saudi Arabia)** suggested that having abolished currency boards on gaining independence, many central banks in ex-British colonies now felt that a currency board might protect them from government predations. **Mr Stals (South Africa)** said that reducing a central bank's powers (to finance deficits) would increase their effectiveness. **HE Sheikh Al-Sabah (Kuwait)** agreed that fiscal discipline was a key factor in ensuring monetary policy. Whilst recognising the thrust of these arguments, **Mr Alam (Bangladesh)** said that his government had behaved better than he had expected in containing expenditure.

66 **Mr Easparathasan (Sri Lanka)** elaborated on the above points, agreeing with the authors that quasi-fiscal subsidies by the central bank to government were less visible than direct budgetary expenditure, which made them attractive to government. But government could not require central banks to hold sub-standard assets for an extended period without having to bail out its central bank. In this context it was important to develop financial markets to encourage savings and in order to reduce the cost of government financing.

67 **Mr Smith (Bahamas)** noted that in the era of high government intervention there had been a degree of indigenisation of the banking system in developing countries. This was now being reduced with the necessary trend towards less government intervention and he felt that the study might cover this point in its examination of a central bank's relationship to the private sector.

68 A fourth theme covered was the use of supervisory tools. **Sir Indur Ramphul (Mauritius)** was keen to counter the authors' description of supervisory tools being used to raise revenue for government. He said that capital adequacy ratios were used to protect the financial system as a whole, and after the introduction of capital adequacy rules, cash reserve and liquidity ratios had been maintained in his country for purely prudential reasons. **HE Sheikh Al-Sabah (Kuwait)** on the other hand was concerned at the potentially detrimental effects to the economy of the use of supervisory tools for monetary purposes in some countries.

69 The Symposium concluded with **Professor Goodhart** thanking the participants for their remarks and welcoming any further comments. **Professor Fry** explained that the discussions had thrown light on two anomalous findings from the study, namely that central banks with government representation on their Boards both appeared to be more conservative and to regard themselves as more independent of government. He now believed that it was the degree of cooperation and mutual education between a central bank and its government that led to a successful monetary policy. He added that a good research department could increase the central bank's influence on this process.

ANNEX A

Central bank participants

Mr Eddie George
Governor
Bank of England

Dr Roque Fernandez
President
Central Bank of Argentina

Mr Bernie Fraser
Governor and Chairman of Board
   of Directors
Reserve Bank of Australia

Mr James Smith
Governor
The Central Bank of the Bahamas

Mr Khorshed Alam
Governor and Chairman of Board
   of Directors
Bangladesh Bank

Mr Calvin Springer
Governor
Central Bank of Barbados

Mr Keith Arnold
Governor and Chairman of Board
   of Directors
Central Bank of Belize

Mr H.C.L. Hermans
Governor and Chairman of Board
   of Directors
Bank of Botswana

Mr Gordon Thiessen
Governor
Bank of Canada

Mr Afxentis Afxentiou
Governor
Central Bank of Cyprus

Mr Dwight Venner
Governor
Eastern Caribbean Central Bank

Mr Junkung Abayo
General Manager
Central Bank of The Gambia

Dr G.K. Agama
Governor
Bank of Ghana

Mr Joseph Yam
Chief Executive
Hong Kong Monetary Authority

Mr Birgir Isleifur Gunnarsson
Chairman of the Board of
   Governors
Bank of Iceland

Dr C. Rangarajan
Governor
Reserve Bank of India

Professor Jacob A. Frenkel
Governor
Bank of Israel

Mr Jacques A. Bussieres
Governor
Bank of Jamaica

HE Dr Mohammed Said Nabulsi
Governor and Chairman of the
  Board of Directors
Central Bank of Jordan

Mr Micah Cheserem
Governor
Central Bank of Kenya

HE Sheikh Salem Abdul Aziz
  Al-Sabah
Governor and Chairman of the
  Board of Directors
Central Bank of Kuwait

Dr A.M. Maruping
Governor
Central Bank of Lesotho

Dr Matthew Chikaonda
Governor and Chairman of the
  Board of Directors
Reserve Bank of Malawi

Mr Ahmad Mohd Don
Governor and Chairman of the
  Board of Directors
Bank Negara Malaysia

Mr Francis J. Vassallo
Governor
Central Bank of Malta

Sir Indur Ramphul
Governor
Bank of Mauritius

Dr Donald Brash
Governor
Reserve Bank of New Zealand

Mr Victor Odozi
Deputy Governor
Central Bank of Nigeria

Dr L. Rutayisire
First Vice-Governor
National Bank of Rwanda

HE Sheikh Hamad Al-Sayari
Governor
Saudi Arabian Monetary Agency

Mrs Yvonne Gibril
Deputy Governor
Bank of Sierra Leone

Mr Lee Ek Tieng
Managing Director
Monetary Authority of Singapore

Mr Rick Houenipwela
Governor
Central Bank of Solomon Islands

Dr Chris Stals
Governor
South African Reserve Bank

Mr S. Easparathasan
Deputy Governor
Central Bank of Sri Lanka

Mr James Nxumalo
Governor and Chairman of the
  Board of Directors
Central Bank of Swaziland

Dr Idris M. Rashidi
Governor
Bank of Tanzania

Mr Thomas Ainsworth Harewood
Governor
Central Bank of Trinidad and
  Tobago

Mr Charles N. Kikonyogo
Governor and Chairman of the
  Board of Directors
Bank of Uganda

HE Sultan Bin Nasser Al-Suwaidi
Governor
Central Bank of United Arab
Emirates

Mr Sampson Ngwele
Governor
Reserve Bank of Vanuatu

Dr Jacob Mwanza
Governor
Bank of Zambia

Dr Leonard L. Tsumba
Governor
Reserve Bank of Zimbabwe

Authors and discussant

Professor Maxwell Fry
The University of Birmingham

Professor Charles Goodhart
London School of Economics and
Political Science

Mr Alvaro Almeida
London School of Economics and
Political Science

Mr Stanley Fischer
First Deputy Managing Director
International Monetary Fund

Observers – Bank of England

Mr Ian Plenderleith
Executive Director

Sir Peter Petrie
Adviser to The Governor

Mr John Townend
Deputy Director

Mr Lionel Price
Director of Central Banking
Studies

Mr John Footman
Secretary of the Bank

Mr David Reid
Head of Supervision and
Surveillance Division

Mr Peter Hayward
Senior Adviser

Mr Tim Smith
Senior Adviser

Ms Victoria Fleming
Manager, Centre for Central
Banking Studies

Observers – overseas

Ms Julia Majaha-Jartby
Acting Deputy Governor
Botswana

Mr Musa Sillah
Principal Economist
The Gambia

Mr Frederick Manning
Deputy Governor
Jamaica

Mr Joseph Kinyua
Director of Research
Kenya

Mrs. N.E. Mashologu
Senior Economist
Lesotho

Mr M. Tabane
Banking Supervision Officer
Lesotho

Mr Udaibir S. Das
Executive Assistant
India

Mr Elias Kambalame
Deputy General Manager
Malawi

Dr Zeti Akhtar Aziz
Manager, Economics
Malaysia

Mr John Agius
Board Secretary
Malta

Mr R. Basant Roi
Director of Research
Mauritius

Mr M.A. Adeoti
Senior Manager
Nigeria

Mr Jo Iyari
Manager
Nigeria

Mr Alhaji M.R. Rasheed
Director
Nigeria

Mr Saeed Al-Qahtani
Director
Public Relations
Saudi Arabian Monetary Agency

Mr Kallay
Division Head
Sierra Leone

Mr C.S. Hugo
Governor's Assistant
South Africa

Dr Charles Kimei
Director
Tanzania

Dr Polycarp Musinguzi
Director, Research
Uganda

Mr T.K. Majero
Deputy General Manager, Human
  Resources
Zimbabwe

BIBLIOGRAPHY

Bailey, Martin J. (1956), 'The Welfare Cost of Inflationary Finance', *Journal of Political Economy*, 64(2), April, pp. 93–110.

Barro, Robert J. (1995), 'Inflation and Economic Growth', *Bank of England Quarterly Bulletin*, 35(2), May, pp. 166–176.

Bisat, Amer, R. Barry Johnston and Venkataraman Sundararajan (1992), 'Issues in Managing and Sequencing Financial Sector Reforms: Lessons from Experiences in Five Developing Countries' (Washington, DC: International Monetary Fund, WP/92/82, October).

Blejer, Mario I. and Silvia B. Sagari (1987), 'The Structure of the Banking Sector and the Sequence of Financial Liberalization' in *Economic Reform and Stabilization in Latin America* edited by Michael Connolly and Claudio Gonzalez-Vega (New York: Praeger), pp. 93–107.

Cagan, Phillip (1956), 'The Monetary Dynamics of Hyperinflation' in *Studies in the Quantity Theory of Money* edited by Milton Friedman (Chicago: University of Chicago Press), pp. 25–117.

Cameron, Rondo, ed. (1972), *Banking and Economic Development: Some Lessons of History* (New York: Oxford University Press).

Cameron, Rondo, Olga Crisp, Hugh T. Patrick and Richard Tilly (1967), *Banking in the Early Stages of Industrialization: A Study in Comparative Economic History* (New York: Oxford University Press).

Caprio, Gerard, Jr., Izak Atiyas and James A. Hanson, eds, (1994), *Financial Reform: Theory and Experience* (Cambridge: Cambridge University Press).

Cottarelli, Carlo (1993), 'Limiting Central Bank Credit to the Government: Theory and Practice' (Washington, DC: International Monetary Fund, Occasional Paper 110, December).

Cottarelli, Carlo (1994), 'Should an Independent Central Bank Control Foreign Exchange Policy?' in *Framework for Monetary Stability: Policy Issues and Country Experiences* edited by Tomás J. T. Baliño and Carlo Cottarelli (Washington, DC: International Monetary Fund), pp. 330–354.

Cukierman, Alex (1992), *Central Bank Strategy, Credibility, and Independence* (Cambridge, Mass.: MIT Press).

Cukierman, Alex, Steven B. Webb and Bilin Neyapti (1992), 'Measuring the Independence of Central Banks and Its Effect on Policy Outcomes', *World Bank Economic Review*, 6(3), September, pp. 353–398.

Cukierman, Alex, Pantelis Kalaitzidakis, Lawrence H. Summers and Steven B. Webb (1993), 'Central Bank Independence, Growth, Investment, and Real Rates', *Carnegie-Rochester Conference Series on Public Policy*, 39, December, pp. 95–140.

De Gregorio, José (1994), 'Inflation, Growth and Central Banks: Theory and Evidence' (Washington, DC: International Monetary Fund, May).

De Gregorio, José and Pablo E. Guidotti (1993), 'Financial Development and Economic Growth' (Washington DC: International Monetary Fund, July).

Dollar, David (1992), 'Outward-Oriented Developing Economies Really Do Grow More Rapidly: Evidence from 95 LDCs, 1976–1985', *Economic Development and Cultural Change*, 40(3), April, pp. 523–544.

Drazen, Allan (1985), 'A General Measure of Inflation Tax Revenues', *Economics Letters*, 17, pp. 327–330.

Easterly, William R., Paolo Mauro and Klaus Schmidt-Hebbel (1995), 'Money Demand and Seigniorage-Maximizing Inflation', *Journal of Money, Credit and Banking*, 27(2), May, pp. 583–603.

Feder, Gershon (1982), 'On Exports and Economic Growth', *Journal of Development Economics*, 12(1–2), February–April, pp. 59–73.

Fischer, Stanley (1982), 'Seigniorage and the Case for a National Money', *Journal of Political Economy*, 90(2), April, pp. 295–313.

Fischer, Stanley (1994), 'Modern Central Banking' in *The Future of Central Banking: The Tercentenary Symposium of the Bank of England* by Forrest Capie, Charles Goodhart, Stanley Fischer and Norbert Schnadt (Cambridge: Cambridge University Press), pp. 262–308.

Friedman, Milton (1971), 'Government Revenue from Inflation', *Journal of Political Economy*, 79(4), July/August, pp. 846–856.

Froyen, Richard T. (1974), 'A Test of the Endogeneity of Monetary Policy', *Journal of Econometrics*, 2(2), July, pp. 175–188.

Fry, Maxwell J. (1973), 'Manipulating Demand for Money' in *Essays in Modern Economics* edited by Michael Parkin (London: Longman), pp. 371–385.

Fry, Maxwell J. (1988), 'Money Supply Responses to Exogenous Shocks in Turkey' in *Liberalization and the Turkish Economy* edited by Tevfik F. Nas and Mehmet Odekon (Westport, Conn.: Greenwood Press), pp. 85–114.

Fry, Maxwell J. (1992), 'Can a Central Bank Go Bust?', *Manchester School of Economic and Social Studies*, 60 (Supplement), June, pp. 85–98.

Fry, Maxwell J. (1995), *Money, Interest, and Banking in Economic Development*, 2nd edn (Baltimore, Md.: Johns Hopkins University Press).

Fry, Maxwell J. and David M. Lilien (1986), 'Monetary Policy Responses to Exogenous Shocks', *American Economic Review*, 76(2), May, pp. 79–83.

Fry, Maxwell J. and R. Basant Roi (1995), 'Monetary Policy-Making in Mauritius', *Bank of Mauritius Quarterly Bulletin*, 35(1), January–March, pp. 11–16.

Gerschenkron, Alexander (1962), *Economic Backwardness in Historical Perspective: A Book of Essays* (Cambridge, Mass.: Harvard University Press).

BIBLIOGRAPHY

Giovannini, Alberto and Martha de Melo (1993), 'Government Revenue from Financial Repression', *American Economic Review*, 83(4), September, pp. 953–963.

Goldsmith, Raymond W. (1969), *Financial Structure and Development* (New Haven, Conn.: Yale University Press).

Hochreiter, Eduard (1994), 'Central Banking in Economies in Transition' (Milan: Bocconi University, Paolo Baffi Centre for Monetary Economics and Finance, July).

Hume, David (1752), 'Of Money' in *Political Discourses*, 2nd edn (Edinburgh: Kincaid and Donaldson), pp. 41–59.

International Monetary Fund (1984), *A Guide to Money and Banking Statistics in* International Financial Statistics (Washington, DC: International Monetary Fund, December).

Jappelli, Tullio and Marco Pagano (1994), 'Saving, Growth, and Liquidity Constraints', *Quarterly Journal of Economics*, 109(1), February, pp. 83–109.

Johnston, Jack (1984), *Econometric Methods*, 3rd edn (New York: McGraw-Hill).

Johnston, R. Barry (1991), 'Sequencing Financial Reform' in *The Evolving Role of Central Banks* edited by Patrick Downes and Reza Vaez-Zadeh (Washington, DC: International Monetary Fund), pp. 295–306.

King, Robert G. and Ross Levine (1993a), 'Finance and Growth: Schumpeter Might Be Right', *Quarterly Journal of Economics*, 108(3), August, pp. 717–737.

King, Robert G. and Ross Levine (1993b), 'Finance, Entrepreneurship, and Growth: Theory and Evidence', *Journal of Monetary Economics*, 32(3), December, pp. 513–542.

Klein, Martin and Manfred J.M. Neumann (1990), 'Seigniorage: What Is It and Who Gets It?', *Weltwirtschaftliches Archiv*, 126(2), pp. 205–221.

Lee, Yang-Pal (1980), 'Inflation Hedges and Economic Growth in a Monetary Economy' (Stanford: Stanford University, Ph.D. thesis).

Liu, Liang-Yn and Wing Thye Woo (1994), 'Saving Behaviour under Imperfect Financial Markets and the Current Account Consequences', *Economic Journal*, 104(424), May, pp. 512–527.

Locke, John (1695), *Further Considerations Concerning Raising the Value of Money*, 2nd edn (London: A.&J. Churchil).

McKinnon, Ronald I. (1973), *Money and Capital in Economic Development* (Washington, DC: Brookings Institution).

McKinnon, Ronald I. (1993), *The Order of Economic Liberalization: Financial Control in the Transition to a Market Economy*, 2nd edn (Baltimore, Md.: Johns Hopkins University Press).

Majumdar, Bani (1974), *Central Banks and Treasuries* (Bombay: Vora).

Mittra, Sid (1978), *Central Bank versus Treasury* (Washington, DC: University Press of America).

Nichols, Donald A. (1974), 'Some Principles of Inflationary Finance', *Journal of Political Economy*, 82(2), March–April, pp. 423–430.

Pagano, Marco (1993), 'Financial Markets and Growth: An Overview', *European Economic Review*, 37(2–3), April, pp. 613–622.

Patrick, Hugh T. (1994), 'Comparisons, Contrasts and Implications' in *The Financial Development of Japan, Korea, and Taiwan: Growth,*

BIBLIOGRAPHY

Repression, and Liberalization edited by Hugh T. Patrick and Yung Chul Park (New York: Oxford University Press), pp. 325–371.

Patrick, Hugh T. and Yung Chul Park, eds (1994), *The Financial Development of Japan, Korea, and Taiwan: Growth, Repression, and Liberalization* (New York: Oxford University Press).

Phelps, Edmund S. (1973), 'Inflation in the Theory of Public Finance', *Swedish Journal of Economics*, 75(1), March, pp. 67–82.

Porzecanski, Arturo (1979), 'Patterns of Monetary Policy in Latin America', *Journal of Money, Credit and Banking*, 11(4), November, pp. 427–437.

Radcliffe Committee (1959), *Report of the Committee on the Working of the Monetary System* (Radcliffe Report) (London: Her Majesty's Stationery Office).

Reuber, Grant L. (1964), 'The Objectives of Canadian Monetary Policy, 1949–61: Empirical "Trade-Offs" and the Reaction Function of the Authorities', *Journal of Political Economy*, 72(2), April, pp. 109–132.

Ricardo, David (1817), *On the Principles of Political Economy, and Taxation* (London: John Murray).

Robinson, David J. and Peter Stella (1988), 'Amalgamating Central Bank and Fiscal Deficits' in *Measurement of Fiscal Impact: Methodological Issues* edited by Mario I. Blejer and Ke-Young Chu (Washington, DC: International Monetary Fund, Occasional Paper 59, June), pp. 20–31.

Schadler, Susan, Maria Carkovic, Adam Bennett and Robert Kahn (1993), 'Recent Experiences with Surges in Capital Inflows' (Washington, DC: International Monetary Fund, Occasional Paper 108, December).

Schumpeter, Joseph A. (1912), *Theorie der wirtschaftlichen Entwicklung* (Leipzig: Duncker & Humblot) [*The Theory of Economic Development; An Inquiry into Profits, Capital, Credit, Interest, and the Business Cycle* translated by Redvers Opie (Cambridge, Mass.: Harvard University Press, 1934)].

Shaw, Edward S. (1973), *Financial Deepening in Economic Development* (New York: Oxford University Press).

Shaw, Edward S. (1975), 'Inflation, Finance and Capital Markets', *Federal Reserve Bank of San Francisco Economic Review*, December, pp. 5–20.

Skanland, Hermod (1984), *The Central Bank and Political Authorities in Some Industrial Countries* (Oslo: Norges Banks Skriftserie No. 13).

Summers, Robert and Alan Heston (1991), 'The Penn World Table (Mark 5): An Expanded Set of International Comparisons, 1950–1988', *Quarterly Journal of Economics*, 106(2), May, pp. 327–368.

Sundararajan, Venkataraman (1992), 'Financial Sector Reforms and their Appropriate Sequencing' (Washington, DC: International Monetary Fund, Monetary and Exchange Affairs Department, September).

Talley, Samuel H. and Ignacio Mas (1992), 'The Role of Deposit Insurance' in *Financial Regulation: Changing the Rules of the Game* edited by Dimitri Vitas (Washington, DC: World Bank, EDI Development Studies), pp. 321–351.

Van Ewijk, Casper and Lambertus J.R. Scholtens (1992), 'The Distribution of Seigniorage in the Netherlands', *De Economist*, 140(2), pp. 446–469.

World Bank (1989), *World Development Report 1989: Financial Systems and Development* (New York: Oxford University Press for the World Bank).

INDEX

Note: Page numbers followed by *t*, *f* or *n* indicate material contained in tables, figures or notes, respectively.

accounting conventions, unique to
   central banking, 31
Africa, countries in Bank of England
   (BoE) group, 2, 2*t*
Argentina
   bank reserves/bank deposits (*R/D*),
     120, 124
   cash reserve ratio, 29
   central bank
     appointment of directors, 110*n*
     independence, 100, 101, 104
     net worth, in 1989, 39
     price stability as objective for, 103
     quasi-fiscal activities, and
       profitability, 40
     statutory objectives, 19
   central bank net credit to
     government/net domestic
     credit to government (*CBCG*),
     121, 125
   central bank profit 1993/GDP, 130
   economic collapse in, 38
   estimated seigniorage revenue in,
     1979–93 (per cent), 130–2
   exchange rate depreciation, 134
   financial markets in, 71*t*, 74*t*
   foreign debt/GDP (*DT/Y*), 121, 124
   foreign exchange regime in, 48, 49*t*,
     50, 51, 55*n*
   government deficit/GDP (*−GS/Y*),
     121, 126
   government domestic debt/GDP, 135
   government revenue/GDP (*GR/Y*),
     121, 126, 130
   inflation (*INF*), 120, 122

inflationary experiences of, 22, 24,
   24*f*, 24*n*, 25*nn*
inflation tax/GDP
   1979–93, 130
   1989–93, 130
inflation tax/government revenue,
   130
macroeconomic and monetary
   characteristics of, 120–6
money (M2)/GDP (*M/Y*), 120, 123
net domestic credit to
   government/aggregate
   domestic credit (CGDC), 121,
   125
payments system in, 58, 59*t*
   reform, 61*t*
per capita income in US dollars,
   alternative measures of, 128
private sector domestic credit/GDP,
   135
reserve money/M2 (*H/M*), 120, 123
trend growth rate in GDP at
   constant prices (*YG*), 120, 122
Asia, countries in Bank of England
   (BoE) group, 2, 2*t*
Asian Development Bank, *Key
   Indicators of Developing Asian
   and Pacific Countries*, 10*n*

Bahamas
   bank loan rate to private sector, 134
   bank reserves/bank deposits (*R/D*),
     120, 124
   cash reserve requirements, 29
   central bank

159

independence, 101
  as regulatory agency, 88n
central bank net credit to
  government/net domestic
  credit to government (CBCG),
  121, 125
central bank profit 1993/GDP, 130
deposit insurance and, 87
estimated seigniorage revenue in,
  1979–93 (per cent), 130–2
exchange rate depreciation, 134
financial markets in, 66, 71t, 74t
  reforms and developments
  underway, 77n
foreign exchange regime in, 49t, 50,
  55n
government bond/bill yield, 134
government deficit/GDP (–GS/Y),
  121, 126
government domestic debt/GDP, 135
government revenue/GDP (GR/Y),
  121, 126, 130
inflation (INF), 120, 122
inflation tax/GDP
  1979–93, 130
  1989–93, 130
inflation tax/government revenue,
  130
liquid asset ratio requirements, 30
macroeconomic and monetary
  characteristics of, 120–6
money (M2)/GDP (M/Y), 120, 123
net domestic credit to
  government/aggregate
  domestic credit (CGDC), 121,
  125
payments system in, 59t
per capita income in US dollars,
  alternative measures of, 128
private sector domestic credit/GDP,
  135
reserve money/M2 (H/M), 120, 123
seigniorage revenue in, 38
subsidy on government debt/GDP,
  135
subsidy on private sector
  borrowing/GDP, 135
trend growth rate in GDP at
  constant prices (YG), 120, 122
US minus exchange rate-adjusted
  government yield, 134
US minus exchange rate-adjusted
  loan rate, 134
Bangladesh

bank loan rate to private sector, 134
bank reserves/bank deposits (R/D),
  120, 124
BCCI débâcle and, 85
central bank, staff recruitment, 91
central bank net credit to
  government/net domestic
  credit to government (CBCG),
  121, 125
central bank profit 1993/GDP, 130
credit allocation to priority sectors,
  30
deposit insurance and, 87
domestic loan guarantees in, 30
estimated seigniorage revenue in,
  1979–93 (per cent), 130–2
exchange rate depreciation, 134
financial markets in, 71t, 74t
foreign debt/GDP (DT/Y), 121, 124
foreign exchange regime in, 49t, 50
government deficit/GDP (–GS/Y),
  121, 126
government domestic debt/GDP, 135
government revenue/GDP (GR/Y),
  121, 126, 130
inflation (INF), 120, 122
inflation tax/GDP
  1979–93, 130
  1989–93, 130
inflation tax/government revenue,
  130
liquid asset ratio requirements, 30
macroeconomic and monetary
  characteristics of, 120–6
money (M2)/GDP (M/Y), 120, 123
net domestic credit to
  government/aggregate
  domestic credit (CGDC), 121,
  125
payments system in, 59t, 77n
per capita income in US dollars,
  alternative measures of, 128
private sector domestic credit/GDP,
  135
reserve money/M2 (H/M), 120, 123
reserve requirements, 29
subsidy on private sector
  borrowing/GDP, 135
trend growth rate in GDP at
  constant prices (YG), 120, 122
US minus exchange rate-adjusted
  loan rate, 134
bank failures, 88, 89n
  fraud and, 83

liquidation and, 85–6
mergers and, 85–6
nationalisation and, 85
questionnaire questions on, 117
recapitalisation and, 85–6
rescue of, 83–6, 142
  lifeboat (loss-sharing)
    arrangements, 86, 85
  restructuring and, 8–86
bank loans
  demand for, 35
  and financial sector growth, 68–9,
    142
  risk-weighted capital-adequacy
    requirements for, 68–9
Bank of England (BoE) group, 2, 2*t*.
  See also specific country
  bank reserves/bank deposits (*R/D*)
    in, 3–4, 4*t*, 8, 8*t*, 9, 28–9
    relation to inflation and
      government deficits, 5, 5*f*
  central banks, statutory objectives,
    19, 25*n*, 103
  economic growth (*YG*) in
    1979–93, 7
    foreign debt (*DT/Y*) and, 5
    government borrowing as
      proportion of total domestic
      credit (*CGDC*) and, 5
    government borrowing from
      central bank (*CBCG*) and, 5, 6*f*
    government deficits (*–GS/Y*) and,
      5, 7*f*
  financial repression in
    estimated revenue from, 1979–93
      (per cent), 134–6
    instruments of, 36
  foreign debt/GDP (DT/Y), 4, 4*t*, 8, 8*t*, 9
  foreign exchange in, 48, 49*t*
    controls, 49*t*, 50, 51
  government deficit/GDP (*–GS/Y*) in,
    4, 4*t*, 8, 8*t*
  government revenue/GDP (*GR/Y*)
    in, 4*t*, 8, 8*t*
  inflation in, 7, 8, 8*t*, 13–14, 14*f*, 29
    consumer price index (CPI), 19, 20*t*
    economic growth (*YG*) and, 5
    government borrowing as
      proportion of total domestic
      credit (*CGDC*) and, 5
    government borrowing from
      central bank (*CBCG*) and, 5, 6*f*
    growth and, statistical
      relationship, 16–19

mean, 19–20, 20*t*
monetary expansion and, 15–16
and in other developing
  countries, comparison, 4, 4*t*,
  138
standard deviation, 19–20, 20*t*
trends in, 19–20, 20*t*, 22
variability, 15, 15*f*
interest rates in, 36
loan rate ceilings in, 36
macroeconomic and monetary
  characteristics of, 1979–93,
  3–10, 4*t*, 5*f*, 6*f*, 7*f*, 8*t*, 119–26
monetary policy reaction functions
  for, 41–5
  estimates, by exchange rate
    regime, 52–5
  money (M2)/GDP (*M/Y*) in, 3–4,
    4*t*, 8, 8*t*
  net domestic credit to
    government/aggregate
    domestic credit (*CGDC*) in, 4*t*,
    8, 8*t*, 9, 28–9
  other developing countries and,
    comparison, 3–4, 4*t*, 7, 138
  reserve money/M2 (*H/M*) in, 3–4, 4*t*,
    8–9, 8*t*, 29
  inflation and government deficits
    and, 5
  seigniorage revenue in, estimated,
    1979–93 (per cent), 34, 130–2
bank reserves, in developing countries,
  27–8
bank reserves/bank deposits (*R/D*)
  in Bank of England (BoE) group,
    3–4, 4*t*, 8, 8*t*, 9, 28–9
    relation to inflation and
      government deficits, 5, 5*f*
  in developing countries vs. OECD
    countries, 3–4, 4*t*
banking habit, development, 63–5, 141
banking systems, domestic, 79
  control over, 79–80, 83–6
  questionnaire questions on, 115
  development
    central banks role in, 58–66
    growth and, 63–4, 63*t*, 64*t*
  indigenisation, in developing
    countries, 150
  liberalisation, 68, 142, 146
Barbados
  bank loan rate to private sector, 134
  bank reserves/bank deposits (*R/D*),
    120, 124

BCCI débâcle and, 85
central bank net credit to
    government/net domestic
    credit to government (*CBCG*),
    121, 125
central bank profit 1993/GDP, 130
deposit insurance in, 87
domestic loan guarantees in, 30
estimated seigniorage revenue in,
    1979–93 (per cent), 130–2
exchange rate depreciation, 134
financial markets in, 66–8, 71*t*, 74*t*
foreign borrowing in, 51
foreign debt/GDP (*DT/Y*), 121, 124
foreign exchange regime in, 49*t*, 50,
    55*n*
government bond/bill yield, 134
government deficit/GDP (*–GS/Y*),
    121, 126
government domestic debt/GDP, 135
government revenue/GDP (*GR/Y*),
    121, 126, 130
inflation (*INF*), 120, 122
inflation tax/GDP
    1979–93, 130
    1989–93, 130
inflation tax/government revenue,
    130
liquid asset ratio requirements, 30
macroeconomic and monetary
    characteristics of, 120–6
net domestic credit to
    government/aggregate
    domestic credit (*CGDC*), 121,
    125
payments system in, 57, 59*t*
per capita income in US dollars,
    alternative measures of, 128
priority sector lending in, 30
private sector domestic credit/GDP,
    135
reserve money/M2 (*H/M*), 120, 123
reserve requirements, 29
subsidy on government debt/GDP,
    135
subsidy on private sector
    borrowing/GDP, 135
trend growth rate in GDP at
    constant prices (*YG*), 120, 122
US minus exchange rate-adjusted
    government yield, 134
US minus exchange rate-adjusted
    loan rate, 134
Barro, Robert J., 143, 146

BCCI, international effects, 83, 85, 86, 88
Belize
    bank loan rate to private sector, 134
    bank reserves/bank deposits (*R/D*),
        120, 124
    central bank
        staff, 95
        statutory objectives, 103
        supervisory functions, 88*n*
    central bank net credit to
        government/net domestic
        credit to government (*CBCG*),
        121, 125
    central bank profit 1993/GDP, 130
    estimated seigniorage revenue in,
        1979–93 (per cent), 130–2
    exchange rate depreciation, 134
    financial markets in, 71*t*, 74*t*
    foreign debt/GDP (*DT/Y*), 121, 124
    foreign exchange guarantees in, 51
    foreign exchange losses in, 37, 51
    foreign exchange regime in, 49*t*, 50,
        55*n*
    government bond/bill yield, 134
    government deficit/GDP (*–GS/Y*),
        121, 126
    government domestic debt/GDP, 135
    government revenue/GDP (*GR/Y*),
        121, 126, 130
    inflation (*INF*), 120, 122
    inflation tax/GDP
        1979–93, 130
        1989–93, 130
    inflation tax/government revenue,
        130
    liquid asset ratio requirements, 30
    macroeconomic and monetary
        characteristics of, 120–6
    money (M2)/GDP (*M/Y*), 120, 123
    net domestic credit to
        government/aggregate
        domestic credit (*CGDC*), 121,
        125
    payments system in, 59*t*
        reform, 61*t*
    per capita income in US dollars,
        alternative measures of, 128
    priority sector lending in, 30
    private sector domestic credit/GDP,
        135
    reserve money/M2 (*H/M*), 120, 123
    seigniorage revenue in, 38
    subsidy on government debt/GDP,
        135

subsidy on private sector
  borrowing/GDP, 135
trend growth rate in GDP at
  constant prices (*YG*), 120, 122
US minus exchange rate-adjusted
  government yield, 134
US minus exchange rate-adjusted
  loan rate, 134
bond market, 69–71
Botswana
  bank loan rate to private sector, 134
  bank reserves/bank deposits (*R/D*),
    120, 124
  BCCI débâcle and, 85
  central bank
    quasi-fiscal activities, and
      profitability, 40
    staff, 95
    staff recruitment, 91
  central bank net credit to
    government/net domestic
    credit to government (*CBCG*),
    121, 125
  central bank profit 1993/GDP, 130
  estimated seigniorage revenue in,
    1979–93 (per cent), 130–2
  exchange rate depreciation, 134
  financial markets in, 71*t*
  foreign debt/GDP (*DT/Y*), 121, 124
  foreign exchange regime in, 49*t*, 50
  government deficit/GDP (–*GS/Y*),
    121, 126
  government revenue/GDP (*GR/Y*),
    121, 126, 130
  inflation (*INF*), 120, 122
  inflation tax/GDP
    1979–93, 130
    1989–93, 130
  inflation tax/government revenue, 130
  interest rates in, 36
  macroeconomic and monetary
    characteristics of, 120–6
  money (M2)/GDP (*M/Y*), 120, 123
  net domestic credit to
    government/aggregate
    domestic credit (*CGDC*), 121,
    125
  payments system in, 59*t*, 61*t*
  per capita income in US dollars,
    alternative measures of, 128
  private sector domestic credit/GDP,
    135
  reserve money/M2 (*H/M*), 120, 123
  subsidy on private sector

borrowing/GDP, 135
trend growth rate in GDP at
  constant prices (*YG*), 120, 122
US minus exchange rate-adjusted
  loan rate, 134
Brazil, interest rate on required
  reserves, 45*n*
Brunei, 2*t*, 10*n*, 26*n*, 46*n*
  central bank
    staff, 95
    staff recruitment, 90
    supervisory authority, 80
  financial markets in, 71*t*
  interest rates in, 36
  payments system in, 59*t*, 77*n*

capital account, controls on, in
  developing countries, 146,
  147. *See also* financial systems,
  liberalisation
capital adequacy ratio requirements,
  29, 150
capital-adequacy requirements,
  risk-weighted, for bank loans,
  68–9
capital flight, foreign debt and, 5, 11*n*
capital inflows, international, with
  liberalised financial system,
  69, 142
CBCG. See central bank net credit to
  government/net domestic
  credit to government
central bank and government
  cooperation, 108–10
central bank net credit to
  government/net domestic
  credit to government (*CBCG*)
  in Bank of England (BoE) group, 4*t*,
    8, 8*t*, 9, 28–9
  in developing and OECD countries,
    4*t*. *See also specific country*
central banks
  balance sheet, 37–8, 39
  in Bank of England (BoE) group
    changing role of, 113
    statutory objectives, 19, 25*n*, 103
  board of directors, government
    representatives on, 28, 46*n*,
    101–3, 103*t*, 106, 108, 151
  effects on government borrowing
    and private sector credit, 43–5,
    139
  constitutional position, 145. *See also*
    independence

inflation and, 143
decision-making powers and, 103–4
directors, appointment of, 101, 110n
domestic role, 137–40
    questionnaire questions on, 115
external role, 47–55, 140
    questionnaire questions on, 116
failures, 39
financing of government deficit, 22,
    105
fiscal activities on behalf of
    government, 33
foreign exchange operations, 47–8
governors, turnover, 100–2, 102f
independence. *See* independence, of
    central banks
insolvent, 40
interest-free loans from, to
    government, 33
losses, 39–40, 139
    from foreign exchange
        operations, 37, 45n
net worth of, 38
objectives of, 9–10
privatisation, 39
profitability
    balance-sheet approach to, 37–8
    in flow terms, 38–9, 139
    inflation and, 39–40
    quasi-fiscal activities and, 37–8, 40
    in stock terms, 39, 139
profits, transfer to government, 33
quasi-fiscal activities, 27–8, 31, 37–8,
    39–40, 140
    monetary activities and, 31–2
research function, 96, 109, 146, 147,
    151
responsibility for monetary control,
    20–2
revenue-raising activities, 30
size, inflation and, 98, 198
staff. *See* professional status, of
    central bank; staff
status. *See* status
as supervisory agent, questionnaire
    questions on, 116–17
supervisory authority, 79, 87–8. *See*
    also supervision
    questionnaire questions on,
    116–17
support operations. *See also* bank
    failures
    expenses, 86
CGDC. See net domestic credit to
    government/aggregate
    domestic credit
Chile
    bank loan rate to private sector, 134
    bank reserves/bank deposits (*R/D*),
        120, 124
    central bank, 100
        independence, 104
        price stability as objective for, 103
        staff, 95
        staff recruitment, 91
        statutory objectives, 19
        support operations, expenses, 86,
            88
    central bank losses in, 39–40
    central bank net credit to
        government/net domestic
        credit to government (*CBCG*),
        121, 125
    central bank profit 1993/GDP, 130
    deposit insurance and, 87
    economic collapse in, 38
    estimated seigniorage revenue in,
        1979–93 (per cent), 130–2
    exchange rate depreciation, 134
    financial markets in, 72t, 74t
    foreign debt/GDP (*DT/Y*), 121, 124
    foreign exchange losses in, 51
    foreign exchange regime in, 49t, 50
    government deficit/GDP (*–GS/Y*),
        121, 126
    government domestic debt/GDP, 135
    government revenue/GDP (*GR/Y*),
        121, 126, 130
    inflation (*INF*), 120, 122
    inflationary experiences of, 22
    inflation tax/GDP
        1979–93, 130
        1989–93, 130
    inflation tax/government revenue, 130
    inflation tax in, 38
    liquid asset ratio requirements, 30
    loan rate ceilings in, 36
    macroeconomic and monetary
        characteristics of, 120–6
    money (M2)/GDP (*M/Y*), 120, 123
    net domestic credit to
        government/aggregate
        domestic credit (*CGDC*), 121,
        125
    payments system in, 57, 59t, 58
        reforms, 58, 61t
    per capita income in US dollars,
        alternative measures of, 128

private sector domestic credit/GDP, 135
reserve money/M2 (*H/M*), 120, 123
reserve requirements, 29
subsidy on private sector
   borrowing/GDP, 135
trend growth rate in GDP at
   constant prices (*YG*), 120, 122
US minus exchange rate-adjusted
   loan rate, 134
commercial banks
   deposit insurance and, 87
   development, 62
   as financial intermediaries, 62–3
   herd instinct and, 68, 77*n*
   supervision of. *See* supervision
credit
   domestic, expansion, and automatic
     government borrowing, 44–5
   private sector, reduction, to
     neutralise government credit
     expansion, 41–5
credit policy
   sectoral, 30, 35–6
   selective, 30, 35–6
Cukierman, Alex, 10, 98–100, 101, 109,
   110, 143
currency issue, central banks'
   monopoly power over,
   32
current account payments, restrictions
   on, 48–50, 49*t*
Cyprus
   bank loan rate to private sector, 134
   bank reserves/bank deposits (*R/D*),
     120, 124
   central bank
     price stability as objective for, 103
     staff, 95
     statutory objectives, 19
   central bank net credit to
     government/net domestic
     credit to government (*CBCG*),
     121, 125
   central bank profit 1993/GDP, 130
   credit allocation to priority sectors,
     30
   deposit insurance and, 87
   estimated seigniorage revenue in,
     1979–93 (per cent), 130–2
   exchange rate depreciation, 134
   financial markets in, 66, 71*t*, 74*t*
   reforms and developments
     underway, 77*n*

foreign borrowing in, 51
foreign exchange guarantees in, 51
foreign exchange regime in, 49*t*, 50,
   55*n*
government deficit/GDP (*–GS/Y*),
   121, 126
government domestic debt/GDP, 135
government revenue/GDP (*GR/Y*),
   121, 126, 130
inflation (*INF*), 120, 122
inflation tax/GDP
   1979–93, 130
   1989–93, 130
inflation tax/government revenue,
   130
liquid asset ratio requirements, 30
loan rate ceilings in, 36
macroeconomic and monetary
   characteristics of, 120–6
money (M2)/GDP (*M/Y*), 120, 123
net domestic credit to
   government/aggregate
   domestic credit (*CGDC*), 121,
   125
payments system in, 59*t*
   reform, 61*t*
per capita income in US dollars,
   alternative measures of, 128
priority sector lending in, 30
private sector domestic credit/GDP,
   135
reserve money/M2 (*H/M*), 120, 123
reserve requirements, 29
subsidy on private sector
   borrowing/GDP, 135
trend growth rate in GDP at
   constant prices (*YG*), 120, 122
US minus exchange rate-adjusted
   loan rate, 134

De Gregorio, José, 10
demand-for-money functions, in
   analysis of development of
   banking habit, 64–5, 67*t*, 141
deposit insurance, 31, 46*n*, 86–7, 89*n*,
   142–3
   questionnaire questions on, 117
developing countries
   central bank net credit to
     government/net domestic
     credit to government (*CBCG*)
     in, 4*t*
   central banks' role in, 2–3
   control group, 3–4, 4*t*, 10*n*–11*n*

foreign debt/GDP (*DT/Y*), 4, 4*t*
government deficit/GDP (*−GS/Y*) in,
   4, 4*t*
government revenue/GDP (*GR/Y*)
   in, 4*t*
macroeconomic and monetary
   characteristics of, 3–4, 4*t*
monetary policy reaction functions
   for, 41–5
net domestic credit to
   government/aggregate
   domestic credit (*CGDC*) in, 4*t*
per capita income in US dollars,
   1992 (*PCY*), 4*t*
dirigism, 112, 138, 144
domestic banking system
   regulation, 1
   supervision, 1
domestic credit, exchange rate regimes
   and, 52
DT/Y. See foreign debt/GDP

East Caribbean
   central bank, staff, 95
   financial markets in, 71*t*, 74*t*
     reforms and developments
     underway, 77*n*
   payments system in, 58
Easterly, William, 34
Eastern Caribbean Central Bank, 10*n*,
   51
   staff, 95
economic growth (*YG*). *See also* gross
     domestic product (GDP),
     trend growth rate in at
     constant prices (*YG*)
   in Bank of England (BoE) group
     1979–1993, 7
   relation to foreign debt (*DT/Y*), 5
   relation to government
     borrowing as proportion of
     total domestic credit (*CGDC*), 5
   relation to government
     borrowing from central bank
     (*CBCG*), 5, 6*f*
   relation to government deficits
     (*−GS/Y*), 5, 7*f*
   and Consumer Price Index (CPI)
     inflation, 13–14, 14*f*
equity market, 69–70
Europe, countries in Bank of England
   (BoE) group, 2, 2*t*
European Central Bank, 32
European System Central Banks

(ESCB), price stability and, 16,
   19
exchange rates
   fixed, 50, 49*t*, 140
     conservative central banks and,
     50–3, 141
     government deficit and, 51
     responses to economic shocks
     and, 52–3
   floating, 50, 49*t*, 48, 51, 140
     government deficit and, 51
     responses to economic shocks
     and, 52–3
   and inflation, 16, 25*n*
   managed, 50, 49*t*, 140
     government deficit and, 51
     responses to economic shocks
     and, 52–3
   regimes
     classification, 48, 49*t*, 140
     economic growth and, 52, 138
     effects of changes in net foreign
     assets on money supply and,
     52–5, 141
     factors affecting choice of, 50–1,
     140
     financial liberalisation and, 146
     foreign debt and, 51–2
     inflation and, 52, 138
     money holdings and, 65, 141
     reserve money/M2 (*H/M*) and,
     52, 55*n*
     sterilisation and neutralisation of
     government borrowing
     requirements and, 52–5, 141
   export proceeds surrender
     requirements, 48–50, 49*t*
   economic growth and, 52

failures, bank. *See* bank failures
Fiji
   bank loan rate to private sector, 134
   bank reserves/bank deposits (*R/D*),
     120, 124
   cash reserve requirements, 29
   central bank, appointment of
     directors, 110*n*
   central bank net credit to
     government/net domestic
     credit to government (*CBCG*),
     121, 125
   central bank profit 1993/GDP, 130
   credit allocation to priority sectors,
     30

estimated seigniorage revenue in, 1979–93 (per cent), 130–2
exchange rate depreciation, 134
financial markets in, 71*t*, 74*t*
  reforms and developments underway, 77*n*
foreign debt/GDP (*DT/Y*), 121, 124
foreign exchange losses in, 37, 51
foreign exchange regime in, 49*t*
government bond/bill yield, 134
government deficit/GDP (*–GS/Y*), 121, 126
government domestic debt/GDP, 135
government revenue/GDP (*GR/Y*), 121, 126, 130
inflation (*INF*), 120, 122
inflation tax/GDP
  1979–93, 130
  1989–93, 130
inflation tax/government revenue, 130
liquid asset ratio requirements, 30
macroeconomic and monetary characteristics of, 120–6
money (M2)/GDP (*M/Y*), 120, 123
net domestic credit to government/ aggregate domestic credit (*CGDC*), 121, 125
payments system in, 59*t*
per capita income in US dollars, alternative measures of, 128
private sector domestic credit/GDP, 135
reserve money/M2 (*H/M*), 120, 123
reserve requirements, 29
subsidy on government debt/GDP, 135
subsidy on private sector borrowing/GDP, 135
trend growth rate in GDP at constant prices (*YG*), 120, 122
US minus exchange rate-adjusted government yield, 134
US minus exchange rate-adjusted loan rate, 134
financial institutions
  fragility, 39–40, 83–86, 142
  insolvent. *See also* bank failures
  central bank rescue of, 39–40, 142
  restricted competition among, and development of indigenous institutions, 142
financial intermediation, 62–3
  discriminatory tax on, 29

financial markets. *See also* bond market; equity market; money market
development
  central banks' role in, 66–76, 142
  impediments to, 72–3, 74*t*–6*t*
  private sector participants and, 73–6, 78*n*
  domestic, questionnaire questions on, 115
  indirect open-market mechanisms, 66, 113, 141
  ranking, 65, 71*t*–2*t*
  reforms, 72, 77*t*–8*t*
financial repression, 35–36, 66, 109, 112, 139
  in Bank of England (BoE) group
    estimated revenue from, 1979–93 (per cent), 134–6
    instruments of, 36
  effects
    on demand for money, 65
    on growth of banking habit, 65
  tax revenue from, 36
financial systems
  domestic, 79, 141–2
  liberalisation, 73–6, 146
  difficulties of, 68–70
  money holdings and, 65, 141
Fischer, Stanley, 45*n*, 96, 145–6
foreign debt
  in Bank of England (BoE) group, and other developing countries, comparison, 138
  capital flight and, 5, 11*n*
  in developing countries, 37
  exchange rate regimes and, 51–2, 52
foreign debt/GDP (*DT/Y*)
  in Bank of England (BoE) group, 4, 4*t*, 8, 8*t*, 9
  in developing countries vs. OECD countries, 4, 4*t*
foreign exchange. *See also* exchange rates
  in Bank of England (BoE) group, 48, 49*t*
  central banks role in, 47–8
  controls
    in Bank of England (BoE) group, 49*t*, 50, 51
    central banks administration of, 51
  guarantees, 51
  losses, by central banks, 51

market making, 48
passive intervention and, 48
regimes, 1
choice of, 27
foreign exchange operations, 37
subsidy elements, 37
tax elements, 37
foreign loans, central banks' role in, 51
forward foreign exchange transactions,
49t, 50
fraud, bank failure and, 83
Froyen, Richard, 41–2
Fry, Maxwell J., 55n, 89n

Gambia
bank loan rate to private sector, 134
bank reserves/bank deposits (R/D),
120, 124
cash reserve ratio, 29
central bank
staff training, 91
specialised supervisory staff, 81
supervisory functions, 88n
central bank net credit to
government/net domestic
credit to government (CBCG),
121, 125
central bank profit 1993/GDP, 130
estimated seigniorage revenue in,
1979–93 (per cent), 130–2
exchange rate depreciation, 134
financial markets in, 71t
foreign debt/GDP (DT/Y), 121, 124
foreign exchange operations, 47
foreign exchange regime in, 49t, 51
government deficit/GDP (–GS/Y),
121, 126
government domestic debt/GDP, 135
government revenue/GDP (GR/Y),
121, 126, 130
inflation (INF), 120, 122
inflation tax/GDP
1979–93, 130
1989–93, 130
inflation tax/government revenue,
130
interest rates in, 36
liquid asset ratio requirements, 30
macroeconomic and monetary
characteristics of, 120–6
money (M2)/GDP (M/Y), 120, 123
net domestic credit to government/
aggregate domestic credit
(CGDC), 121, 125

payments system in, 59t
per capita income in US dollars,
alternative measures of, 128
private sector domestic credit/GDP,
135
reserve money/M2 (H/M), 120, 123
subsidy on private sector
borrowing/GDP, 135
trend growth rate in GDP at
constant prices (YG), 120, 122
US minus exchange rate-adjusted
loan rate, 134
Ghana
bank loan rate to private sector, 134
bank reserves/bank deposits (R/D),
120, 124
central bank net credit to
government/net domestic
credit to government (CBCG),
121, 125
estimated seigniorage revenue in,
1979–93 (per cent), 130–2
exchange rate depreciation, 134
foreign debt/GDP (DT/Y), 121, 124
foreign exchange regime in, 49t
government bond/bill yield, 134
government deficit/GDP (–GS/Y),
121, 126
government domestic debt/GDP, 135
government revenue/GDP (GR/Y),
121, 126, 130
inflation (INF), 120, 122
inflation tax/GDP
1979–93, 130
1989–93, 130
inflation tax/government revenue, 130
macroeconomic and monetary
characteristics of, 120–6
money (M2)/GDP (M/Y), 120, 123
net domestic credit to government/
aggregate domestic credit
(CGDC), 121, 125
payments system in, 59t
per capita income in US dollars,
alternative measures of, 128
private sector domestic credit/GDP,
135
reserve money/M2 (H/M), 120, 123
subsidy on government debt/GDP,
135
subsidy on private sector
borrowing/GDP, 135
trend growth rate in GDP at
constant prices (YG), 120, 122

US minus exchange rate-adjusted
government yield, 134
US minus exchange rate-adjusted
loan rate, 134
Giovannini, Alberto, 36
government, central banks' relationship
with, 22, 27–46, 138–40
constitutional interrelationships and,
143
stock and flow variables in, 37–40,
139
government borrowing, 144
automatic, 104
domestic credit expansion and,
44–5
from central banks, 28–9
crowding out of private sector
borrowing, 145
exchange rate regimes and, 52
level playing field concept, 109–10
neutralisation, by reduced private
sector credit, 41–5
government debt, marketable, 109–10
government deficit
in Bank of England (BoE) group,
and other developing
countries, comparison, 138
central banks' financing of, 22, 104
exchange rates and, 25n, 51
interest rates and, 25n
noninflationary finance of, 38
output growth and, 25n
primary, reduction, 33
government deficit/GDP (–GS/Y)
in Bank of England (BoE) group, 4,
4t, 8, 8t
in developing and OECD countries,
4, 4t. See also specific country
government finance, noninflationary, 38
government financing, 1
government revenue/GDP (GR/Y)
in Bank of England (BoE) group, 4t,
8, 8t
in developing and OECD countries,
4t. See also specific country
gross domestic product (GDP), trend
growth rate in at constant
prices (YG)
in Bank of England (BoE) group, 4t,
8t
in developing and OECD countries,
4t. See also specific country
growth. See economic growth (YG);
monetary expansion

monetisation and, 63–4, 63t, 64t
GR/Y. See government revenue/GDP
–GS/Y. See government deficit/GDP
Guyana
bank loan rate to private sector, 134
bank reserves/bank deposits (R/D),
120, 124
cash reserve ratio, 29
central bank, supervisory functions,
88n
central bank losses in, 39–40
central bank net credit to
government/net domestic
credit to government (CBCG),
121, 125
central bank profit 1993/GDP, 130
estimated seigniorage revenue in,
1979–93 (per cent), 130–2
exchange rate depreciation, 134
financial markets in, 71t, 74t
reforms and developments
underway, 77n
foreign debt/GDP (DT/Y), 121, 124
foreign exchange guarantees in, 51
foreign exchange losses in, 37, 51
foreign exchange regime in, 49t
government bond/bill yield, 134
government deficit/GDP (–GS/Y),
121, 126
government domestic debt/GDP, 135
government revenue/GDP (GR/Y),
121, 126, 130
inflation (INF), 120, 122
inflation tax/GDP
1979–93, 130
1989–93, 130
inflation tax/government revenue, 130
inflation tax in, 38
interest rates in, 36
liquid asset ratio requirements, 30
macroeconomic and monetary
characteristics of, 120–6
money (M2)/GDP (M/Y), 120, 123
net domestic credit to
government/aggregate
domestic credit (CGDC), 121,
125
payments system in, 59t
per capita income in US dollars,
alternative measures of, 128
private sector domestic credit/GDP,
135
reserve money/M2 (H/M), 120, 123
reserve requirements, 29

subsidy on government debt/GDP, 135
subsidy on private sector borrowing/GDP, 135
trend growth rate in GDP at constant prices (*YG*), 120, 122
US minus exchange rate-adjusted government yield, 134
US minus exchange rate-adjusted loan rate, 134

Heston, Alan. *See* Summers, Robert, and Alan Heston
H/M. See reserve money/M2
Hong Kong, 26*n*, 46*n*
bank loan rate to private sector, 134
bank reserves/bank deposits (*R/D*), 120, 124
bond market in, 70–2
central bank
appointment of directors, 110*n*
independence, 101
staff recruitment, 90
supervisory authority, specialised staff for, 80, 81
central bank net credit to government/net domestic credit to government (*CBCG*), 121, 125
central bank profit 1993/GDP, 130
data for, sources, 10*n*
deposit insurance and, 87
estimated seigniorage revenue in, 1979–93 (per cent), 130–2
exchange rate depreciation, 134
financial markets in, 69, 71*t*, 72*t*, 74*t*
reforms and developments underway, 77*n*
foreign exchange regime in, 49*t*, 50, 51, 55*n*
government deficit/GDP (–*GS/Y*), 121, 126
government revenue/GDP (*GR/Y*), 121, 126, 130
inflation (*INF*), 120, 122
inflation tax/GDP
1979–93, 130
1989–93, 130
inflation tax/government revenue, 130
liquid asset ratio requirements, 30
macroeconomic and monetary characteristics of, 120–6
money (M2)/GDP (*M/Y*), 120, 123

net domestic credit to government/aggregate domestic credit (*CGDC*), 121, 125
payments system in, 57, 59*t*, 77*n*
reform, 61*t*
per capita income in US dollars, alternative measures of, 128
private sector domestic credit/GDP, 135
reserve money/M2 (*H/M*), 120, 123
reserve requirements, 29
seigniorage revenue in, 38
subsidy on private sector borrowing/GDP, 135
trend growth rate in GDP at constant prices (*YG*), 120, 122
US minus exchange rate-adjusted loan rate, 134
Hume, David, 13

independence, of central banks, 10, 31–2, 98–108, 143, 146
central banks self-assessment of, 104–6, 104*t*, 143–4, 151
inflation and, 104–106, 144
recruitment of skilled staff and, 93, 98
growth and, 145
inflation and, 98–101
India
bank loan rate to private sector, 134
bank reserves/bank deposits (*R/D*), 120, 124
cash reserve ratio, 29
central bank
appointment of directors, 110*n*
quasi-fiscal activities, and profitability, 40
central bank net credit to government/net domestic credit to government (*CBCG*), 121, 125
central bank profit 1993/GDP, 130
credit allocation to priority sectors, 30
deposit insurance and, 87
estimated seigniorage revenue in, 1979–93 (percent), 130–2
exchange rate depreciation, 134
financial markets in, 71*t*, 72*t*
reforms and developments underway, 77*n*
foreign debt/GDP (*DT/Y*), 121, 124
foreign exchange losses in, 37, 51

foreign exchange regime in, 49*t*, 50
government deficit/GDP (*–GS/Y*), 121, 126
government domestic debt/GDP, 135
government revenue/GDP (*GR/Y*), 121, 126, 130
inflation (*INF*), 120, 122
inflation in, 144
inflation tax/GDP
    1979–93, 130
    1989–93, 130
inflation tax/government revenue, 130
liquid asset ratio requirements, 30
liquid asset ratios in, 45*n*
loan rate ceilings in, 36
macroeconomic and monetary characteristics of, 120–6
money (M2)/GDP (*M/Y*), 120, 123
net domestic credit to government/aggregate domestic credit (*CGDC*), 121, 125
payments system in, 58, 59*t*, 77*n*
    reform, 61*t*
per capita income in US dollars, alternative measures of, 128
priority sector lending in, 30
private sector domestic credit/GDP, 135
reserve money/M2 (*H/M*), 120, 123
subsidy on private sector borrowing/GDP, 135
trend growth rate in GDP at constant prices (*YG*), 120, 122
US minus exchange rate-adjusted loan rate, 134
Indonesia, monetary policy reaction functions for, 41
INF. See inflation
inflation (*INF*), 9
    in Bank of England (BoE) group, 7, 8, 8*t*, 13–14, 14*f*, 29, 88
        economic growth (*YG*) and, 5, 145–6, 148–9
        government borrowing as proportion of total domestic credit (*CGDC*) and, 5
        government borrowing from central bank (*CBCG*) and, 5, 6*f*, 149–50
        monetary expansion and, 15–16
        and other developing countries, comparison, 4, 4*t*, 138

trends in, 19–20, 20*t*, 22
    variability, 15, 15*f*
central bank profitability and, 39–40
central banks' independence and, 98–101, 144
Consumer Price Index (CPI)
    in Bank of England (BoE) group, 19, 20*t*
    in developing countries, 28
    economic growth and, 13–14, 14*f*
    and its standard deviation, 15, 15*f*
    in OECD countries, 28
in developing countries, 144, 145
government revenue from, 34
and growth, 13–24, 138, 145–6, 148–9
    statistical relationship for Bank of England (BoE) group, 16–19, 138
interest rate ceilings and, 35–6
mean
    in Bank of England (BoE) group, 19–20, 20*t*
    and coefficient of variation, 24*n*–25*n*
    and standard deviation, 24*n*–5*n*
median, in Bank of England (BoE) group, 19–20, 20*t*
monetary expansion and, 20, 21*f*, 21*t*
monetary growth and, relationship refined, 22–24
in OECD countries, 4*t*, 88
    trends in, 22
standard deviation, 15, 15*f*
    in Bank of England (BoE) group, 19–20, 20*t*
status of central bank and, 105–8, 107*t*
inflation tax, 38, 139
    on currency holdings, 35
interest rates
    in Bank of England (BoE) group, 36
    ceilings, 35–6
    controls, 30
    domestic, questionnaire questions on, 115–16
    and inflation, 16, 25*n*, 138
    liberalisation, 68
    on required reserves, 34
International Monetary Fund
    Article VIII agreement on currency convertibility, 48, 145
    Exchange Arrangements and Exchange Restrictions: Annual Report 1994, 55*n*

International Financial Statistics
  (*IFS*), 1, 3
  reserve money in, 45*n*
investment culture, in private sector,
  73–6
Israel
  bank loan rate to private sector, 134
  bank reserves/bank deposits (*R/D*),
    120, 124
  central bank
  independence, 110
  staff, 91
  central bank net credit to
    government/net domestic
    credit to government (*CBCG*),
    121, 125
  central bank profit 1993/GDP, 130
  estimated seigniorage revenue in,
    1979–93 (per cent), 130–2
  exchange rate depreciation, 134
  financial markets in, 66, 71*t*, 72, 72*t*,
    74*t*
  foreign exchange regime in, 48, 49*t*,
    50, 49*t*
  government bond/bill yield, 134
  government deficit/GDP (*–GS/Y*),
    121, 126
  government domestic debt/GDP, 135
  government revenue/GDP (*GR/Y*),
    121, 126, 130
  inflation (*INF*), 120, 122
  inflation tax/GDP
    1979–93, 130
    1989–93, 130
  inflation tax/government revenue,
    130
  liquid asset ratio requirements, 30
  macroeconomic and monetary
    characteristics of, 120–6
  money (M2)/GDP (*M/Y*), 120,
    123
  net domestic credit to
    government/aggregate
    domestic credit (*CGDC*), 121,
    125
  payments system in, 57, 59*t*
    reform, 61*t*
  per capita income in US dollars,
    alternative measures of, 128
  private sector domestic credit/GDP,
    135
  reserve money in, 45*n*
  reserve money/M2 (*H/M*), 120, 123
  reserve requirements, 29

  subsidy on government debt/GDP,
    135
  subsidy on private sector
    borrowing/GDP, 135
  trend growth rate in GDP at
    constant prices (*YG*), 120, 122
  US minus exchange rate-adjusted
    government yield, 134
  US minus exchange rate-adjusted
    loan rate, 134

Jamaica
  bank loan rate to private sector, 134
  bank reserves/bank deposits (*R/D*),
    120, 124
  cash reserve ratio, 29
  central bank, staff training, 91
  central bank losses in, 39–40
  central bank net credit to
    government/net domestic
    credit to government (*CBCG*),
    121, 125
  central bank profit 1993/GDP, 130
  estimated seigniorage revenue in,
    1979–93 (per cent), 130–2
  exchange rate depreciation, 134
  financial markets in, 71*t*
  foreign debt/GDP (*DT/Y*), 121, 124
  foreign exchange losses in, 37, 51
  foreign exchange regime in, 49*t*, 51
  government bond/bill yield, 134
  government deficit/GDP (*–GS/Y*),
    121, 126
  government domestic debt/GDP, 135
  government revenue/GDP (*GR/Y*),
    121, 126, 130
  inflation (*INF*), 120, 122
  inflation tax/GDP
    1979–93, 130
    1989–93, 130
  inflation tax/government revenue,
    130
  liquid asset ratio requirements, 30
  macroeconomic and monetary
    characteristics of, 120–6
  money (M2)/GDP (*M/Y*), 120, 123
  net domestic credit to
    government/aggregate
    domestic credit (*CGDC*), 121,
    125
  payments system in, 59*t*
    reforms, 58, 61*t*
  per capita income in US dollars,
    alternative measures of, 128

private sector domestic credit/GDP, 135
reserve money/M2 (*H/M*), 120, 123
subsidy on government debt/GDP, 135
subsidy on private sector borrowing/GDP, 135
trend growth rate in GDP at constant prices (*YG*), 120, 122
US minus exchange rate-adjusted government yield, 134
US minus exchange rate-adjusted loan rate, 134
Jordan
  bank loan rate to private sector, 134
  bank reserves/bank deposits (*R/D*), 120, 124
  central bank
    quasi-fiscal activities, and profitability, 40
    staff, 95
  central bank net credit to government/net domestic credit to government (*CBCG*), 121, 125
  central bank profit 1993/GDP, 130
  deposit insurance and, 87
  estimated seigniorage revenue in, 1979–93 (per cent), 130–2
  exchange rate depreciation, 134
  financial markets in, 71*t*, 74*t*
  foreign debt/GDP (*DT/Y*), 121, 124
  foreign exchange regime in, 49*t*, 50
  government deficit/GDP (–*GS/Y*), 121, 126
  government domestic debt/GDP, 135
  government revenue/GDP (*GR/Y*), 121, 126, 130
  inflation (*INF*), 120, 122
  inflation tax/GDP
    1979–93, 130
    1989–93, 130
  inflation tax/government revenue, 130
  liquid asset ratio requirements, 30
  macroeconomic and monetary characteristics of, 120–6
  money (M2)/GDP (*M/Y*), 120, 123
  net domestic credit to government/aggregate domestic credit (*CGDC*), 121, 125
  payments system in, 58, 59*t*
    reform, 61*t*

per capita income in US dollars, alternative measures of, 128
priority sector lending in, 30
private sector domestic credit/GDP, 135
reserve money/M2 (*H/M*), 120, 123
subsidy on private sector borrowing/GDP, 135
trend growth rate in GDP at constant prices (*YG*), 120, 122
US minus exchange rate-adjusted loan rate, 134
Kenya
  bank loan rate to private sector, 134
  bank reserves/bank deposits (*R/D*), 120, 124
  central bank net credit to government/net domestic credit to government (*CBCG*), 121, 125
  estimated seigniorage revenue in, 1979–93 (per cent), 130–2
  exchange rate depreciation, 134
  foreign debt/GDP (*DT/Y*), 121, 124
  foreign exchange regime in, 49*t*
  government bond/bill yield, 134
  government deficit/GDP (–*GS/Y*), 121, 126
  government domestic debt/GDP, 135
  government revenue/GDP (*GR/Y*), 121, 126, 130
  inflation (*INF*), 120, 122
  inflation tax/GDP
    1979–93, 130
    1989–93, 130
  inflation tax/government revenue, 130
  macroeconomic and monetary characteristics of, 120–6
  money (M2)/GDP (*M/Y*), 120, 123
  net domestic credit to government/ aggregate domestic credit (*CGDC*), 121, 125
  payments system in, 59*t*
  per capita income in US dollars, alternative measures of, 128
  private sector domestic credit/GDP, 135
  reserve money/M2 (*H/M*), 120, 123
  subsidy on government debt/GDP, 135
  subsidy on private sector borrowing/GDP, 135

trend growth rate in GDP at
 constant prices (*YG*), 120, 122
US minus exchange rate-adjusted
 government yield, 134
US minus exchange rate-adjusted
 loan rate, 134
Klein, Martin, 32
Korea, monetary policy reaction
 functions for, 41
Kuwait
 banking system, reorganisation after
  Iraqi invasion, 85, 88
 bank loan rate to private sector, 134
 bank reserves/bank deposits (*R/D*),
  120, 124
 cash reserve requirements, 29
 central bank
  staff recruitment, 91
  support operations, expenses, 86
 central bank net credit to
  government/net domestic
  credit to government (*CBCG*),
  121, 125
 central bank profit 1993/GDP, 130
 deposit insurance in, 87
 estimated seigniorage revenue in,
  1979–93 (per cent), 130–2
 exchange rate depreciation, 134
 financial markets in, 71*t*, 74*t*
  reforms and developments
  underway, 77*n*
 foreign borrowing in, 51
 foreign exchange regime in, 49*t*, 50
 government bond/bill yield, 134
 government deficit/GDP (*−GS/Y*),
  121, 126
 government domestic debt/GDP, 135
 government revenue/GDP (*GR/Y*),
  121, 126, 130
 inflation (*INF*), 120, 122
 inflation tax/GDP
  1979–93, 130
  1989–93, 130
 inflation tax/government revenue, 130
 liquid asset ratio requirements, 30
 loan rate ceilings in, 36, 45*n*
 macroeconomic and monetary
  characteristics of, 120–6
 money (M2)/GDP (*M/Y*), 120, 123
 net domestic credit to government/
  aggregate domestic credit
  (*CGDC*), 121, 125
 payments system in, 59*t*
  reform, 61*t*

per capita income in US dollars,
 alternative measures of, 128
private sector domestic credit/GDP,
 135
reserve money/M2 (*H/M*), 120, 123
reserve requirements, 29
seigniorage revenue in, 38
subsidy on private sector
 borrowing/GDP, 135
trend growth rate in GDP at
 constant prices (*YG*), 120, 122
US minus exchange rate-adjusted
 government yield, 134
US minus exchange rate-adjusted
 loan rate, 134

Lesotho
 bank loan rate to private sector, 134
 bank reserves/bank deposits (*R/D*),
  120, 124
 cash reserve ratio, 29
 central bank
  staff, 95
  supervisory authority, 80
 central bank net credit to
  government/net domestic
  credit to government (*CBCG*),
  121, 125
 central bank profit 1993/GDP, 130
 estimated seigniorage revenue in,
  1979–93 (per cent), 130–2
 exchange rate depreciation, 134
 financial markets in, 71*t*, 74*t*
 foreign debt/GDP (*DT/Y*), 121, 124
 foreign exchange regime in, 49*t*, 50,
  55*n*
 government bond/bill yield, 134
 government deficit/GDP (*−GS/Y*),
  121, 126
 government domestic debt/GDP, 135
 government revenue/GDP (*GR/Y*),
  121, 126, 130
 inflation (*INF*), 120, 122
 inflation tax/GDP
  1979–93, 130
  1989–93, 130
 inflation tax/government revenue, 130
 macroeconomic and monetary
  characteristics of, 120–6
 money (M2)/GDP (*M/Y*), 120, 123
 net domestic credit to
  government/aggregate
  domestic credit (*CGDC*), 121,
  125

payments system in, 59*t*
per capita income in US dollars,
    alternative measures of, 128
private sector domestic credit/GDP,
    135
reserve money/M2 (*H/M*), 120, 123
subsidy on government debt/GDP,
    135
subsidy on private sector
    borrowing/GDP, 135
trend growth rate in GDP at
    constant prices (*YG*), 120, 122
US minus exchange rate-adjusted
    government yield, 134
US minus exchange rate-adjusted
    loan rate, 134
lifeboat rescue, of failed banks, 85, 86
Lilien, David, 55*n*
liquid asset ratio requirements, 29–30
liquid asset ratios, inclusive of cash
    reserves, 45*n*
loan guarantee programmes, 30, 31
loan rate ceilings, in Bank of England
    (BoE) group, 36
Locke, John, 15

Maastricht Treaty, price stability and, 16
Malawi
    bank loan rate to private sector, 134
    bank reserves/bank deposits (*R/D*),
        120, 124
    central bank
        independence, 145
        staff, 95
        supervisory authority, 80
        supervisory methodology for, 82
    central bank net credit to
        government/net domestic
        credit to government (*CBCG*),
        121, 125
    central bank profit 1993/GDP, 130
    estimated seigniorage revenue in,
        1979–93 (per cent), 130–2
    exchange rate depreciation, 134
    financial markets in, 71*t*, 74*t*
        reforms and developments
        underway, 78*n*
    foreign borrowing in, 51
    foreign debt/GDP (*DT/Y*), 121, 124
    foreign exchange regime in, 49*t*, 51
    government bond/bill yield, 134
    government deficit/GDP (–*GS/Y*),
        121, 126
    government domestic debt/GDP, 135

government revenue/GDP (*GR/Y*),
    121, 126, 130
inflation (*INF*), 120, 122
inflation in, 145
inflation tax/GDP
    1979–93, 130
    1989–93, 130
inflation tax/government revenue,
    130
liquid asset ratio requirements, 30
liquid asset ratios in, 45*n*
macroeconomic and monetary
    characteristics of, 120–6
money (M2)/GDP (*M/Y*), 120, 123
net domestic credit to
    government/aggregate
    domestic credit (*CGDC*), 121,
    125
payments system in, 59*t*
per capita income in US dollars,
    alternative measures of, 128
private sector domestic credit/GDP,
    135
reserve money/M2 (*H/M*), 120, 123
subsidy on government debt/GDP,
    135
subsidy on private sector
    borrowing/GDP, 135
trend growth rate in GDP at
    constant prices (*YG*), 120, 122
US minus exchange rate-adjusted
    government yield, 134
US minus exchange rate-adjusted
    loan rate, 134
Malaysia
    bank loan rate to private sector, 134
    bank reserves/bank deposits (*R/D*),
        120, 124
    central bank
        staff training, 91, 110*n*
        supervisory authority, 80
        support operations, expenses, 86, 88
    central bank losses in, 39–40
    central bank net credit to
        government/net domestic
        credit to government (*CBCG*),
        121, 125
    central bank profit 1993/GDP, 130
    credit allocation to priority sectors,
        30
    estimated seigniorage revenue in,
        1979–93 (per cent), 130–2
    exchange rate depreciation, 134
    financial markets in, 71*t*, 72*t*, 74*t*, 77*n*

reforms and developments
underway, 78n
foreign borrowing in, 51
foreign debt/GDP (*DT/Y*), 121, 124
foreign exchange losses in, 37
foreign exchange regime in, 49t, 50
government deficit/GDP (−*GS/Y*),
121, 126
government domestic debt/GDP, 135
government revenue/GDP (*GR/Y*),
121, 126, 130
inflation (*INF*), 120, 122
inflation tax/GDP
1979–93, 130
1989–93, 130
inflation tax/government revenue,
130
liquid asset ratio requirements, 30
macroeconomic and monetary
characteristics of, 120–6
monetary policy reaction functions
for, 41
money (M2)/GDP (*M/Y*), 120, 123
net domestic credit to
government/aggregate
domestic credit (*CGDC*), 121,
125
payments system in, 59t
reform, 61t
per capita income in US dollars,
alternative measures of, 128
private sector domestic credit/GDP,
135
reserve money/M2 (*H/M*), 120, 123
subsidy on private sector
borrowing/GDP, 135
trend growth rate in GDP at
constant prices (*YG*), 120, 122
US minus exchange rate-adjusted
loan rate, 134
Malta
bank loan rate to private sector, 134
bank reserves/bank deposits (*R/D*),
120, 124
cash reserve requirements, 29
central bank, staff training, 91
central bank net credit to
government/net domestic
credit to government (*CBCG*),
121, 125
central bank profit 1993/GDP, 130
deposit insurance and, 87
estimated seigniorage revenue in,
1979–93 (per cent), 130–2

exchange rate depreciation, 134
financial markets in, 66, 71t, 74t
reforms and developments
underway, 78n
foreign debt/GDP (*DT/Y*), 121, 124
foreign exchange guarantees in, 51
foreign exchange losses in, 37, 51
foreign exchange regime in, 49t, 50
government bond/bill yield, 134
government deficit/GDP (−*GS/Y*),
121, 126
government domestic debt/GDP, 135
government revenue/GDP (*GR/Y*),
121, 126, 130
inflation (*INF*), 120, 122
inflation tax/GDP
1979–93, 130
1989–93, 130
inflation tax/government revenue,
130
loan rate ceilings in, 36
macroeconomic and monetary
characteristics of, 120–6
money (M2)/GDP (*M/Y*), 120, 123
net domestic credit to
government/aggregate
domestic credit (*CGDC*), 121,
125
payments system in, 59t
reform, 61t
per capita income in US dollars,
alternative measures of, 128
private sector domestic credit/GDP,
135
reserve money/M2 (*H/M*), 120, 123
reserve requirements, 29
subsidy on government debt/GDP,
135
subsidy on private sector
borrowing/GDP, 135
trend growth rate in GDP at
constant prices (*YG*), 120, 122
US minus exchange rate-adjusted
government yield, 134
US minus exchange rate-adjusted
loan rate, 134
Mas, Ignacio, 89n
Mauritius
bank loan rate to private sector, 134
bank reserves/bank deposits (*R/D*),
120, 124
BCCI débâcle and, 85
central bank, supervisory functions,
88n

central bank and government
cooperation in, 108–10
central bank net credit to
government/net domestic
credit to government (*CBCG*),
121, 125
central bank profit 1993/GDP, 130
estimated seigniorage revenue in,
1979–93 (per cent), 130–2
exchange rate depreciation, 134
financial markets in, 66, 71*t*, 74*t*
reforms and developments
underway, 78*n*
foreign debt/GDP (*DT/Y*), 121, 124
foreign exchange regime in, 49*t*
government deficit/GDP (*–GS/Y*),
121, 126
government domestic debt/GDP, 135
government revenue/GDP (*GR/Y*),
121, 126, 130
inflation (*INF*), 120, 122
inflation tax/GDP
1979–93, 130
1989–93, 130
inflation tax/government revenue,
130
interest rates in, 36
liquid asset ratio requirements, 30
liquid asset ratios in, 45*n*
macroeconomic and monetary
characteristics of, 120–6
monetary policy reaction function
in, 41
money (M2)/GDP (*M/Y*), 120, 123
net domestic credit to ·
government/aggregate
domestic credit (*CGDC*), 121,
125
payments system in, 59*t*
reform, 61*t*
per capita income in US dollars,
alternative measures of, 128
private sector domestic credit/GDP,
135
reserve money/M2 (*H/M*), 120, 123
subsidy on private sector
borrowing/GDP, 135
trend growth rate in GDP at
constant prices (*YG*), 120, 122
US minus exchange rate-adjusted
loan rate, 134
Mauro, Paolo, 34
McKinnon, Ronald, 112
Melo, Martha de, 36

Mexico
bank loan rate to private sector, 134
bank reserves/bank deposits (*R/D*),
120, 124
central bank
appointment of directors, 110*n*
price stability as objective for, 103
staff recruitment, 90
statutory objectives, 19
central bank net credit to
government/net domestic
credit to government (*CBCG*),
121, 125
central bank profit 1993/GDP, 130
Comisión Nacional Bancaria, 79, 88*n*
deposit insurance and, 87
estimated seigniorage revenue in,
1979–93 (per cent), 130–2
exchange rate depreciation, 134
financial markets in, 72*t*
foreign debt/GDP (*DT/Y*), 121, 124
foreign exchange regime in, 48, 49*t*,
51, 49*t*, 55*n*
government bond/bill yield, 134
government deficit/GDP (*–GS/Y*),
121, 126
government domestic debt/GDP, 135
government revenue/GDP (*GR/Y*),
121, 126, 130
inflation (*INF*), 120, 122
inflationary experiences of, 22
inflation tax/GDP
1979–93, 130
1989–93, 130
inflation tax/government revenue,
130
inflation tax in, 38
interest rates in, 36
macroeconomic and monetary
characteristics of, 120–6
monetary policy reaction function
for, 53
money (M2)/GDP (*M/Y*), 120, 123
net domestic credit to
government/aggregate
domestic credit (*CGDC*), 121,
125
payments system in, 57, 59*t*
reform, 61*t*
per capita income in US dollars,
alternative measures of, 128
private sector domestic credit/GDP,
135
reserve money/M2 (*H/M*), 120, 123

subsidy on government debt/GDP,
135
subsidy on private sector
borrowing/GDP, 135
trend growth rate in GDP at
constant prices (*YG*), 120, 122
US minus exchange rate-adjusted
government yield, 134
US minus exchange rate-adjusted
loan rate, 134
Middle East, countries in Bank of
England (BoE) group, 2, 2*t*
monetary expansion, inflation and, 20,
21*f*, 21*t*
relationship refined, 22–4
monetary policy, 45*n*
exchange rate policy and, 45*n*
fiscal content of, 28
implementation, 1, 3
indirect market-based instruments,
66, 113, 138
reserve requirements and, 144
monetary policy committee, 108–9
monetary policy reaction function, 40–5
for Bank of England (BoE) group,
41–5
estimates by exchange rate
regime, 52–5, 141
estimates by independence, 41–3,
139
monetisation, and growth, 63–4, 63*t*,
64*t*, 141
money demand function, 22–4
money (M2)/GDP (*M/Y*), 11*n*–12*n*
in Bank of England (BoE) group,
3–4, 4*t*, 8, 8*t*
in developing countries vs. OECD
countries, 3–4, 4*t*
money/income ratio
in developing countries, 3–4, 4*t*
in OECD countries, 3, 4*t*
money market, 69–71
M/Y. See money (M2)/GDP

Namibia, 26*n*, 46*n*
bank loan rate to private sector, 134
central bank, staff recruitment, 91
central bank net credit to
government/net domestic
credit to government (*CBCG*),
121, 125
central bank profit 1993/GDP, 130
estimated seigniorage revenue in,
1979–93 (per cent), 130–2

exchange rate depreciation, 134
financial markets in, 71*t*, 74*t*
foreign borrowing in, 51
foreign exchange regime in, 49*t*, 50,
55*n*
government bond/bill yield, 134
government deficit/GDP (−*GS/Y*),
121, 126
government domestic debt/GDP, 135
government revenue/GDP (*GR/Y*),
121, 126, 130
inflation (*INF*), 120, 122
inflation tax/GDP
1979–93, 130
1989–93, 130
interest rates in, 36
liquid asset ratio requirements, 30
macroeconomic and monetary
characteristics of, 120–6
net domestic credit to government/
aggregate domestic credit
(*CGDC*), 121, 125
payments system in, 59*t*
per capita income in US dollars,
alternative measures of, 128
private sector domestic credit/GDP,
135
reserve requirements, 29
seigniorage revenue in, 38
subsidy on government debt/GDP,
135
subsidy on private sector
borrowing/GDP, 135
trend growth rate in GDP at
constant prices (*YG*), 120, 122
US minus exchange rate-adjusted
government yield, 134
US minus exchange rate-adjusted
loan rate, 134
net domestic credit to
government/aggregate
domestic credit (*CGDC*)
in Bank of England (BoE) group, 4*t*,
8, 8*t*, 9, 28–9
in developing and OECD countries,
4*t. See also specific country*
Neumann, Manfred, 32
New Zealand, central bank, 100
Nigeria
bank loan rate to private sector, 134
bank reserves/bank deposits (*R/D*),
120, 124
central bank, appointment of
directors, 110*n*

central bank net credit to government/net domestic credit to government (*CBCG*), 121, 125
central bank profit 1993/GDP, 130
credit allocation to priority sectors, 30
deposit insurance and, 87
domestic loan guarantees in, 30
estimated seigniorage revenue in, 1979–93 (per cent), 130–2
exchange rate depreciation, 134
financial markets in, 71t, 74t
foreign debt/GDP (*DT/Y*), 121, 124
foreign exchange regime in, 48, 49t, 51
government deficit/GDP (*–GS/Y*), 121, 126
government domestic debt/GDP, 135
government revenue/GDP (*GR/Y*), 121, 126, 130
inflation (*INF*), 120, 122
inflation tax/GDP
 1979–93, 130
 1989–93, 130
inflation tax/government revenue, 130
liquid asset ratio requirements, 30
loan rate ceilings in, 36
macroeconomic and monetary characteristics of, 120–6
money (M2)/GDP (*M/Y*), 120, 123
net domestic credit to government/aggregate domestic credit (*CGDC*), 121, 125
payments system in, 58, 59t
 reform, 61t
per capita income in US dollars, alternative measures of, 128
private sector domestic credit/GDP, 135
reserve money/M2 (*H/M*), 120, 123
reserve requirements, 29
subsidy on private sector borrowing/GDP, 135
trend growth rate in GDP at constant prices (*YG*), 120, 122
US minus exchange rate-adjusted loan rate, 134

OECD. *See* Organisation for Economic Co-operation and Development

oil prices, 53, 55n
Organisation for Economic Co-operation and Development countries
 bank reserves/bank deposits (*R/D*) in, 3–4, 4t
 and developing countries, comparison, 3, 4t, 137, 147
 foreign debt/GDP (*DT/Y*), 4, 4t
 government deficit/GDP (*–GS/Y*) in, 4t
 government revenue/GDP (*GR/Y*) in, 4t
 list of, 10n
 macroeconomic and monetary characteristics of, 3–4, 4t
 net domestic credit to government/aggregate domestic credit (CGDC) in, 4t
 per capita income in US dollars, 1992 (*PCY*), 4t
 reserve money/M2 (*H/M*) in, 3–4, 4t

Pacific Basin developing countries, monetary policy reaction functions for, 41, 44, 53
Pakistan
 bank loan rate to private sector, 134
 bank reserves/bank deposits (*R/D*), 120, 124
 BCCI débâcle and, 85
 central bank
  appointment of directors, 110n
  quasi-fiscal activities, and profitability, 40
  staff recruitment, 91
 central bank net credit to government/net domestic credit to government (*CBCG*), 121, 125
 central bank profit 1993/GDP, 130
 credit allocation to priority sectors, 30
 deposit insurance and, 87
 domestic loan guarantees in, 30
 estimated seigniorage revenue in, 1979–93 (per cent), 130–2
 exchange rate depreciation, 134
 financial markets in, 71t, 74t, 77n
 foreign debt/GDP (*DT/Y*), 121, 124
 foreign exchange guarantees in, 51
 foreign exchange losses in, 37, 51
 foreign exchange regime in, 49t, 50
 government deficit/GDP (*–GS/Y*), 121, 126

government domestic debt/GDP, 135
government revenue/GDP (*GR/Y*),
　　121, 126, 130
inflation (*INF*), 120, 122
inflation tax/GDP
　　1979–93, 130
　　1989–93, 130
inflation tax/government revenue,
　　130
liquid asset ratio requirements, 30
macroeconomic and monetary
　　characteristics of, 120–6
money (M2)/GDP (*M/Y*), 120, 123
net domestic credit to
　　government/aggregate
　　domestic credit (*CGDC*), 121,
　　125
payments system in, 58, 59*t*
　　reform, 61*t*
per capita income in US dollars,
　　alternative measures of, 128
private sector domestic credit/GDP,
　　135
reserve money/M2 (*H/M*), 120, 123
subsidy on private sector
　　borrowing/GDP, 135
trend growth rate in GDP at
　　constant prices (*YG*), 120, 122
US minus exchange rate-adjusted
　　loan rate, 134
Papua New Guinea
bank loan rate to private sector, 134
bank reserves/bank deposits (*R/D*),
　　120, 124
central bank net credit to
　　government/net domestic
　　credit to government (*CBCG*),
　　121, 125
estimated seigniorage revenue in,
　　1979–93 (per cent), 130–2
exchange rate depreciation, 134
foreign debt/GDP (*DT/Y*), 121, 124
foreign exchange regime in, 49*t*
government bond/bill yield, 134
government deficit/GDP (*–GS/Y*),
　　121, 126
government domestic debt/GDP, 135
government revenue/GDP (*GR/Y*),
　　121, 126, 130
inflation (*INF*), 120, 122
inflation tax/GDP
　　1979–93, 130
　　1989–93, 130
inflation tax/government revenue, 130

macroeconomic and monetary
　　characteristics of, 120–6
money (M2)/GDP (*M/Y*), 120, 123
net domestic credit to government/
　　aggregate domestic credit
　　(*CGDC*), 121, 125
payments system in, 59*t*
per capita income in US dollars,
　　alternative measures of, 128
private sector domestic credit/GDP,
　　135
reserve money/M2 (*H/M*), 120, 123
seigniorage revenue in, 38
subsidy on government debt/GDP,
　　135
subsidy on private sector
　　borrowing/GDP, 135
trend growth rate in GDP at
　　constant prices (*YG*), 120, 122
US minus exchange rate-adjusted
　　government yield, 134
US minus exchange rate-adjusted
　　loan rate, 134
payments system, domestic, 79
average settlement delay, 58, 60*f*, 65
clearance system, 57–8, 65
daily turnover, 57–8, 58*t*
development, central banks' role in,
　　56–58, 141
questionnaire questions on, 115
reforms, 58, 61*t*–2*t*
PCY. See per capita income in US
　　dollars, 1992
per capita income in US dollars (*PCY*)
adjusted for purchasing-power
　　parity (PPP), 12*n*, 127–8
alternative measures of, 7–8, 12*n*,
　　127–128
in developing and OECD countries.
　　See also specific country
　　1992, 4*t*
exchange-rate based estimates
　　(Summers and Heston), 12*n*,
　　127–8
Philippines, monetary policy reaction
　　functions for, 41
Phillips curve, 148
expectations-augmented, 13–14, 138
pi (π), 34
population
central banks' total staff and, 97
concentration, and money holdings,
　　65
Porzecanski, Arturo, 53

price stability, 1, 9, 32
   as central banks' objective, 79, 138,
      147, 148
   in Bank of England (BoE) group,
      19
   in OECD countries, 16
   statutory, 16, 103
private sector
   central bank and, 1, 56–78, 79, 141–4
   investment culture in, 73–6, 78n
professional status, of central bank,
      90–111
   questionnaire questions on, 117
public expenditure, quality of, in
   developing countries, 147–8

questionnaire, for Bank of England
   (BoE) group, xi, 2, 114–18
   responses, confidentiality, 10n

R/D. See Bank reserves/bank deposits
   (R/D)
rediscount policy, preferential, 39–40
reforms
   in Bank of England (BoE) group, 113
   in financial markets, 72, 77t–8t
   in payments system, 58, 61t–2t
regulation
   central banks' role in, 79–89
   questionnaire questions on, 116
   definition, 79
reserve money
   definition, 11n
   in *International Financial Statistics*
      (*IFS*), 45n
   monetary and fiscal aspects of
      issuing, 32
   tax on, 34
reserve money/M2 (*H/M*)
   in Bank of England (BoE) group,
      3–4, 4t, 8–9, 8t, 29
   exchange rate regimes and, 52,
      55n
   inflation and government deficits
      and, 5
   in developing countries vs. OECD
      countries, 3–4, 4t
reserve requirement tax, 35
reserve requirements, 29, 144. *See also*
   financial repression
   noninterest, 29
Reuber, Grant, 41–2
Ricardo, David, 5, 11n

St Kitts, 10n
St Lucia, 10n
   bank loan rate to private sector, 134
   bank reserves/bank deposits (R/D),
      120, 124
   central bank net credit to
      government/net domestic
      credit to government (*CBCG*),
      121, 125
   central bank profit 1993/GDP, 130
   domestic loan guarantees in, 30
   estimated seigniorage revenue in,
      1979–93 (per cent), 130–2
   exchange rate depreciation, 134
   foreign debt/GDP (*DT/Y*), 121, 124
   foreign exchange regime in, 49t, 50,
      55n
   government bond/bill yield, 134
   government deficit/GDP (–*GS/Y*),
      121, 126
   government domestic debt/GDP, 135
   government revenue/GDP (*GR/Y*),
      121, 126, 130
   inflation (*INF*), 120, 122
   inflation tax/GDP
      1979–93, 130
      1989–93, 130
   inflation tax/government revenue, 130
   macroeconomic and monetary
      characteristics of, 120–6
   net domestic credit to government/
      aggregate domestic credit
      (*CGDC*), 121, 125
   payments system in, 57, 59t
      reform, 61t
   per capita income in US dollars,
      alternative measures of, 128
   private sector domestic credit/GDP,
      135
   reserve money/M2 (H/M), 120, 123
   subsidy on government debt/GDP,
      135
   subsidy on private sector
      borrowing/GDP, 135
   trend growth rate in GDP at
      constant prices (*YG*), 120, 122
   US minus exchange rate-adjusted
      government yield, 134
   US minus exchange rate-adjusted
      loan rate, 134
Saudi Arabia
   bank reserves/bank deposits (R/D),
      120, 124

central bank
  independence, 104
  staff recruitment, 91
  supervisory functions, 88*n*
central bank net credit to
  government/net domestic
  credit to government (*CBCG*),
  121, 125
central bank profit 1993/GDP, 130
estimated seigniorage revenue in,
  1979–93 (per cent), 130–2
exchange rate depreciation, 134
financial markets in, 71*t*, 74*t*
reforms and developments
  underway, 78*n*
foreign borrowing in, 51
foreign exchange regime in, 49*t*, 50,
  55*n*
inflation (*INF*), 120, 122
inflation tax/GDP
  1979–93, 130
  1989–93, 130
liquid asset ratio requirements, 30
macroeconomic and monetary
  characteristics of, 120–6
money (M2)/GDP (*M/Y*), 120, 123
net domestic credit to government/
  aggregate domestic credit
  (*CGDC*), 121, 125
payments system in, 60*t*
  reform, 61*t*
per capita income in US dollars,
  alternative measures of, 128
private sector domestic credit/GDP,
  135
reserve money/M2 (*H/M*), 120, 123
reserve requirements, 29
seigniorage revenue in, 38
trend growth rate in GDP at
  constant prices (*YG*), 120, 122
Schmidt-Hebbel, Klaus, 34
Scholtens, Lambertus, 32
seigniorage, 30, 32–5
  government appropriation of, 33
  measurement, 146
    on cash flow basis, 33
    fiscal approach to, 33
  revenue
    in Bank of England (BoE) group,
      estimated, 1979–93 (per cent),
      34, 130–2
    central bank profits and, 39–40
    from currency and bank reserves,
      comparison, 34

estimation, 46*n*
  in flow terms, 38
  generated by central bank, 32–5
  as government nontax revenue,
    33
  as percentage of GDP, 34
  as percentage of government's
    current revenue, 34
  as tax, 32
Shaw, Edward, 112
Sierra Leone
  bank loan rate to private sector, 134
  bank reserves/bank deposits (*R/D*),
    120, 124
  central bank
    staff recruitment, 91
    specialised supervisory staff, 81
    supervisory functions, 88*n*
  central bank losses in, 39–40
  central bank net credit to
    government/net domestic
    credit to government (*CBCG*),
    121, 125
  central bank profit 1993/GDP, 130
  estimated seigniorage revenue in,
    1979–93 (per cent), 130–2
  exchange rate depreciation, 134
  financial markets in, 71*t*, 74*t*
  foreign debt/GDP (*DT/Y*), 121, 124
  foreign exchange regime in, 49*t*, 51
  government bond/bill yield, 134
  government deficit/GDP (*–GS/Y*),
    121, 126
  government domestic debt/GDP, 135
  government revenue/GDP (*GR/Y*),
    121, 126, 130
  inflation (*INF*), 120, 122
  inflation tax/GDP
    1979–93, 130
    1989–93, 130
  inflation tax/government revenue,
    130
  inflation tax in, 38
  liquid asset ratio requirements, 30
  liquid asset ratios in, 45*n*
  macroeconomic and monetary
    characteristics of, 120–6
  money (M2)/GDP (*M/Y*), 120, 123
  net domestic credit to government/
    aggregate domestic credit
    (*CGDC*), 121, 125
  payments system in, 60*t*
  per capita income in US dollars,
    alternative measures of, 128

private sector domestic credit/GDP, 135
reserve money/M2 (*H/M*), 120, 123
subsidy on government debt/GDP, 135
subsidy on private sector borrowing/GDP, 135
trend growth rate in GDP at constant prices (*YG*), 120, 122
US minus exchange rate-adjusted government yield, 134
US minus exchange rate-adjusted loan rate, 134
Singapore
  bank loan rate to private sector, 134
  bank reserves/bank deposits (*R/D*), 120, 124
  cash reserve requirements, 29
  central bank
    appointment of directors, 110*n*
    staff training, 91
    specialised supervisory staff, 80
    supervisory authority, 80
  central bank net credit to government/net domestic credit to government (*CBCG*), 121, 125
  central bank profit 1993/GDP, 130
  estimated seigniorage revenue in, 1979–93 (per cent), 130–2
  exchange rate depreciation, 134
  financial markets in, 71*t*, 72*t*, 77*n*
  foreign exchange guarantees in, 51
  foreign exchange regime in, 48, 49*t*
  government deficit/GDP (*–GS/Y*), 121, 126
  government revenue/GDP (*GR/Y*), 121, 126, 130
  inflation (*INF*), 120, 122
  inflation tax/GDP
    1979–93, 130
    1989–93, 130
  inflation tax/government revenue, 130
  liquid asset ratio requirements, 30
  macroeconomic and monetary characteristics of, 120–6
  money (M2)/GDP (*M/Y*), 120, 123
  net domestic credit to government/aggregate domestic credit (*CGDC*), 121, 125
  payments system in, 57, 60*t*
    reform, 61*t*

per capita income in US dollars, alternative measures of, 128
priority sector lending in, 30
private sector domestic credit/GDP, 135
reserve money/M2 (*H/M*), 120, 123
subsidy on private sector borrowing/GDP, 135
trend growth rate in GDP at constant prices (*YG*), 120, 122
US minus exchange rate-adjusted loan rate, 134
Solomon Islands
  bank loan rate to private sector, 134
  bank reserves/bank deposits (*R/D*), 120, 124
  central bank
    independence, 101
    supervisory functions, 80, 88*n*
  central bank net credit to government/net domestic credit to government (*CBCG*), 121, 125
  central bank profit 1993/GDP, 130
  domestic loan guarantees in, 30
  estimated seigniorage revenue in, 1979–93 (per cent), 130–2
  exchange rate depreciation, 134
  financial markets in, 71*t*
  foreign debt/GDP (*DT/Y*), 121, 124
  foreign exchange losses in, 37, 51
  foreign exchange regime in, 49*t*, 50
  government bond/bill yield, 134
  government deficit/GDP (*–GS/Y*), 121, 126
  government domestic debt/GDP, 135
  government revenue/GDP (*GR/Y*), 121, 126, 130
  inflation (*INF*), 120, 122
  inflation tax/GDP
    1979–93, 130
    1989–93, 130
  inflation tax/government revenue, 130
  loan rate ceilings in, 36
  macroeconomic and monetary characteristics of, 120–6
  money (M2)/GDP (*M/Y*), 120, 123
  net domestic credit to government/aggregate domestic credit (*CGDC*), 121, 125
  payments system in, 58, 60*t*
    reform, 61*t*

per capita income in US dollars, alternative measures of, 128

private sector domestic credit/GDP, 135

reserve money/M2 (*H/M*), 120, 123

subsidy on government debt/GDP, 135

subsidy on private sector borrowing/GDP, 135

trend growth rate in GDP at constant prices (*YG*), 120, 122

US minus exchange rate-adjusted government yield, 134

US minus exchange rate-adjusted loan rate, 134

South Africa
  bank loan rate to private sector, 134
  bank reserves/bank deposits (*R/D*), 120, 124
  central bank
    independence, 101
    specialised supervisory staff, 81
    supervisory functions, 88*n*
  central bank net credit to government/net domestic credit to government (*CBCG*), 121, 125
  central bank profit 1993/GDP, 130
  deposit insurance and, 87
  estimated seigniorage revenue in, 1979–93 (per cent), 130–2
  exchange rate depreciation, 134
  financial markets in, 71*t*, 72, 72*t*, 74*t*
  foreign exchange regime in, 49*t*, 50, 51
  government bond/bill yield, 134
  government deficit/GDP (*–GS/Y*), 121, 126
  government domestic debt/GDP, 135
  government revenue/GDP (*GR/Y*), 121, 126, 130
  inflation (*INF*), 120, 122
  inflation tax/GDP
    1979–93, 130
    1989–93, 130
  inflation tax/government revenue, 130
  liquid asset ratio requirements, 30
  loan rate ceilings in, 36
  macroeconomic and monetary characteristics of, 120–6
  money (M2)/GDP (*M/Y*), 120, 123
  net domestic credit to government/ aggregate domestic credit (*CGDC*), 121, 125

payments system in, 57, 60*t*
  reform, 61*t*

per capita income in US dollars, alternative measures of, 128

private sector domestic credit/GDP, 135

reserve money/M2 (*H/M*), 120, 123

reserve requirements, 29

subsidy on government debt/GDP, 135

subsidy on private sector borrowing/GDP, 135

trend growth rate in GDP at constant prices (*YG*), 120, 122

US minus exchange rate-adjusted government yield, 134

US minus exchange rate-adjusted loan rate, 134

Sri Lanka
  bank loan rate to private sector, 134
  bank reserves/bank deposits (*R/D*), 120, 124
  BCCI débâcle and, 85
  cash reserve ratio, 29
  central bank, staff, 91
  central bank net credit to government/net domestic credit to government (*CBCG*), 121, 125
  central bank profit 1993/GDP, 130
  deposit insurance in, 87
  domestic loan guarantees in, 30
  estimated seigniorage revenue in, 1979–93 (per cent), 130–2
  exchange rate depreciation, 134
  financial markets in, 71*t*, 74*t*
  reforms and developments underway, 78*n*
  foreign debt/GDP (*DT/Y*), 121, 124
  foreign exchange regime in, 49*t*, 50
  government bond/bill yield, 134
  government deficit/GDP (*–GS/Y*), 121, 126
  government domestic debt/GDP, 135
  government revenue/GDP (*GR/Y*), 121, 126, 130
  inflation (*INF*), 120, 122
  inflation tax/GDP
    1979–93, 130
    1989–93, 130
  inflation tax/government revenue, 130
  liquid asset ratio requirements, 30
  macroeconomic and monetary characteristics of, 120–6

money (M2)/GDP (*M/Y*), 120, 123
net domestic credit to
    government/aggregate
    domestic credit (*CGDC*), 121,
    125
payments system in, 57, 60*t*, 58
    reform, 62*t*
per capita income in US dollars,
    alternative measures of, 128
private sector domestic credit/GDP,
    135
reserve money/M2 (*H/M*), 120, 123
subsidy on government debt/GDP,
    135
subsidy on private sector
    borrowing/GDP, 135
trend growth rate in GDP at
    constant prices (*YG*), 120, 122
US minus exchange rate-adjusted
    government yield, 134
US minus exchange rate-adjusted
    loan rate, 134
staff, central bank
    graduate intake for, 91–3, 92*f*, 94*t*, 96
    graduate/postgraduate ratio, 93–5,
        95*f*, 96
    nonsupervisory, size, and
        population, 97–8, 99*t*
    pay scales for, 90–1
        civil service, 90–1
    postgraduate intake for, specialised
        skills and, 93–5, 96*f*
    questionnaire questions on, 117
    recruitment, 90–3, 143
    size
        banks' independence and, 93, 98
        determinants, 97–8, 143
        foreign exchange operations and,
            98
        number of branches and, 98
    skilled
        hiring, 90–3, 143
        recruitment, and banks'
            self-assessment of
            independence, 93, 96
        use of, by central banks, 90–7
    specialist, for supervision, 80–2, 81*f*,
        82*f*, 88*n*, 143
        bank deposits and, ratio of, 81–3,
            84*t*
        supervisory methods and, 81–3, 143
    training programmes for, 91, 93
status, of central bank, 90–111, 143
    government financing and, 104

inflation and, 105–8, 107*t*
    questionnaire questions on, 117
Summers, Robert, and Alan Heston,
    per capita income in US
    dollars (*PCY*), exchange-rate
    based estimates, 12*n*, 127–8
supervision
    central banks' role in, 79–89, 150
    questionnaire questions on, 116
    definition, 79
    methods used, 81–3
Swaziland
    bank loan rate to private sector, 134
    bank reserves/bank deposits (*R/D*),
        120, 124
    central bank, staff recruitment, 91
    central bank net credit to
        government/net domestic
        credit to government (*CBCG*),
        121, 125
    central bank profit 1993/GDP, 130
    domestic loan guarantees in, 30
    estimated seigniorage revenue in,
        1979–93 (per cent), 130–2
    exchange rate depreciation, 134
    financial markets in, 71*t*, 74*t*
    foreign debt/GDP (*DT/Y*), 121, 124
    foreign exchange guarantees in, 51
    foreign exchange losses in, 37, 51
    foreign exchange regime in, 49*t*, 50,
        55*n*
    government bond/bill yield, 134
    government deficit/GDP (*–GS/Y*),
        121, 126
    government domestic debt/GDP, 135
    government revenue/GDP (*GR/Y*),
        121, 126, 130
    inflation (*INF*), 120, 122
    inflation tax/GDP
        1979–93, 130
        1989–93, 130
    inflation tax/government revenue,
        130
    liquid asset ratio requirements, 30
    macroeconomic and monetary
        characteristics of, 120–6
    money (M2)/GDP (*M/Y*), 120, 123
    net domestic credit to
        government/aggregate
        domestic credit (*CGDC*), 121,
        125
    payments system in, 60*t*
    per capita income in US dollars,
        alternative measures of, 128

private sector domestic credit/GDP, 135
reserve money/M2 (*H/M*), 120, 123
reserve requirements, 29
subsidy on government debt/GDP, 135
subsidy on private sector borrowing/GDP, 135
trend growth rate in GDP at constant prices (*YG*), 120, 122
US minus exchange rate-adjusted government yield, 134
US minus exchange rate-adjusted loan rate, 134
Symposium on Central Banking in Developing Countries, Bank of England, 9 June 1995
  authors and discussants, 153
  central bank participants, 151–3
  minutes, 137–51
  observers
    Bank of England, 153
    overseas, 153–4

Taiwan, monetary policy reaction functions for, 41
Talley, Samuel, 89*n*
Tanzania
  bank loan rate to private sector, 134
  bank reserves/bank deposits (*R/D*), 120, 124
  central bank net credit to government/net domestic credit to government (*CBCG*), 121, 125
  estimated seigniorage revenue in, 1979–93 (per cent), 130–2
  exchange rate depreciation, 134
  foreign debt/GDP (*DT/Y*), 121, 124
  foreign exchange regime in, 49*t*
  government deficit/GDP (–*GS/Y*), 121, 126
  government domestic debt/GDP, 135
  government revenue/GDP (*GR/Y*), 121, 126, 130
  inflation (*INF*), 120, 122
  inflation tax/GDP
    1979–93, 130
    1989–93, 130
  inflation tax/government revenue, 130
  macroeconomic and monetary characteristics of, 120–6

money (M2)/GDP (*M/Y*), 120, 123
net domestic credit to government/aggregate domestic credit (*CGDC*), 121, 125
payments system in, 60*t*
per capita income in US dollars, alternative measures of, 128
private sector domestic credit/GDP, 135
reserve money/M2 (*H/M*), 120, 123
subsidy on private sector borrowing/GDP, 135
trend growth rate in GDP at constant prices (*YG*), 120, 122
US minus exchange rate-adjusted loan rate, 134
terms of trade, exchange rate regimes and, 52
Thailand, monetary policy reaction functions for, 41
trade unions, and central bank staff hiring, 110*n*
treasury bill auctions, 109–10
Trinidad and Tobago
  bank loan rate to private sector, 134
  bank reserves/bank deposits (*R/D*), 120, 124
  cash reserve ratio, 29
  central bank net credit to government/net domestic credit to government (*CBCG*), 121, 125
  central bank profit 1993/GDP, 130
  deposit insurance and, 87
  estimated seigniorage revenue in, 1979–93 (per cent), 130–2
  exchange rate depreciation, 134
  financial markets in, 66, 71*t*, 77*n*
  foreign debt/GDP (*DT/Y*), 121, 124
  foreign exchange regime in, 49*t*
  government bond/bill yield, 134
  government deficit/GDP (–*GS/Y*), 121, 126
  government domestic debt/GDP, 135
  government revenue/GDP (*GR/Y*), 121, 126, 130
  inflation (*INF*), 120, 122
  inflation tax/GDP
    1979–93, 130
    1989–93, 130
  inflation tax/government revenue, 130
  interest rates in, 36

macroeconomic and monetary
    characteristics of, 120–6
money (M2)/GDP (*M/Y*), 120, 123
net domestic credit to
    government/aggregate
    domestic credit (*CGDC*), 121,
    125
payments system in, 60*t*
    reform, 62*t*
per capita income in US dollars,
    alternative measures of, 128
private sector domestic credit/GDP,
    135
reserve money/M2 (*H/M*), 120, 123
subsidy on government debt/GDP,
    135
subsidy on private sector
    borrowing/GDP, 135
trend growth rate in GDP at
    constant prices (*YG*), 120, 122
US minus exchange rate-adjusted
    government yield, 134
US minus exchange rate-adjusted
    loan rate, 134
Turkey
    central bank, foreign exchange risk
        insurance scheme, 45*n*
    interest rates in, 45*n*
    monetary policy reaction function
        for, 54

Uganda
    bank loan rate to private sector, 134
    bank reserves/bank deposits (*R/D*),
        120, 124
    central bank, supervisory authority,
        specialised staff for, 81
    central bank losses in, 39–40
    central bank net credit to
        government/net domestic
        credit to government (*CBCG*),
        121, 125
    central bank profit 1993/GDP, 130
    deposit insurance and, 87
    domestic loan guarantees in, 30
    estimated seigniorage revenue in,
        1979–93 (per cent), 130–2
    exchange rate depreciation, 134
    financial markets in, 71*t*, 74*t*
        reforms and developments
        underway, 78*n*
    foreign debt/GDP (*DT/Y*), 121, 124
    foreign exchange losses in, 37
    foreign exchange regime in, 49*t*, 51

government bond/bill yield, 134
government deficit/GDP (*–GS/Y*),
    121, 126
government domestic debt/GDP, 135
government revenue/GDP (*GR/Y*),
    121, 126, 130
inflation (*INF*), 120, 122
inflation tax/GDP
    1979–93, 130
    1989–93, 130
inflation tax/government revenue,
    130
liquid asset ratio requirements, 30
macroeconomic and monetary
    characteristics of, 120–6
money (M2)/GDP (*M/Y*), 120, 123
net domestic credit to government/
    aggregate domestic credit
    (*CGDC*), 121, 125
payments system in, 58, 60*t*
    reform, 62*t*
per capita income in US dollars,
    alternative measures of, 128
private sector domestic credit/GDP,
    135
reserve money/M2 (*H/M*), 120, 123
subsidy on government debt/GDP,
    135
subsidy on private sector
    borrowing/GDP, 135
trend growth rate in GDP at
    constant prices (*YG*), 120, 122
US minus exchange rate-adjusted
    government yield, 134
US minus exchange rate-adjusted
    loan rate, 134
United Arab Emirates
    bank reserves/bank deposits (*R/D*),
        120, 124
    central bank, appointment of
        directors, 110*n*
    central bank net credit to
        government/net domestic
        credit to government (*CBCG*),
        121, 125
    central bank profit 1993/GDP, 130
    estimated seigniorage revenue in,
        1979–93 (per cent), 130–2
    exchange rate depreciation, 134
    financial markets in, 71*t*
    foreign exchange regime in, 49*t*, 50,
        55*n*
    government deficit/GDP (*–GS/Y*),
        121, 126

government domestic debt/GDP, 135
government revenue/GDP (*GR/Y*),
    121, 126, 130
inflation tax/GDP
    1979–93, 130
    1989–93, 130
inflation tax/government revenue, 130
liquid asset ratio requirements, 30
macroeconomic and monetary
    characteristics of, 120–6
money (M2)/GDP (*M/Y*), 120, 123
net domestic credit to government/
    aggregate domestic credit
    (*CGDC*), 121, 125
payments system in, 58, 60*t*
    reform, 62*t*
per capita income in US dollars,
    alternative measures of, 128
private sector domestic credit/GDP,
    135
reserve money/M2 (*H/M*), 120, 123
seigniorage revenue in, 38
trend growth rate in GDP at
    constant prices (*YG*), 120, 122
United States
    deposit insurance and, 87
    savings-and-loan débâcle, 46*n*

Van Ewijk, Casper, 32
Venezuela
    foreign exchange rate guarantee
        scheme, 46*n*
    monetary policy reaction function
        for, 53
western hemisphere, countries in Bank
    of England (BoE) group, 2, 2*t*
World Bank, *Socio-economic
    Time-series Access and
    Retrieval System: World Tables*,
    1, 3
YG. See economic growth; gross
    domestic product (GDP),
    trend growth rate in at
    constant prices

Zambia
    bank loan rate to private sector, 134
    bank reserves/bank deposits (*R/D*),
        120, 124
    central bank
        quasi-fiscal activities, and
            profitability, 40
        support operations, 88
    central bank net credit to

government/net domestic
    credit to government (*CBCG*),
    121, 125
central bank profit 1993/GDP, 130
estimated seigniorage revenue in,
    1979–93 (per cent), 130–2
exchange rate depreciation, 134
financial markets in, 71*t*, 74*t*
    reforms and developments
        underway, 78*n*
foreign borrowing in, 51
foreign debt/GDP (*DT/Y*), 121, 124
foreign exchange losses in, 37, 51
foreign exchange regime in, 49*t*, 51
government bond/bill yield, 134
government deficit/GDP (–*GS/Y*),
    121, 126
government domestic debt/GDP, 135
government revenue/GDP (*GR/Y*),
    121, 126, 130
inflation (*INF*), 120, 122
inflation tax/GDP
    1979–93, 130
    1989–93, 130
inflation tax/government revenue, 130
interest rates in, 36
liquid asset ratio requirements, 30
macroeconomic and monetary
    characteristics of, 120–6
money (M2)/GDP (*M/Y*), 120, 123
net domestic credit to government/
    aggregate domestic credit
    (*CGDC*), 121, 125
payments system in, 60*t*
per capita income in US dollars,
    alternative measures of, 128
private sector domestic credit/GDP,
    135
reserve money/M2 (*H/M*), 120, 123
subsidy on government debt/GDP,
    135
subsidy on private sector
    borrowing/GDP, 135
trend growth rate in GDP at
    constant prices (*YG*), 120, 122
US minus exchange rate-adjusted
    government yield, 134
US minus exchange rate-adjusted
    loan rate, 134
Zimbabwe
    bank loan rate to private sector, 134
    bank reserves/bank deposits (*R/D*),
        120, 124
    cash reserve ratio, 29

central bank
  quasi-fiscal activities, and
    profitability, 40
  as supervisory authority, 80, 88*n*
central bank net credit to
    government/net domestic
    credit to government (*CBCG*),
    121, 125
central bank profit 1993/GDP, 130
domestic loan guarantees in, 30
estimated seigniorage revenue in,
    1979–93 (per cent), 130–2
exchange rate depreciation, 134
financial markets in, 71*t*, 74*t*
foreign debt/GDP (*DT/Y*), 121, 124
foreign exchange regime in, 49*t*
government bond/bill yield, 134
government deficit/GDP (*–GS/Y*),
    121, 126
government domestic debt/GDP, 135
government revenue/GDP (*GR/Y*),
    121, 126, 130
inflation (*INF*), 120, 122
inflation tax/GDP
  1979–93, 130
  1989–93, 130

inflation tax/government revenue,
    130
macroeconomic and monetary
    characteristics of, 120–6
money (M2)/GDP (*M/Y*), 120, 123
net domestic credit to
    government/aggregate
    domestic credit (*CGDC*), 121,
    125
payments system in, 57, 60*t*
  reform, 62*t*
per capita income in US dollars,
    alternative measures of, 128
private sector domestic credit/GDP,
    135
reserve money/M2 (*H/M*), 120, 123
subsidy on government debt/GDP,
    135
subsidy on private sector
    borrowing/GDP, 135
trend growth rate in GDP at
    constant prices (*YG*), 120, 122
US minus exchange rate-adjusted
    government yield, 134
US minus exchange rate-adjusted
    loan rate, 134